STOP THE PRESS

STOP
THE
PRESS

How the Mormon Church Tried to
Silence the *Salt Lake Tribune*

JAMES W. URE

Prometheus Books

59 John Glenn Drive
Amherst, New York 14228

Published 2018 by Prometheus Books

Stop the Press: How the Mormon Church Tried to Silence the Salt Lake Tribune. Copyright © 2018 by James W. Ure. All rights reserved. No part of this publication may be reproduced, stored in a retrieval system, or transmitted in any form or by any means, digital, electronic, mechanical, photocopying, recording, or otherwise, or conveyed via the Internet or a website without prior written permission of the publisher, except in the case of brief quotations embodied in critical articles and reviews.

Image of Mormon Temple in Salt Lake City, Utah © Media Bakery
Newspaper print image © MaryValery/Shutterstock
Cover design by Liz Mills
Cover design © Prometheus Books

Salt Lake Tribune Bones of Contention series reprinted with permission © *Salt Lake Tribute.*

Trademarked names appear throughout this book. Prometheus Books recognizes all registered trademarks, trademarks, and service marks mentioned in the text.

The Internet addresses listed in the text were accurate at the time of publication. The inclusion of a website does not indicate an endorsement by the author(s) or by Prometheus Books, and Prometheus Books does not guarantee the accuracy of the information presented at these sites.

Inquiries should be addressed to
Prometheus Books
59 John Glenn Drive
Amherst, New York 14228
VOICE: 716–691–0133 • FAX: 716–691–0137
WWW.PROMETHEUSBOOKS.COM

22 21 20 19 18   5 4 3 2 1

Library of Congress Cataloging-in-Publication Data Pending

Printed in the United States of America

To the first reporter who scratched in stone, "the king is naked."
To the first editor who decided "nude" fit better in a headline.
To the legions of reporters and editors who have worked so hard
to describe the king's clothes.

Congress shall make no law respecting an establishment of religion, or prohibiting the free exercise thereof; or abridging the freedom of speech, or of the press; or the right of the people to assemble, and to petition the government for a redress of grievances.

—First Amendment, Constitution of the United States

CONTENTS

NOTE TO THE READER

"Mormon," "LDS," "Saints," and "Latter-day Saints" are used interchangeably in this book, but all refer to the Church of Jesus Christ of Latter-day Saints. We have used "Mountain Meadows," although it is sometimes seen elsewhere as "Mountain Meadow," singular.

Chapter 1

BOMBSHELL

Revenge proves its own executioner.

—John Ford

To live in Salt Lake City you must choose sides.

You are either a "good" and obedient Mormon or else you join the side of the dissidents, dropouts, and non-Mormons. Termed the "Great Divide" in the nineteenth century, choosing sides is part of living in this city.

The conflicts between the two sides are historical, bitter, and even bloody. In this work they are seen through the prism of its two competing daily newspapers. This book sheds light on how the church influences and manages the politics, business, and the institutional ethos of the state of Utah.

The *Deseret News* was founded in 1850 by the Church of Jesus Christ of Latter-day Saints (known as Mormons from their bible, the Book of Mormon).[1] The *News* is a faith-promoting publication of the church and is embraced by active Mormons. Its editorial material is kept within the firm boundaries of mainstream Mormon thought. It represents the conservative Mormon establishment.

The *Deseret News* is the voice of a church founded in 1830. The Mormon Church has striven for recognition as a mainstream religion, surviving and thriving on the uniqueness of its founding, its past, and its beliefs.

The *Salt Lake Tribune*, founded in 1871 by active but dissident Mormons and owned for over a century by a Catholic family, had been the secular, critical watchdog of the Mormon Church. It won a Pulitzer Prize in 1957 and had grown in editorial stature and advertising lineage to become the newspaper of record for the city.[2]

The *Tribune* had been called "the balance wheel of Utah causing it to take leadership in, or join, every cause that advanced the economic social and cultural welfare of Utah to the benefit of all Utahns—Mormon and gentile alike."[3] The *Tribune*'s circulation had traditionally been about twice that of the *Deseret News*. The *Tribune* is a more liberal voice in a state often considered the reddest of the red.

The two dailies represented the opposing sides of the Great Divide, yet since 1952 they worked profitably as partners in a joint operating agreement (JOA). This agreement to combine printing, circulation, and advertising departments under a JOA brought together the leaders of both factions. Non-Mormons (called gentiles by members of the LDS Church) joined Mormons in the 1990s to secure the 2002 Winter Olympics. A feeling of conditional goodwill settled like a warm blanket over both sides of the divide. Most Salt Lakers thought the bitter history had reached détente.

They were wrong. As we shall see, the Mormon Church's resentment toward the *Tribune* had smoldered for years.

At least as early as 1995 the Mormon Church was secretly maneuvering to acquire the *Tribune*. A nasty legal fight ensued, and by 2000 the *Tribune*'s Catholic owners were dismayed when a court case turned the newspaper over to a Mormon-friendly media conglomerate, MediaNews Group.[4] After a series of financial and legal missteps by the MediaNews Group, Alden Global Capital had come to own the *Salt Lake Tribune*. The New York–based Alden in 2012 was called the "grandfather of vulture investing" by the *New York Post*.[5]

In 2013 the church saw an opening in the JOA that might enable it to take down the paper once and for all. In the autumn of that year the church made a secret deal with Alden to buy assets of the *Tribune*. The Mormon Church would then bleed the *Tribune* to death.

Alden was paid $23 million; in return, Alden gave the church's *Deseret News* 70 percent of the profits from a long-standing JOA with the *Tribune*, cutting the *Tribune* to a slender 30 percent. For most of the sixty-one years of joint operation, the *Tribune* was allocated 58 percent of the profits and the *News* 42 percent, based on each paper's circulation. On the JOA ledger sheet of November 2013, the transaction is listed as "(Gain) Loss on sale of Newspaper ($23,000,000)."[6]

The secret 2013 deal made certain that the *Tribune*—with nearly double the hard copy circulation (about 73,000 daily versus 37,500 at the *News*) and the more profitable of the two papers—would starve to death, leaving Utahns with the Mormon Church's single voice of news and opinion.

The agreement was secret until seven months later when unsigned notes in unmarked envelopes were opened by *Tribune* reporters Tom Harvey, Robert Gehrke, and columnist Paul Rolly in the City Room of the *Tribune*.[7]

"Church and John Paton are renegotiating JOA. Tribune will be left with very little. Deal is Tribune for cash." It was written in a ragged scrawl meant to disguise the handwriting.

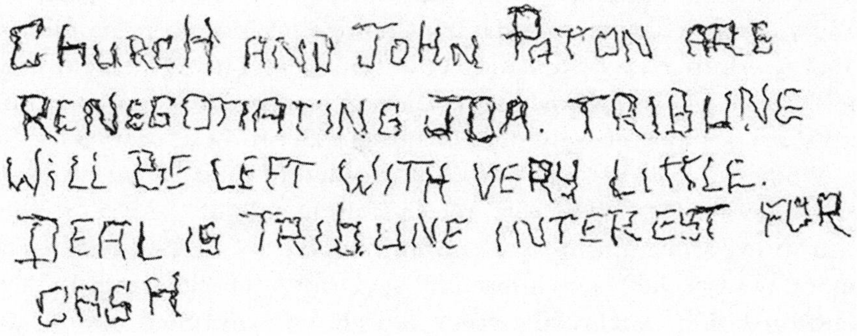
CHURCH AND JOHN PATON ARE
RENEGOTIATING JOA. TRIBUNE
WILL BE LEFT WITH VERY LITTLE.
DEAL IS TRIBUNE INTEREST FOR
CASH

Fig. 1.1. The "Note," arrived in the *Salt Lake Tribune* newsroom anonymously.

The Mormons were ready to sit back and watch their 144-year-old nemesis die from lack of revenue. Furthermore, a clause in the contract allowed the church to veto any prospective purchaser of the paper. The deal appeared to guarantee the demise of the *Tribune*. Even its publisher said it was in a "death spiral."[8]

The Mormon Church, with a history of vengeance and a long memory, had been lying in wait for this moment.

In 1997 the *Tribune* had been sold for more than $730 million.[9] In 2016 the *Tribune* was valued at $5 million and sinking. The church argued that its 2013 deal was magnanimous in giving the *Tribune* 100 percent of any digital revenues it could generate, and the church claimed that all printed newspapers were dying and news was going all digital. But,

Tribune publisher Terry Orme asked, if you slash revenues by half, where would the resources come from to develop a robust, competitive digital presence?[10]

Historically, the *Tribune* had been a large and prickly burr under the saddle of Mormonism. From its founding in 1871, the *Tribune* frequently called attention to acts and beliefs embarrassing to the Mormons, especially polygamy. The *Tribune* called for the separation of church and state when they were one in the same (and mostly still are in Utah). It called for open records in a place where most government office holders are Mormon and many deals are done, Mormon-to-Mormon, out of public sight.

In 1924, recognizing the economic value of détente with the large Mormon business community, the *Tribune* dialed down the tone of its criticism of the church. In 1952 the two papers signed the JOA, creating a company called Newspaper Agency Corporation to handle the ad sales, printing, and circulation of both papers. This agreement saved the *Deseret News* from perishing, according to historians.[11] For the next sixty years both papers would enjoy substantial profits as partners.

While the *Tribune* and *Deseret News* worked in their partnership, the *Tribune* served its readers with the dissenting side of the major issues confronting Mormonism—the church's opposition to the Equal Rights Amendment, its failure to fully church African Americans until 1978, its stand on homosexuality, the contorted church-controlled liquor laws, and the church's denying its women the priesthood or a significant voice in church affairs. However, it was, as one former staffer called it, "soft reporting."[12]

In 1991 the *Tribune* got a new and assertive editor, James E. "Jay" Shelledy. Described as "pugnacious," he encouraged his reporters to take a more aggressive stance in covering the Mormon Church.[13]

For the next decade the *Tribune* took the gloves off in its stories about the church. The façade of Mormonism remained placid in the face of Shelledy's uncompromising direction, but beneath the surface the Mormon leaders were boiling mad and secretly working to buy the *Tribune* and extinguish or mute its voice.[14]

The Mormon hierarchy was most bitter about the *Tribune's* reporting in 2000 of the archeological details revealed during an excavation at the site of the infamous Mountain Meadows Massacre of 1857, a unique event of monstrous proportion that was ordered at the highest levels of the church. It was this three-part series (see appendix for full articles) that intensified the church's determination to kill the *Tribune*.

The revelation of the deal to cut the *Tribune*'s revenues brought a roar of dismay from Utah's dissident Mormons and its non-Mormons, the independents and liberals who represent at least about half the population of Salt Lake City. Says a Mormon Church insider who asked not to be identified, "The church wanted the *Tribune* dead. They just didn't want their fingerprints on the knife."[15]

Just as the knife was about to be plunged, it looked as if a small cadre of Davids had brought the giant church Goliath to its knees, and a long-time suitor stepped up to make an offer.

Retribution and revenge are part and parcel of the history of Mormonism, and there is little doubt that the 2013 deal made by the *Deseret News* was revenge for more than a century of perceived slights.

Chapter 2

DEEP AND HISTORICAL RESENTMENTS

The world is full of magic things, patiently waiting for our senses to grow sharper.

—W. B. Yeats

To understand the twenty-first century conflict between Mormons, dissidents, and non-Mormons as reflected in the newspaper struggle, it is necessary to explore the intriguing origins and growth of the Church of Jesus Christ of Latter-day Saints. Peggy Fletcher Stack, the *Salt Lake Tribune*'s religion writer, and herself an active Mormon, wrote, "The tales of Joseph Smith's founding of the LDS Church have been repeated across the globe by generations of Latter-day Saints, as well as Mormon missionaries, eager to convert others to what they believe.

"Trouble is, the real history is much more nuanced, complicated and even contradictory."[1]

Founded in 1830, the young and fragile Mormon Church loathed and decried public criticism from earliest days, assuming a defensive posture that has never changed. "Like many new faiths, nineteenth century Mormonism had a dark side of violence and fanaticism," wrote Will Bagley in his *Blood of the Prophets: Brigham Young and the Massacre at Mountain Meadows*.[2]

About the only noncontroversial facts of founder Joseph Smith's early life are that he was born on December 23, 1805, in Sharon, Vermont, to Lucy Mack Smith and her husband, Joseph. Due to crop failures in Vermont, his family in 1816 moved to Palmyra in western New York. They arrived during the "Second Great Awakening"; the region was a hotbed of religious enthusiasm.[3]

At this point Joseph's story becomes more opaque. Joseph and some members of his family participated in religious folk magic, a fairly common practice at the time. Now the mists of history begin swirling with claims and counterclaims. There seem to be many versions of the truth of the origins of the Book of Mormon.

Joseph claimed to have had a vision in 1820, when he was fourteen or fifteen, in which God told him that all contemporary churches had turned aside from the gospel. This "First Vision" is considered the basis for the foundation of Mormonism.[4] Joseph described this vision differently on separate occasions.[5]

The next act in the drama came in 1823. While praying for redemption for his sins, he said he was visited by an angel named Moroni. Joseph said Moroni revealed the location of a book of golden plates.

Meanwhile, he was making money as a "treasure seeker" for local property owners; Joseph claimed he could look into seer stones for directions to treasure.[6] He formed a company or partnership based on these alleged abilities. In 1826, Joseph was brought before a Chenango County court for "glass-looking," or pretending to find lost treasure.[7]

In 1827, Joseph eloped with Emma Hale (her father disapproved of his treasure-hunting ways) and returned to Manchester, Vermont. Joseph claimed to have changed, and instead of material pursuits, he was using seer stones in acts of spirituality.[8]

Joseph said that he made his last annual visit to the hill in Manchester on September 22, 1827, taking Emma with him. He claimed to have found the golden plates and hidden them. Several days later he retrieved them. He said the angel commanded him not to show the plates to anyone else but to publish their translation, a religious record of indigenous Americans.[9]

Richard Lyman Bushman, in his laudable book, *Joseph Smith: Rough Stone Rolling*, wrote of the golden plates, "For most modern readers, the plates are beyond belief, a phantasm, yet the Mormon sources accept them as fact."[10] For those strong in the faith, the story resonates with spiritual significance.

Joseph, who at this point did not know how to write, transcribed the characters that he said were engraved on the plates. Joseph dictated a translation to his wife using what he called the Urim and Thummim, a pair of "three-cornered diamonds" bound like spectacles in silver bows.[11]

In February 1828, Martin Harris began assisting Joseph in tran-
scribing. A blanket was raised on a rope dividing Joseph from Harris.
Joseph would place the seer stones in the bottom of a tall hat, and then
he would read out his translation of what he termed "Reformed Egyptian." Joseph warned Harris that if he dared look at him or examine the
plates that God would strike him down.[12]

Joseph, using the Urim and Thummim, continued to dictate to
Harris until mid-June 1828, when Harris began having doubts about
the project. Harris convinced Joseph to let him take the existing 116
pages of manuscript to Palmyra to show a few family members. Harris
promptly lost the manuscript (or possibly his disbelieving wife destroyed
it), and there was no other copy.[13]

Joseph said that as punishment for losing the manuscript the angel
took away the plates and revoked his ability to translate. However, miraculously, Joseph announced that the angel returned the plates to him
on September 22, 1828, and he resumed dictation in April 1829, with a
man named Oliver Cowdery, who replaced Harris as his scribe. The pace
of the work picked up, and the 275,000-word book, which Mark Twain
called "chloroform in print," was finished on April 7, 1829. The book is
difficult reading. The phrase "and it came to pass" is used more than two
thousand times.[14]

Still, it is the work of an inspired and creative mind.

There were eleven witnesses who initially claimed to have seen the
golden plates.[15] According to Joseph, the angel Moroni took back the
plates once he finished his translating. A Palmyra lawyer asked Martin
Harris, "Did you see the plates and the engravings upon them with
your bodily eyes?" Harris replied, "I did not see them as I do that pencil
case, yet I saw them with the eye of faith."[16] The completed Book of
Mormon was published in Palmyra on March 26, 1830, paid for by
Martin Harris, who had to mortgage his farm to meet the costs. On
April 6, 1830, Joseph and his followers formally organized the Church
of Christ. The Book of Mormon brought Smith a kind of fame as well
as opposition from those who remembered his money digging and the
1826 Chenango County trial. He was again arrested and brought to
trial as a disorderly person. He was acquitted, but both he and Cowdery
had to flee to escape a mob.[17]

The Mormons were in conflict with traditional Christianity, and

Mormonism claimed exclusivity as the only true church. For some, this exclusiveness was attractive, and they embraced it with fervor. The church grew.

Joseph moved to Kirtland, Ohio, in 1831. Here religious fervor was in the form of fits, trances, speaking in tongues, and rolling on the ground.[18] It was fertile territory for his new religion. Converts poured in.

In 1832 an angry group of Ohio Mormons (led by the Johnson brothers), fearing his growing power, tarred and feathered Joseph and Sidney Rigdon, his devoted counselor and partner. Joseph was left for dead. It would take Rigdon weeks to recover.[19]

The worst was still to come. Wherever the Mormons went there seemed to be trouble, and with the blindness of sanctimony they blamed their problems on others, "outsiders," on "them."[20]

Joseph adopted communalism, called the United Order, a collectivist program in which members of the church held all things in common.[21] Undeterred by criticism, he built a temple in Kirtland, Ohio, created a bank, and may have had an affair with a serving girl, Fanny Alger. The bank went broke within a month, leaving many Mormons in poverty. He survived accusations of an affair.

After a warrant for banking fraud was issued for his arrest in January 1838, Joseph prudently fled Ohio for Missouri.[22]

Chapter 3

MISSOURI MASSACRE

We can take persecution because we know the purpose
behind it. The purpose is to glorify God.

—Billy Graham

Their church renamed the Church of Jesus Christ of Latter-day Saints, many of the band settled in Caldwell County, Missouri, and established the town of Far West, the "City of Zion." Disputes erupted between the Mormons and their Missouri neighbors when the Mormons gained political power and began to settle in the surrounding counties.[1] "Few episodes in American religious history parallel the barbarism of the anti-Mormon persecutions" in Missouri, wrote Fawn McKay Brodie.[2]

The church's growing problems may have been due to the fact that the Mormons were going against the American grain. Politically, Joseph Smith would build a large following and announce his intention to run for president, a threat to the established political order. Religiously, the Mormon upstarts claimed to be the one true religion and had a corner on God's own truth. Morally, they would face extreme censure for polygamy.

The church's website has a different explanation: it blames Joseph's persecution on the belief that he *did* have a corner on the truth.[3]

A series of escalating conflicts followed the Mormons wherever they went. The governor of Missouri, Lilburn Boggs, called out 2,500 state militiamen to put down what he alleged to be a "Mormon rebellion." Boggs issued Missouri Executive Order 44, a document known to Mormons as the "Extermination Order." This order was issued on October 27, 1838, and decreed that "the Mormons must be treated as enemies, and must be exterminated or driven from the State if necessary for the public peace—their outrages are beyond all description."[4] A number of Mormons died at the hands of Missouri mobs, including eighteen at the Haun's Mill Massacre in Missouri in 1838. Joseph was imprisoned, charged with treason, and sentenced to death for exhorting his followers to fight. He and his brother Hyrum eventually bribed a sheriff with a jug of honeyed wine and $800 and escaped.[5]

During Joseph's months in prison, Brigham Young, then president of the church's Quorum of the Twelve Apostles, rose to prominence among the Mormon faithful when he organized the move of about fourteen thousand Saints to Illinois and eastern Iowa.[6] Many of the Mormons in Missouri were forced to sign over their property in Far West in Caldwell County to pay for the militia muster. They were then ordered to leave the state.

Around June 1838, a recent Mormon convert named Sampson Avard formed a covert organization called the Danites or Destroying Angels to intimidate Mormon dissenters and oppose Missouri's anti-Mormon militia. In his book *Rough Stone Rolling*, Bushman writes that the Danites were a secret society, several hundred strong. "Some historians depict the Danites as Joseph's private army, dispatched at his command to expunge enemies of the Church." Bushman goes on to say that many Mormons, even today, blame Avard for the excesses of Danite revenge.[7] The role and extent of this protective vigilance society is still debated, although a number of murders of Mormon enemies are attributed to its members. One of the most prominent of the Danites was Orrin Porter Rockwell, who served as a personal bodyguard both to Joseph and his successor, Brigham Young.

In 1842, as the hated Lilburn Boggs read a newspaper in his home, someone (probably Rockwell) fired through his window and put four balls of buckshot into him, including one to the head. He miraculously survived, but Rockwell was arrested and spent a year in jail under accusations of the attempted assassination of Governor Boggs. Rockwell was released for lack of evidence.[8]

Though it is unclear how much Joseph knew of the Danites' activities, Joseph clearly approved of those of which he did know. After Sidney Rigdon delivered a sermon that implied dissenters had no place in the Mormon community, the Danites forcibly expelled them.[9]

The seeds of martyrdom and being misunderstood were planted especially deep in Missouri, and they would be nurtured to serve the purposes of the church into the twenty-first century.

Chapter 4

GOLDEN PLATES AGAIN

In our cynical world, where suspicion is a necessity, insisting
that something is true is not nearly as powerful as suggesting
that something might be true.

—Thomas King

The golden plates from which the Book of Mormon had been translated now reentered the picture.

Joseph's assertion that the golden plates were written in "Reformed Egyptian" haunt Mormonism to the present day. Reformed Egyptian became problematic in 1835 when a traveling exhibit of Egyptian mummies came to Kirtland. Since Joseph claimed to have translated Reformed Egyptian to produce the Book of Mormon, and claimed to be a seer who could translate all ancient records, he was approached to translate a few characters from the papyri that accompanied the mummies. Joseph set to work.

"That is the handwriting of Abraham, Father of the Faithful," Joseph wrote.[1]

But trouble lay ahead.

The Rosetta Stone, the key to translating Egyptian hieroglyphics, had been discovered in 1799, and by 1837 it had been fully deciphered by Champollion.[2]

In 1858, the Philomathean Society of Philadelphia printed the first translation of texts from the Rosetta Stone.[3] Fourteen Egyptologists examined Joseph's "Abraham" papyri. Their conclusions all lead to one answer: Joseph Smith was ignorant of the Egyptian script.

In 1967 eleven fragments of Joseph's papyri made their way to the Metropolitan Museum in New York City. They were again examined, and scholars confirmed the earliest appraisals: these were simple funerary documents found in thousands of Egyptian graves.[4]

Egyptologists identified them as documents from the Book of the Dead, hence the reason the papyri were found in coffins. The papyri are dated about 1,500 years after Abraham's time. However, Joseph's translation of the "Abraham Roll" continues to be published as the "Book of Abraham" in one of the church's sacred canons, the Pearl of Great Price.[5]

In 2014, an online essay by the LDS Church obfuscates the issue. It claimed that since most of the papyri had long ago vanished and are presumed destroyed, it is impossible to prove or disprove whether it is a translation from the Book of Abraham, as claimed by Joseph Smith.[6]

Bushman, in *Rough Stone Rolling*, wrote of Joseph, "The signal feature of his life was his sense of being guided by revelation. Only a Mormon reader would say bluntly, 'God revealed a heaven with three degrees of glory,' without any disclaimer. Out of respect for the varied opinions of readers, it would seem judicious to compromise with 'Joseph Smith *purportedly* received a revelation about a heaven with three degrees of glory.'"[7]

Chapter 5

POLYGAMY AND BAPTISM FOR THE DEAD

So many times in the history of Mormon polygamy, the outside world thought it had the movement on the ropes only to see it flourish anew.

—Scott Anderson

The Mormons were driven from various communities in Ohio, Missouri, and Illinois, often with bloodshed. Opposition was regarded as proof of their righteousness. With the excesses of the Missouri government and the Haun's Mill Massacre of Mormons in 1838, many American newspapers were sympathetic to the Mormons.[1]

Joseph moved his flock to Commerce, Illinois, in 1839. The church purchased land and renamed the city Nauvoo (from the Hebrew "beautiful plantation").[2] From Nauvoo, Brigham Young and other Mormons were sent to Europe where they found fertile fields in proselytizing among the poor.[3]

By 1844 Nauvoo had a population of twelve thousand, about the same as Chicago.[4]

Meanwhile, a wealthy and influential convert, Illinois quartermaster general John C. Bennett, used his connections in the Illinois legislature to obtain an unusually liberal charter for the new city. The charter granted the city virtual autonomy. Joseph made Bennett assistant president of the church, and Bennett was elected Nauvoo's first mayor.[5]

The charter also authorized the Nauvoo Legion, an autonomous Mormon militia whose actions were limited only by state and federal constitutions. "Lieutenant General" Smith and "Major General" Bennett became its commanders, thus controlling by far the largest body of armed men in Illinois.[6]

In 1841, Joseph began revealing the doctrine of plural marriage to a few of his closest male associates, including Bennett, who used it as an excuse to seduce numerous women. When embarrassing rumors of "spiritual wifery" got out, Joseph forced Bennett's resignation as mayor. In retaliation, Bennett wrote lurid exposés of life in Nauvoo.[7]

During this period Joseph married at least thirty-three women, including Helen Mar Kimball, a girl of fourteen. He lied to his wife Emma about it, but rumors persisted and contributed to her unhappiness, although she stood by him until his death.[8]

Joseph manifested a number of new doctrines during his busy first years in Nauvoo, including baptism for the dead, an indispensable requirement for the departed to enter the Kingdom of God. Among the first to be baptized in this way were the signers of the Declaration of Independence.[9] (Adolf Hitler was baptized by proxy on December 10, 1993, and sealed to his parents, Alois Hitler and Klara Poelzl, on March 12, 1994.)[10]

Joseph flexed his political muscle while in Nauvoo. He petitioned Congress to make the city an independent territory with the right to call out federal troops in its defense. When unsatisfied with answers from politicians regarding defending the Mormons, he announced his own third-party candidacy for president. He wanted a theocracy, which he called a "Theodemocracy, where God and people hold the power to conduct the affairs of men in righteousness."[11]

His presidential platform included freeing the slaves, turning prisons into institutions of higher learning, and, instead of jail sentences, putting scofflaws to work building roads and on public works. He advocated diminishing the size of Congress while reducing their pay to that of a farmer.[12]

In the spring of 1844 Joseph appeared to be riding high. His candidacy for president seemed to lift him above the church's internal conflicts and politics.[13]

Hidden in the faith-promoting work of many Mormon scholars is the fact that dissidents within his ranks were dealt with harshly by Joseph. Sensitive to criticism, Joseph excommunicated all the counselors in the First Presidency, the faith's highest-ranking leaders, except for his brother, Hyrum. The message was clear: don't cross the boss. As Will Bagley has written, frontier Mormonism feared dissent as much as it valued unity. There are estimates that nearly one-half of all those converting to Mormonism in the early days were apostates who turned elsewhere for spiritual succor.[14]

Chapter 6

A PRESS DESTROYED AND PERIL TO THE PROPHET

Censorship is to art as lynching is to justice.
—Henry Louis Gates Jr.

Danger awaited, and Joseph had fed its flames. The doctrine of plural marriage was about to bring the house of Nauvoo down.

William Law was Joseph's first counselor and was "as steadfast and incorruptible as John C. Bennett had been treacherous and dissolute," according to Fawn McKay Brodie.[1] Law had come from Canada and had money. He poured it into construction and steam mills, doing more than anyone to help build the city. For a time he swallowed his resentment over Joseph's monopoly of managing Nauvoo real estate. Law thought it unseemly for a man alleging to be a prophet of God to threaten excommunication for any who would purchase land without his consent. Law became convinced Joseph was using church funds to buy more land, which he then sold to converts at inflated prices. Law came to mistrust Joseph's business sense and refused to invest in Joseph's plan to publish a revised version of the Bible.[2]

An economic rift became a theocratic one. He watched with alarm as Joseph increased his number of wives. The final fracture may have been when Joseph approached Law's wife, Jane, to join him in spiritual marriage. Law called for reformation of the church and threatened to quit unless Joseph went before the High Council and confessed his sins and promised repentance.

"I'll be damned before I do," Law quoted Joseph's response.[3]

Law was told privately that the Danites, the Destroying Angels, were going to get him.[4]

There were other disgruntled Mormons, especially those whose wives had been approached by Joseph and proposed to for marriage. Law joined this group, perhaps in part to insure his own safety. The schism grew. The dissidents began meeting (Joseph inserted his spies among them). Lawsuits flew and so did the mud. Joseph had weathered storms of internal dissent before, and he was certain this one would pass, too.[5]

But Law and Dr. Robert Foster had bought a printing press. In an effort to reform the church, they created a newspaper called the *Nauvoo Expositor*. On June 7, 1844, they published their one and only issue.[6]

Its main story was that of an English girl who had converted to Mormonism and who had then been indoctrinated into polygamy by Joseph. The newspaper attacked on other fronts. It opposed Joseph's attempt to unite the church and state, was against his grasping for political power, and was against his financial maneuverings. Finally, the *Expositor* alleged Joseph had approached Law's wife and some teenage girls.[7] Nauvoo held its breath.

Joseph ordered that the newspaper be taken to trial. This was not a trial by jury. Joseph's city council supporters stood up one after another and accused the publishers of seduction, pandering, counterfeiting, and thievery. The council declared that the press be destroyed.[8]

A portion of the Nauvoo Legion marched to the *Expositor*, wrecked the press, and burned the remaining issues of the paper.[9]

It would not be the only time a leader of the church called for burning of printed material that did not keep with the prophet's beliefs. Brigham Young called on church members to burn copies of *Biographical Sketches of Joseph Smith the Prophet, and his Progenitors*, written by Joseph's mother, Lucy Mack Smith, and published in 1853.[10]

The fires burning in the offices of the *Expositor* set off conflagrations of political fury among the Illinois anti-Mormons, who had been waiting for just such a breach of the First Amendment.[11]

The dissident Mormon publishers, fearing for their lives, fled to Warsaw and Carthage, Illinois. One of them gave a detailed story of the destruction of the press to Thomas Sharp, editor of the virulently anti-Mormon Warsaw *Signal*, adding to it the sensational news that Orrin Porter Rockwell had been the shooter of Governor Boggs in Missouri and that there had been the seduction of many young Mormon women done by the Mormon hierarchy in the name of God.[12]

Sharp's headlines on June 12 stated, "War and Extermination Inevitable. CITIZENS ARISE, ONE AND ALL!!! Can you stand by and suffer such INFERNAL DEVILS! to rob men of their property and Rights, without avenging them? We have no time for comments; every man will make his own. LET it be made with POWDER AND BALLS!!!"[13]

Couriers brought word from Warsaw and Carthage that angry crowds were gathering.

Joseph assembled thousands of loyal Mormons, whom he asked, "Will you stand by me to the death?"

"Aye," came the answer in unison.[14]

As would happen so often in years to come, including into the twenty-first century, the church leaders failed to see the implications that would follow their acts of suppression.

Or did they?

In fact, some sociologists have suggested that the church thrives because it perceives itself to be embattled. Without conflict, tension, and threat, Mormonism would lose its identity and purpose.[15]

When Thomas Ford, the Illinois governor, decided to investigate the burning of the *Expositor*, he found that outside militias had already gathered under local constables and were preparing to attack Nauvoo. Ford demanded that Joseph and everyone else involved in the destruction of the paper be taken by a constable and placed in the Carthage jail to await trial.[16]

Around noon on June 24, 1844, Joseph and Hyrum and a handful of other Mormons started for Carthage where Joseph was to be tried. They were accompanied by non-Mormon militia from McDonough County, who met them en route.[17]

When they arrived in Carthage, the scene turned ugly. The McDonough County militia fell away, and the Mormons were surrounded by troops from Warsaw and Carthage, who taunted with epithets and derision.

"Stand away, you McDonough boys, and let us shoot the damned Mormons!"

"God damn you, Old Joe, we've got you now."[18]

Governor Ford was worn down. He was dealing with both flooding on the Mississippi as well as insurrection and a serious breach of the First Amendment.

The two Smith brothers were immediately placed in a large cell on the second floor of the Carthage Jail.[19] Governor Ford came to the jail and talked with Joseph for several hours, according to the eyewitness reports of John Bernhisel and John Taylor. The governor and Joseph came to an agreement on everything but the wrecking of the *Expositor*. "The press in the United States is looked upon as the great bulwark of American freedom," Governor Ford insisted, "and its destruction in Nauvoo was represented and looked upon as a high-handed measure, and manifests to the people a disposition on your part to suppress the liberty of speech and of the press."[20]

Joseph protested that his women had been slandered and called the *Expositor* an "infamous and filthy sheet."[21] Ford told Joseph he would go to Nauvoo to address the Mormons and agreed to take Joseph with him, since the prophet feared that only the governor stood between him and the angry militia outside the jail.[22]

The next day Governor Ford was warned that real trouble was brewing, but the governor dismissed it. Breaking his promise to Joseph, he decided to go to Nauvoo without him. He ordered the troops disbanded.[23]

Willard Richards and John Taylor, both staunch pillars of the Mormon community, were allowed in the jail, and Richards told Joseph that the governor had broken his word. Joseph quickly dashed off a note to assemble the Nauvoo Legion and come and break him out of jail "at all costs." He gave it to Jonathan Dunham and expected him to speed the fifteen miles to Nauvoo. In fact, for inexplicable reasons, Dunham never delivered the message.[24]

Meanwhile, Joseph sent for some wine and sipped a little. Outside the jail they heard shouts and shots. Instead of the Nauvoo Legion coming like the cavalry, it was the Warsaw Militia, fury in their eyes and murder in their hearts. With arms smuggled in by friends, Joseph had a revolver and Hyrum a single-barrel pistol. Taylor and Richards were unarmed. The four men pushed to keep the heavy door of the cell shut, but when a bullet pierced the door, they stood back. The door was forced open. Hyrum was immediately shot in the nose, shouting, "I am a dead man!" as he fell. Four more shots from the militia's muzzles struck his body.[25]

Joseph now fired all six shots at the onrushers. Three misfired, but three struck home. Lead poured into the cell. John Taylor was hit by five bullets, but a potentially fatal shot struck his vest pocket watch, saving his life. Willard Richards, a big man, somehow dodged every shot fired at him and remained unscathed. His pistol empty, Joseph flung it at the oncoming men, crying, "There. Defend yourselves as well as you can."[26] He sprang to the open window of the cell.

"Is there no help for a widow's son?" he cried out.[27]

A ball from a militiaman's musket took him in the back, and he slowly pitched forward. He hung to the sill for an instant. Below, Levi Williams, the colonel in charge of the Warsaw Militia, shouted, "Shoot him! God damn him! Shoot the damned rascal."[28]

Joseph was heard to say, "Oh Lord, my God!" and he fell to the ground.[29]

A militiaman dragged a still-living Joseph against a well in the yard. Colonel Williams ordered four men to fire. As the balls struck, Joseph winced and fell forward, landing on his face. The same militiaman who had propped him against the well came at Joseph with a knife, intending to cut off his head. It is Mormon legend that at that moment the clouds parted and the late-evening sun sent a beam down on the prophet as he lay bleeding. "The arm of the ruffian that held the knife fell powerless," said William Daniels, a witness who eventually joined the Mormon Church. "The muskets of the four who fired fell to the ground, and they all stood like marble statues, not having power to move a single limb of their bodies. By this time most of the men had fled in great disorder. I never saw so frightened a set of men before."[30]

Joseph's death would come to be known as "the martyrdom."[31]

How to define the founder of Mormonism has been a question with a thousand different answers since his death. Perhaps the best one is, "Joseph Smith did not offer himself as an exemplar of virtue," wrote Bushman in *Rough Stone Rolling*. Rather, "it was his iron will that brought the church, the cities and the temples into existence."[32]

The murder of Joseph Smith was due to his destruction of a newspaper.

Brigham Young, successor to Smith, vowed that it was inevitable that Joseph Smith's blood, and the blood of all martyrs to the faith, would be atoned for. Their blood, he said, was "crying to God, day and night, for vengeance."[33]

An oath of vengeance was sworn by every Mormon beginning in 1845 if they went through the temple endowment ceremony. It was not until 1930 that the temple endowment ceremony was changed to exclude the blood atonement ritual.[34]

"Modern Mormon authorities insist blood atonement was a 'rhetorical device' and 'has never been practiced by the Church at any time,' but historian Juanita Brooks concluded that blood atonement was a 'literal and terrible reality.[35] Brigham Young advocated it and preached it without compromise,'" wrote Will Bagley in *Blood of the Prophets*.[36]

Blood atonement illustrated the depth of anger held by the church toward its enemies.

Chapter 7

BRIGHAM YOUNG TAKES THE REINS OF A CHURCH IN CHAOS

If your actions inspire others to dream more, learn more, do more and become more, you are a leader.

—John Quincy Adams

Brigham Young had achieved unique status among the Mormon hierarchy, but he was away from Nauvoo on a political mission at the time of Joseph's murder. Meanwhile, thousands of Mormons in Nauvoo were being tugged and pulled by men claiming to be the next leader of the church.

Brigham returned and convinced most of Nauvoo's Mormons to accept the Twelve Apostles as collective leaders. He headed the Twelve.[1]

He had to unite two distinct factions: the supporters of polygamy and the anti-polygamists. Brigham, devoted to Joseph and his ideals, was determined to carry out the martyred prophet's plans to complete the Nauvoo Temple, expand the practice of polygamy, and establish a politically autonomous Kingdom of God on Earth.[2]

Many saw Brigham Young as a usurper. It was inevitable that schisms would cleft the youthful religion, left in a power void upon the death of Joseph. Brigham moved quickly to consolidate his leadership in light of claims to the presidency of the church by Mormons like Samuel Smith, the prophet's brother, who died of unknown causes within several weeks. Another brother of the prophet, William, accused Brigham of poisoning Samuel. Young had been away on the mission at the time of Samuel's death, so it seemed unlikely that he'd been able to connive to have him killed.[3]

Joseph Smith and Brigham Young were a study in contrasts. Joseph was tall, athletic, with a prominent nose and a retreating forehead. In dress he was a dandy. His rhetoric could soar. Brigham was shorter and barrel-chested. In spite of his forty-plus years, Brigham had a full shock of sandy red hair. Brigham's speech was simple, direct, and forceful. At times it could be coarse. Wisely, he chose not to emulate Joseph.[4]

Brigham still publicly denied that polygamy was being practiced. A pattern of dissent met by excommunication was firming Brigham's hand and would form the basis for keeping the flock in line to the present day.

Brigham bought arms for his military organization, and they were prepared to use them. He conducted surveillance on visitors and ejected dissenters. The threat of impending warfare bonded the Mormons of Nauvoo and consolidated Brigham's position.[5]

Brigham had become his people's leader. He was "passionately devoted to the martyred prophet, and his life's work became carrying out the prophet's plans."[6]

In August 1845, in a protest against a huge win by Mormons in the local elections, mobs began burning Mormon homes in a nearby part of the county. The violence escalated. Time was running out for the Mormons in Nauvoo, and everyone knew it. A delegation from Governor Ford, including Congressman Stephen Douglas, put pressure on Brigham to leave Illinois quickly and peacefully in the spring of 1846. In return, the Mormons were promised protection from their threatening neighbors. Brigham hoped for a reasonable settlement on the sale of Mormon-owned property, but that would not happen.[7]

The Mormons displayed enough willingness to fight that the mobs had backed off. Everyone waited anxiously. As John G. Turner wrote, "Young knew when to cut his losses. The Latter-day Saints would be driven, but their expulsion felt like a deliverance from a far worse fate."[8] Young was ready to lead the Mormons from their Egypt, and he set about making plans.

By 1845 Brigham was thinking of Upper California as a new Zion for Mormonism. This was a vast slab of geography claimed by Mexico— present-day California, Nevada, Arizona, and Utah. The Mormons decided to go.[9]

In December 1845, a grand jury in Springfield, Illinois, after hearing persistent reports of counterfeiting by the Mormons, indicted Brigham and eleven other church members. The church probably was counterfeiting. Clearly, cash was hard to come by in Nauvoo.[10]

The law came calling again, determined to arrest Brigham. In an act Brigham would love to tell in later years, William Miller, an early convert to Mormonism, appeared outside the temple and deceived the officers into believing he was Brigham Young. They arrested Miller and took him to Carthage before a former member of the church revealed the error.[11]

Brigham wanted to complete the Nauvoo Temple before leaving and rushed the work throughout the fall and winter of 1845. By early December the temple rooms were ready.[12]

"For Young, the Nauvoo Temple was central to his furtherance of Joseph Smith's theology, built around sealing together patriarchal families headed by faithful saints exalted as priests, kings, and—one day—gods," according to Turner.[13]

Brigham was furious when the secrets of the temple ceremony—including "grips and tokens"—were publicly displayed as he was greeted on the street by those who had been part of the temple rituals. The penalty for revealing the ceremonies was "gruesome death."[14]

Brigham could blast his flock with criticism, but he also had a playful side and was not above joking with his followers. He encouraged the presence of music, dancing, and spiritual beauty in the temple. On December 17, having completed the day's rituals, "[w]hile under the power of animation," Young "danced before the Lord." Young was torn about combining merriment with spiritual zeal, but dancing, plays, and music would become part of the heritage of the church.[15]

As the days in Nauvoo dwindled, Brigham stepped up his courtship and secretly began adding more wives.[16] Young's fifty-five wives ranged in age from sixteen to sixty, and he continued marrying until 1872. He had fifty-six children by sixteen of his wives, of which forty-six lived to adulthood. Not all of his marriages resulted in sexual liaisons; some of his wives were widows in need.[17]

Interestingly, in 1845, John D. Lee (who will later figure prominently in this narrative) vied with Brigham for the hands in marriage of two sisters, Louisa and Emmeline Free. Brigham saw Emmeline and fell in love with her. Lee would tell a council that "Brigham told him if he would give up Emeline [sic] to him he would uphold him in time and eternity & he never should fail, but that he would sit at his right hand in his kingdom."[18] Swapping the sexual for the spiritual was good enough for Lee. Brigham married the pretty Emmeline when she was nineteen, and Lee apparently had no resentments, as he came to view Brigham as a surrogate father.[19]

Chapter 8

WESTWARD HO

For West is where we all plan to go some day.

—Robert Penn Warren

"We will go to a land where there are at last no old settlers to quarrel with us," Young prophesied.[1]

He would leave to create an empire and take a stand in the unsettled West. He wanted to be "500 miles from here" ten days hence. In fact, three hundred miles of mud lay between him and the next place where they would temporarily settle on the Missouri River.[2]

For the several months thousands of Mormons straggled out of Nauvoo and slogged west through the churned-up mud, pursued by vigilantes, with some Mormons being whipped. They sold their homes for pennies on the dollar, and many gave them without recompense as they fled in haste and fear. Their Illinois neighbors who descended on Nauvoo took over their homes and remaining property.[3]

As they headed west, a new chapter was about to begin in the turbulent relationship between the Church of Jesus Christ of Latter-day Saints and the federal government. It has been carried into the twenty-first century.

Brigham Young, contrary to some Mormon apocrypha, knew exactly where he was taking his flock. Young and other apostles had pored over maps of the American West. They studied John C. Fremont's narratives of his travels to California, which included a section of what he called the Great Interior Basin, part of Mexico's Upper California. Fremont described a vast land of mountain ranges and sage valleys, a "region peopled . . . miserably and sparsely."[4] By early 1846 Brigham knew where they would settle—a valley near Utah Lake.[5]

The Mormon leaders wanted a sanctuary free of white settlements. They'd learn to deal with nature and the elements. In the Great Basin the Mormons could establish an autonomous religious and political society. It was as far away from the federal government in the District of Columbia as it was from its Mexican landlord. Brigham hoped to make it to the Great Basin in the fall of 1846.[6]

The Mormon refugees began crossing the Mississippi on February 6, 1846. For weeks they straggled across southern Iowa, the wagons like a string of ants between the Mississippi and the Missouri Rivers.[7]

Progress of the demoralized Mormons was slow. The weather was terrible; hunger and disease beset the pioneers. Brigham realized that the snow and mud of late winter and spring would prevent the wagons from reaching the Great Basin that year.[8]

Along the trail, Brigham goaded his struggling flock with patience and good humor—or spiritual bullying. At one point he threatened dissenters with a "slap of revelation."[9] He brooked no challenges to his leadership. William Clayton observed with jealousy how much lumber Brigham and other top leaders received to build their comfortable wagons, but he wisely kept his anger to himself. Brigham Young was an outstanding organizer, and it was this attribute that finally allowed him to consolidate his leadership, leaving behind any doubt about who should replace Joseph Smith.[10]

The Mormons saw much of this arduous trial through the prism of the Old Testament. Brigham was their Moses. The hard-frozen Mississippi River enabled many to cross with ease; there was also the Miracle of the Quail, in which many wild birds (possibly passenger pigeons) settled among the Mormons and were easily subdued and eaten by the starving pioneers. They were like ancient Israelites, and they literally believed the blood of Israel flowed in their veins (Mormon admiration for Israel and the Jews is founded in this belief). They were God's chosen, and that sustained them during the toilsome path.[11]

By spring 1846, more than 3,500 Mormons straggled into the area around Council Bluffs, Iowa, living in tents and wagons.[12] They were soon to have another miracle of sorts, and it came in the form of an emissary from the US government. Captain James Allen of the US Army arrived in Missouri in June 1846, representing Colonel Stephen Kearny's Army of the West. He brought with him news that the United States was at war with Mexico. President James Polk was in an expansionist mood. He'd secured through treaty a large portion of the Oregon Territory from Great Britain and was set upon acquiring California. Polk ordered American soldiers to advance on New Mexico and Upper California. Captain Allen wanted to recruit five hundred Mormons to join the army. The president authorized him to enlist Mormons in order to "conciliate them, attach them to our country and prevent them from taking part against us."[13]

Distrust ran deep about Captain Allen's mission. Many saw it as a ploy to draw off the strongest males in the Mormon contingent. Brigham, however, saw it as an opportunity. He negotiated with the army to winter on Indian land across the Missouri in what is now part of the community of Florence in North Omaha. They called it Winter Quarters, and from here they would jump off to begin the crossing of the plains.[14]

The church was deeply in debt, and the offer of $30,000 for Mormon soldiers clinched the deal. The enlistees would turn much of the cash over to Brigham in return for his promise to care for their families in their absence. Brigham's powers of persuasion resulted in the creation of the Mormon Battalion, and five hundred Mormon men set off for Fort Leavenworth.[15]

America's one and only exclusively religious army made an arduous march to California, fought a battle in which they killed a dozen cattle at the San Pedro River in Arizona, captured Tucson, and suffered no casualties.[16] Most returned to Great Salt Lake City in 1847–48, but a few stayed to work the gold fields in the Sierra Nevada.

Meanwhile, at Winter Quarters, Brigham was consolidating his wives into a family of sorts. It was like herding cats; some chose to leave him. In one case he pushed one from the fold for revealing to others of the temple ceremony, calling her mouth "an open sepulcher."[17]

Polygamy, called celestial marriage, was discreetly practiced but was common knowledge among the Mormons. For the public at large it was kept a secret.[18] The world had yet to hear the announcement that God had condoned plural wives for members of the Church of Jesus Christ of Latter-day Saints.

+++

About four hundred Saints died during the winter of 1846–47.[19] Life in rude huts and shelters at Winter Quarters was miserable. They fought disease, cattle theft by Indians, and browbeating by Brigham who told them to stop complaining or else they could decamp and go back to Missouri, a notion that shook even the hardiest of Mormon pioneers.

Finally on April 16, they got underway with 143 men and three women, plodding along barely fifteen miles a day. Brigham's train had started earlier than most of the four thousand emigrants who would take the Oregon Trail west during the summer of 1847. The "Mormon Moses" also traveled along the less used north bank of the Platte River.[20] They met the occasional trader and sighted Pawnee and Sioux Indians. The Pawnees stole some of their horses, but while they lived in fear of Indian attacks, none materialized.[21]

In early June they reached Fort Laramie, six hundred miles from Winter Quarters. They pushed on soon after arriving, hoping to stay ahead of the rush of emigrants who would be using the grass near the trail needed for the livestock, including the oxen necessary for pulling the wagons.[22]

The band crossed the Continental Divide at South Pass, Wyoming, and pushed on. In late June the party encountered two seasoned western mountain men, Jim Bridger and Moses Harris. Both knew the region better than anyone, excluding Indians.[23]

Bridger recommended that the party make for the area between Utah Lake and Great Salt Lake. Harris suggested they'd do better in the area of the Bear River's Cache Valley northeast of Great Salt Lake.[24] Brigham took Bridger's advice—mostly. He wanted to avoid agitating the Ute Indians who had winter encampments around Utah Lake. So he chose the area around Great Salt Lake and urged his oxen forward.

They crossed the Green River four hundred miles from Fort Laramie and met up with Sam Brannan, who had been dispatched by sea from New York with a group of 230 Mormons to explore and perhaps colonize California. He had come across the Great Basin to meet the incoming party. He encouraged Brigham to move on to California, but Brigham wanted nothing to do with a country already populated and governed by the United States.[25]

They stopped at the rudimentary Fort Bridger, then began one of the most difficult legs of the journey. They followed in the mountainous tracks of the ill-fated Donner Party, which had passed the year before and had become stranded in the early snows in California's Sierras. The Donners had resorted to cannibalism before at last being rescued.[26]

Brigham's party was forced to crisscross streams, climb steep hills, and lock their wheels to creep down steep washes.[27] Brigham became ill on this last leg of the journey. On July 12, he took to his bed in his wagon. His apostles took charge.[28]

An advance party reached Salt Lake Valley on July 22. Brigham arrived on July 24, 1847, a date celebrated in Utah as Pioneer Day. The state flag bears both the date of Mormon arrival in Salt Lake as well as the date Utah was admitted to the union, 1896. It is a symbol of the melding of church and state.[29]

Brigham, now recovered, considered the efforts of the Saints both prophetic and practical. He set up work parties, built houses, rebaptized everyone in the first wagon party to arrive, and encouraged the Mormons to avoid commerce with outsiders. They would grow and make everything they would need.

He was still fighting a rearguard action with some of his apostles. He had to reassert his power. Orson Pratt claimed the apostles could overrule Brigham. Brigham became agitated. Pratt likened the apostles to Congress. "Shit on Congress," said Brigham.[30]

Ultimately the apostles confirmed the existence of a First Presidency, with Brigham as president supported by two counselors.[31]

By the fall of 1848, four thousand Mormons had settled in the Great Basin, the majority a few miles distant from the eastern shore of the Great Salt Lake.[32]

Seven clear, cold creeks flowed into the valley from heavily timbered Wasatch Mountains, and the river bottoms in the valley contained stands of cottonwood, willow, box elder, and gamble oak.

It was at the mouth of City Creek Canyon that Brigham built the Lion House and the Beehive House, and it was from this point that he would lay out the city with wide streets and lots big enough for a house and a garden. The Mormons believed the Wasatch Mountains provided a ten-thousand-foot-tall bulwark against the encroachment of the hated gentiles and the federal government.

John Pulsipher wrote in 1848, "The Lord Almighty is preparing a scourge for this nation. The blood of the Saints is crying out from the ground for vengeance on that wicked nation. . . . We are glad the mountain valies [sic] are so far off as they are."[33]

Word had come in 1848 that Utah was no longer a Mexican territory. The Treaty of Guadalupe-Hidalgo ceded "Upper California" to the United States, and Brigham found himself serving as governor under an "irredeemably corrupt government," wrote historian John G. Turner.[34]

The mountains would not stop the rush of forty-niners, nor would they prove insurmountable to the federal government and the long arm of the law. Even newspapermen would make it over the rocky passes and narrow clefts.

In order to secure the Mormons' geopolitical power in the Great Basin, Brigham sent settlers as far as Las Vegas Springs and San Bernardino to the south, north and west to Yellowstone country in Idaho, Wyoming, and Montana, and onto the western slope of the Rockies in Colorado. Brigham never again wanted Mormon towns to be surrounded by gentile communities. The hostility the Saints had endured in Ohio and Missouri was a strong and bitter memory. Within a few years the Mormons had laid claim to a thousand-mile corridor of colonies and forts in the American West. These included the Iron Mission west of Cedar City, and the Cotton Mission in St. George.[35] Both towns would be implicated in the Mountain Meadows Massacre of 1857.

Chapter 9

PAIUTE INDIANS

> Yet only the atrocities of the conquered are referred to as criminal acts; those of the conqueror are justified as necessary, heroic, and even worse, as the fulfillment of God's will.
>
> —Jim Fergus

An important part of the work of these colonizers was to evangelize the Lamanites, the term the Book of Mormon applied to Native Americans. Brigham is famously noted for his comment, "It's better to feed them than fight them."[1] In fact his policy, as BYU historian Howard Christy calls it, was an "open hand and mailed fist."[2] The Indians had the choice of becoming enemies or dependent on the Mormons.

It had been Joseph Smith's dream to form a union between the Saints and the Indians. Together they would move on the wicked world and "put to flight those that have Oprest them."[3] The intent of the golden plates was to bring knowledge of their ancestors to American Indians. This would bring them to believe in Mormon gospel and Jesus Christ. Until changes made in 1981, the Book of Mormon assured the dark-skinned Indians that once they repented and became righteous, they would become "a white and delightsome people again."[4]

Wrote Historian Will Bagley, "The Mormons faced no greater challenge than that posed by their Ute, Paiute, Goshute and Shoshoni neighbors."[5] As they settled the fertile valleys, they pushed out the Indians.

The act creating Utah Territory specified that the governor would serve as ex-officio superintendent of Indian affairs. That would be Brigham Young. The federal government appointed three agents in 1851 to work under Brigham's supervision.[6]

The agents didn't like the way Brigham did things with the Indians. The Mormons "at first conciliated the Indians by kind treatment; but once they got a foothold they began to force their way. The consequence was a war with the Indians, and in many instances, a most brutal butchery," wrote subagent Jacob H. Holeman.[7] "At best, any money Brigham spent on the Indians was to proselytize them and to promote the interests of the church," according to Holeman.[8]

John D. Lee's angry memoir says, "The only money [Brigham] ever spent on the Indians was when we were at war with them."[9]

And yet, Mormons had come to believe that the Indians, the bad Lamanites who fought the good Nephites in the Book of Mormon, would be their foremost allies. Indians would be a fearsome weapon against their enemies. Within six months of Joseph Smith's death the Saints were asserting that Indians would play a major role in avenging the death of Joseph.[10]

Brigham vowed that the Mormons and the Indians would join forces and bring vengeance on the persecuting gentiles, a theme to which he would return again and again for the first ten years the settlers were in Utah.[11] The Indians viewed the Mormons as visitors, bound to leave sooner or later.

In southern Utah lived a tribal band called Nuwuvi or Paiutes. Most of them lived along the Santa Clara, Virgin, and Muddy Rivers. They lived in small family groups raising corn, squash, beans, melons, sunflowers, gourds, and wheat in small plots. Hunter-gatherers, they moved with the seasons.[12]

Magotsu Creek, which flows through Mountain Meadows in the southwest corner of Utah, was named for the country of the Matootshats band of Paiutes, who headquartered south of Mountain Meadows at a hot spring near present Veyo. We will return to them later.

Brigham never forgot the prophecy of the Indians partnering to defeat the gentiles, but he declared that they were "hopeless cases and would die and be damned."[13] At a meeting of the Council of Fifty on May 12, 1849, he dropped any pretext of a practical approach to the local tribes. They would never be converted to Mormonism. It didn't matter "whether they kill one another off or Some body else do[es] it."[14] In fact, he wanted them moved to a reservation, preferably on the eastern slope of the Sierra Nevada some three hundred miles west.[15]

The Indians were soon the subject of complaints by the Mormons. Campsites and water sources were points of conflict, and skirmishes soon turned bloody.

Brigham sent John M. Higbee and thirty-three men to build a settlement at the mouth of the Provo River where it entered Utah Lake. This was traditional Ute fishing ground. A young Indian met the settlers and blocked the trail with his horse. The settlers pleaded that they should try to live together. The young Indian made them take a vow that the white people would not take any of their rights or try to drive them away.[16]

The settlers broke the vow. Tensions grew, and several Mormon men brutally killed an Indian who caught them poaching a deer. At a council held in Great Salt Lake City on January 31, 1850, Parley Pratt, whom we will visit later in this narrative, thought it would be best to kill all the Indians. It was put to a vote. Every hand went up in a vote to exterminate them.[17]

Shortly after, a battle raged on the shore of Utah Lake. One Mormon man was fatally shot, and another man was wounded. Seventeen Ute prisoners were executed on the ice of Utah Lake, and their wives and children were taken as slaves.[18]

Some idea of the treatment of some Indians was noted in the *Deseret News* of 1852, part of a series of letters by Mrs. B. G. Ferris, a Mormon:

> They [the settlers] came to an open rupture with these miserable natives in the winter of 1850, and killed some of them in various skirmishes. He said it was very similar to chasing wild beasts, and that they would often stumble upon the poor creatures while burrowed, as it were, in the thick grass and concealed in clumps of willows. They captured quite a number of squaws and children, and provided for them till spring—some of the squaws, however, stole away and lay in the hot-spring lake, near the city, to keep warm—just keeping their heads out of water, and in this condition they would catch the wild fowl swimming around them and devour them raw.[19]

Brigham acknowledged that the Mormons were on Indian land, using their water and grass, and growing crops on Indian soil. But his policy toward the Indians continued unabated. Indians could surrender and supplicate or resist and be killed.

In late 1849 Apostle Parley Pratt was sent south from Great Salt Lake City with twelve wagons and fifty-two Mormon men. With him was a diarist,

Isaac C. Haight, who noted that the Ute Indian response to a measles epidemic was to shoot "a small Pah Uta boy as a sacrifice that the sickness must stop."[20] As with others, we will return to Haight and his role at Mountain Meadows in 1857.

The party crossed over the rim of the Great Basin into a landscape the likes of which the Mormons had never seen before. It was rough, with jumbled mountains, grassless plains, and perpendicular beds of sandstone.[21]

Then they ascended the Santa Clara River from its confluence with the Virgin River, coming upon Mountain Meadows. It was fertile, studded with pinion and juniper trees, a fine, clear stream, and rolling pastures. Haight called it one of the loveliest places in the Great Basin.[22]

The Paiutes in the area were solicitous. They offered to trade a vast tract of land for a knife if the Mormons would settle among them and help them raise corn, although the Mormons found dams, irrigated fields, and stands of corn eleven feet high.[23]

After returning to Salt Lake, Pratt told Brigham of the nearby abundance of iron ore and coal, resulting in Brigham dispatching 120 men to establish the Iron Mission under the command of Apostle George A. Smith, a cousin of the prophet Joseph. He'd earned the affectionate rubric of the "Potato Saint" during the difficult winter of 1847 when he discovered that raw potatoes would prevent scurvy among the shivering pioneers at Winter Quarters.[24] He looked like a potato himself, tall, weighing over three hundred pounds, round, and awkward. George A Smith was also known for his fiery rhetoric that could inflame the passions of the faithful. In spite of his inability to mount a horse, he would eventually be named brigadier general commanding the Nauvoo Legion in southern Utah. The Potato Saint knew he was ugly, but he was also vain. Outlandish clothes and a poor-fitting red wig completed his exhibition of bad taste. When he took out his false teeth, observant Indians dubbed him "Man Who Comes Apart." George would also play a role in the drama that would unfold in the next few years.[25]

The Iron Mission settlers founded a village called Cedar Fort, which would in a short time be renamed Cedar City. They also founded and built Fort Louisa, which would become Parowan. Nearby coal outcroppings were mined to smelt the iron ore.[26]

Pretty much everyone hated being part of the Iron Mission. John

D. Lee offered $2,000 to be released from the mission, but Brigham declined it.[27]

The Iron Mission turned out a low-grade pig iron beginning in 1852. For six more years they struggled to produce iron under the direction of the inexperienced but willing Isaac Haight. They were never able to produce enough to make the mission economical.[28]

It brought the Mormons into closer contact with the Southern Paiutes, who were grateful when the Mormons halted the ceaseless raids on their band by Utes and Mexicans looking for slaves. In a kind of quid pro quo, Brigham decided that he would send missionaries to the Southern Paiutes.[29]

Dimick Huntington was among those charged with learning the Southern Paiute dialect. Huntington had solid ties to the Mormon leadership. He had sealed (married) two of his sisters to Joseph Smith. The sisters married Brigham Young and Apostle Heber Kimball after Joseph's death. In 1857 Huntington was the official federal government interpreter for the territory, a job that paid the princely sum of five dollars a day in gold. Huntington handled Brigham's "most dangerous and delicate" Indian problems.[30]

Brigham, as Indian superintendent for the territory, also appointed John D. Lee as farmer to the Indians, a federal government post requiring that Lee protect the Southern Paiutes and emigrants from each other. He was to teach them to farm and distribute goods to the Indians.[31]

John D. Lee was born in Illinois in 1812. He had a difficult early life. He was left to a nurse after his alcoholic father abandoned him in 1815, and was cared for by Catholic relatives who took his inheritance (such as it was). At sixteen he became a frontier courier and then a fireman on a Mississippi boat. He fought in the Black Hawk War.[32]

Married in 1833, he was reading the Book of Mormon the night of his daughter's death of scarlet fever in 1837. He moved from Fayette County, Illinois, to be with Joseph Smith in Far West, Missouri. Far West became the headquarters of the Latter-day Saint movement in early 1838 when the prophet Joseph Smith and Sidney Rigdon relocated to the town from the previous church headquarters in Kirtland, Ohio. After Lee became a Mormon, he went on a mission in 1838, preaching the gospel in Ohio, Kentucky, and Tennessee and converting entire families and congregations with his eloquence and passion.[33]

When the anti-Mormon religious wars broke out in Missouri in 1838, Lee heard Rigdon's impassioned speech threatening a "war of extermination."[34] Like other true believers, Lee felt the Mormons were invincible because of the righteousness of their cause. When Brigham took over as president after Joseph's death, Lee was one of those appointed to replace Brigham's opponents on the Council of Fifty. He became clerk for the council as it planned the move west.

Later that year Lee received his patriarchal blessing, a special benediction that traces the recipient's lineage from the Tribes of Israel. It is also a blessing in which the future of its supplicant is predicted.[35]

For Lee, he would have luxuries and power over his enemies. If he lived righteously he would rise on the morning of the first day of the resurrection.[36]

But as Bagley noted, "The blessing carried an odd qualifier: the only act that could prevent Lee's salvation was 'the shedding of innocent blood or consenting thereto.'"[37]

Through the Law of Adoption, a Mormon temple ritual (since abandoned), every member of the priesthood was adopted into the extended families of Mormon authorities. Lee had been sealed to Brigham and in pride began signing his name "J. D. L. Young."[38]

Patriarchal blessing or not, Lee went into the Nauvoo Temple in 1845 for a "second anointing,"[39] which was ever more sacrosanct than the standard endowment. Brigham had added a Pledge of Vengeance to the second anointing ceremony, one in which Lee promised, "I will pray, and never cease to pray, and never cease to importune high heaven to avenge the blood of the Prophets on this nation, and I will teach this to my children, and my children's children unto the third and fourth generations."[40]

In this ceremony, Brigham would "swear by the eternal Heavens . . . I have unsheathed my sword, and will never return it until the blood of the Prophet Joseph and Hyrum, and those who were slain in Missouri, is avenged."[41] For Lee this oath was the more sacred obligation than his patriarchal blessing.

After arriving in Utah, Lee was faced with the previously mentioned dilemma over whether to surrender Emmeline Free to Brigham. Brigham promised Lee that if he'd give up Emmeline, he would uphold Lee "in time and eternity."[42] He was told he would sit at Brigham's right hand in his kingdom. Lee loved Emmeline dearly, according to Bagley, and he reluctantly gave her up to Brigham. She became one of Brigham's favorite wives and bore him ten children.[43]

Bowed but unbroken, Lee took Louisa Free, sister to Emmeline, as one of his nineteen wives. Lee later boasted to George Grant, like a teenage boy, that "he frigged Louisa Free 20 times in one night."[44] He carried on about his sexual prowess, and Grant would later testify that Lee "believed he had the Devil in him."[45] Lee's nineteen wives would give him fifty-six children.

As we shall see, Lee's role as Indian agent would have fatal consequences.

There were sixteen bands of Southern Paiutes as Lee's wards. The largest, the Tonaquints, who numbered about eight hundred, lived on the Santa Clara River. The nominal leader of this band was Tutsegabit. Most of them were older, their children having been taken as slaves by the Utes and Mexicans or otherwise sold.[46] The Mormons may have purchased some, as indicated by this ad from the *Deseret News* of September 18, 1852:

> RAN AWAY from the Subscriber, an Indian BOY, about 12 years old; speaks a little English. Supposed to have gone back to Parowan. Any person giving information where said Boy may be found, or returning him to me, shall be liberally rewarded.
> —CHRISTOPHER MERKLEY, 19TH Ward.[47]

The disorganized Paiutes fought among themselves, sometimes brutally. Jacob Hamblin, a pioneer Mormon living in southern Utah, told how the Santa Clara band avenged the killing of one of their women by the Moapats: "[They] took a Moapats woman, fastened her to a tree, and burnt her."[48]

Hamblin was liked by the Southern Paiutes. He made mush for them. He danced with them. He was a very effective missionary, and Brigham felt they had established a rapport.

Tutsegabit wasn't so sure: "We cannot be good, we must be Paiutes. . . . We want to follow our old customs."[49]

Outsiders visiting the Southern Paiutes saw ominous signs of an alliance with the Mormons. Lieutenant Sylvester Mowry wrote that the Santa Clara band had arms and ammunition, including good rifles. Two years before they had had only bows and arrows. Mowry believed that unless the federal government took steps, the Southern Paiutes would become formidable allies of the Mormons.[50]

In fact, Brigham was not arming all the Indians, only a select few to curry favor. He had laid down the law to the Mormons that guns, powder, and lead were not to be given by the Mormons to any Indians.[51]

The success of the Southern Indian Mission led Brigham to hope that other tribes could be converted and consolidated in the effort to overthrow the federal government in the coming apocalypse. Missionaries were sent to the Crow, Cheyenne, Cherokee, Choctaw, Creek, Hopi, Shoshoni, Navajo, Bannock, and Nez Perce, in addition to all of the Utah tribes.[52]

Brigham said, "The day has come to turn the key of the gospel against the gentiles and open it to the remnant of Israel."[53]

The blood boiled still in some Saints who remembered their treatment in Nauvoo and in Missouri. Patriarchal blessings—blessings bestowed upon the worthy—promised they would lead Indian armies in the Last Days and avenge the blood of the prophets.

As Bagley wrote, "For the Saints, the war at the end of time had already begun."[54]

Chapter 10

A NEW MORMON NEWSPAPER

[H]ostile newspapers are more to be feared than a thousand bayonets.

—Napoléon Bonaparte

WANTED, at our office, flour, wheat, cornmeal, butter, cheese, tallow and pork in exchange for the *NEWS*.[1]

So read the first advertisement in the first issue of the Mormon Church's *Deseret News*, published on June 15, 1850. This time Brigham would control the news the church saw fit to disseminate. There would be no more runaway dissidents scribbling on pages read by the faithful.

Nearly three years after the burning of the Nauvoo *Expositor*, the Quorum of Twelve Apostles, still at Winter Quarters, authorized William W. Phelps to buy a printing press to be taken to their new Great Basin home. Phelps went to Boston and bought a wrought-iron Ramage hand-press, type, and other equipment. In April 1849, the large, heavy press was loaded onto ox-drawn wagons and traveled along the Mormon Trail. In Great Salt Lake City it was set up on the church block just west of Brigham's Beehive and Lion Houses, and was first used to print legal documents necessary in setting up the provisional state of Deseret.[2]

"Deseret" is a term used in the Book of Mormon and is said to mean "honeybee" in the language of the Jaredites, who Mormons believe came to America about the time of the Tower of Babel's construction.[3] The ubiquitous bee and hive are symbols of the church found on the state flag and on public buildings. Numerous businesses carry the name, signifying they are Mormon, or are soliciting Mormon business.

The first issue of the *Deseret News* was eight pages. It included the paper's prospectus, along with news from Congress and a report on the 1849 Christmas Eve fire in San Francisco. Its motto was "Truth and Liberty." In the beginning it was published once a week on Saturdays. The subscription cost $2.50 for six months.[4] Its first editor was Apostle Willard Richards, who had escaped unhurt from the Carthage jail when Joseph was killed.

The Ramage press was also set up so the *News* could print books, booklets, handbills, broadsides, etc. for paying customers and other publishers. The Saints donated old paper and cloth to be recycled into paper for the venture. In the summer of 1854 the first issues of the *News* were published on locally made paper. It was thick and gray. Eventually, Brigham would establish a Rag Gathering Mission and this helped keep the paper going, at least most of the time.[5]

Occasionally an extra would be published, usually displaying a sermon or edict considered important to the brethren.

+++

With the discovery of gold at Sutter's Mill in the foothills of California's Sierra Nevada, Utah became a path heavily beaten by forty-niners headed for the placers and mines. For the impoverished pioneers it was both a bane and a blessing.

The bane: Brigham hated the effect the stream of travelers had on the community. It was hard to keep his flock from joining them. The visitors could be rowdy. Gentiles established businesses in Great Salt Lake City. Worse, disaffected brethren and some Mormon women left with the travelers for the Sierras. Too many brethren were talking of leaving for California, so the boss, as he was known with varying degrees of affection, came down hard.

"There were plenty of 'devils' in the valley . . . that deserved death and should leave before meeting their end," he warned. "Gold seekers and fornicators, leave the valley. . . . [Y]ou are in danger of more than you think of."[6]

Brigham was uneasy; he had expected to rule without interference from gentiles, non-Mormon settlers or the US government, yet he was inundated and his people were distracted during a time when he insisted they concentrate on farming and building a new Zion.

The blessing lay in the fact that the gold seekers had seven hundred desolate miles to travel from Salt Lake to Sutter's Mill and its gold-bearing hills, and they needed to resupply in Great Salt Lake City. The Mormons bought worn horses from the travelers for pennies on the dollar and sold fresh ones for greatly inflated prices. Storekeepers did a booming business selling foodstuffs, clothing, and tack to the stream of California-bound men. The hard currency could not have come at a better time, and it helped keep the creaky Utah economy going during a period of hardship.[7]

Brigham was set on keeping his flock in line and keeping them from the ills that accompanied the boom-and-bust of mining. The Great Basin was an Eden, he said, suitable for building a Mormon community based on agriculture and light manufacturing. He warned the Saints not to go mining. Self-sufficiency was of paramount importance, and he preached it regularly from the pulpit.[8]

"Gold will sink a man to hell," he said.[9]

Brigham was an outstanding organizer, partly because with his left hand he held a carrot and in his right a stick.

By 1850 he had seen to the establishment of an education system, including the University of Utah. A substantial library was established. Mills were built on the creeks running into the valley, and experiments to make sugar and molasses from beets were proving successful. Spinning wheels and carding machines were turning out material for fabric; tanneries were making leather from beef, calf, sheep, and dog skins. Pottery was manufactured. After the difficult early years, when some Mormons resorted to foraging for wild-growing tubers and berries, large fields of grain yielded harvests to sustain the Saints with bread. A foundry was built.[10]

City fathers repealed all licenses for selling beer and intoxicating liquors. However, Brigham owned a distillery that put out a whiskey that Mark Twain called Valley Tan in his book *Roughing It*.[11] Brigham considered it a medicine. The Word of Wisdom—that Saints shall drink no alcohol, tea, or coffee and shall smoke no tobacco—had only been loosely enforced until the Mormons arrived in the Great Basin. Under Brigham it would move from moderate use to abstinence. Brigham's distillery provided medicinal whiskey, but apparently some was consumed for sport.[12]

The tranquility of life in Utah was frequently interrupted by skirmishes with the Indians, especially the Utes under Chief Wakara (Walker). Wakara had organized a tribal cavalry and was skilled at raiding. He spoke English, as well as several Indian dialects. He raided as far west as El Cajon, California, where he stole hundreds—if not thousands—of horses.[13]

It was during this period that Captain John W. Gunnison's Pacific Railroad survey party was exploring west of Fillmore, Utah. On October 26, 1853, a band of Utes massacred Gunnison and eight of his twelve men. Searchers found the mutilated bodies and buried them at the site.[14]

Brigham urged settlers not to go into the canyons alone or "bye places where an Indian can lurk unseen by you, without first exploring and ascertaining that all is safe."[15]

That same year Brigham broke ground for the Salt Lake Temple. Plans were made to dig a canal to carry building stone from a quarry twenty miles away, near the mouth of Little Cottonwood Canyon. It would take forty years for the completion of the building.[16]

Chapter 11

SCAPEGOATING

The search for a scapegoat is the easiest of all hunting expeditions.

—Dwight D. Eisenhower

The LDS Church can never see its wounds as being self-inflicted. Therefore it has a history of scapegoating. An example was its Willie-Martin handcart party disaster.

Today you can drive on good highways about five hours from Salt Lake City to South Pass, Wyoming. This was the portal through which most western-bound wagon parties crossed the Continental Divide.

Leave South Pass and drive eight miles southeast on the Lewiston Road, a well-marked dirt track through rolling sagebrush hills marked with stands of aspen trees. Antelope bark if approached by humans on foot. Golden eagles soar overhead.

You'll arrive at the Willie Handcart Memorial site. Under US Bureau of Land Management supervision, it is maintained by the LDS Church, and members of the church do frequent reenactments of a trek that killed more than two hundred Mormons pulling handcarts. They died because of poor foresight and mismanagement.

Mormon converts, who lacked funds for wagons and oxen in order to come to Utah, were encouraged to use handcarts, beginning in 1856. About three thousand converts from England, Wales, and Scandinavia would make their way across the plains from Iowa City, Iowa (the terminus of the railroad), to Utah in ten different handcart companies. The church established its Perpetual Emigration Fund to provide money for poor emigrants, and Brigham advanced the idea of having the poorer converts come west by pulling handcarts.[1] The cost to bring emigrants to Utah in this way was about one-third of the cost of wagons and teams of oxen or horses.

Built to Brigham Young's specifications, the handcarts had two wheels five feet in diameter and a single axle four and a half feet wide. Empty, each weighed about sixty pounds. Running along the sides of the bed were seven-foot pull shafts ending with a three-foot crossbar at the front. The crossbar allowed the carts to be pushed or pulled. Cargo was carried in a box about three feet by four feet with eight-inch walls. The handcarts generally carried up to 250 pounds of supplies and luggage, though they were capable of handling loads as heavy as five hundred pounds. The handcart companies were organized using the handcarts and sleeping tents as the primary units. Five persons were assigned per handcart, with each individual limited to seventeen pounds of clothing and bedding. Each round tent, supported by a center pole, housed twenty occupants and was supervised by a tent captain. Provisions for each group of one hundred emigrants were carried in an ox wagon.[2]

Two of the companies ran into trouble nearly from the beginning.

The Willie Company and the Martin Company got a late start. In early October the two companies reached Fort Laramie, Wyoming, where they expected to be restocked with provisions. There were no provisions there for them. They cut back food rations, hoping that their supplies would last until help could be sent from Utah. To lighten their loads, the Martin Company cut the luggage allowance to ten pounds per person, discarding clothing and blankets that soon would be desperately needed.[3] A company of returning missionaries passed the party and reached Great Salt Lake City with a message of their distress. Brigham ordered the Saints to mount a rescue mission. On October 7, 1856, the first wagons headed east from Salt Lake to meet the two parties.

Early snow began to fall, fast and thick—a real blizzard that stopped the companies in their tracks. The Willie and Martin companies were running out of food. Temperatures were bitterly cold. The Willie Company was along the Sweetwater River approaching the Continental Divide near South Pass.

The members of the Willie Company began slaughtering the handful of broken-down cattle that still remained. Meanwhile the human death toll mounted.

On October 21 Brigham's advance rescue party reached the company and provided them with food and assistance. Half of the rescue party remained to assist the Willie Company while the other half pressed forward to assist the Martin Company.[4]

The difficulties of the handcart pioneers were not yet over. On October 23, the second day after the main rescue party had arrived, the Willie Company faced the most difficult section of the trail—the ascent up Rocky Ridge. The climb took place during a howling snowstorm through knee-deep snow. That night thirteen emigrants died.[5]

On October 19, the Martin Company was about 110 miles farther east, making its last crossing of the North Platte River near present-day Casper, Wyoming. Shortly after completing the crossing, the blizzard hit them. Many members of the company suffered from hypothermia or frostbite after wading through the frigid river. They set up camp at Red Bluffs, unable to continue forward through the snow.[6]

The Martin Company remained in their camp at Red Bluffs for nine days until three scouts finally arrived on October 28. By the time the scouts arrived, fifty-six members of the company had died. Three days later the main rescue party arrived and helped them on to Devil's Gate.[7]

+++

George D. Grant, who headed the rescue party, reported to President Young,

> It is not of much use for me to attempt to give a description of the situation of these people, for this you will learn from [others]; but you can imagine between five and six hundred men, women and children, worn down by drawing hand carts through snow and mud; fainting by the wayside; falling, chilled by the cold; children crying, their limbs stiffened by cold, their feet bleeding and some of them bare to snow and frost. The sight is almost too much for the stoutest of us; but we go on doing all we can, not doubting nor despairing.[8]

The rescue parties escorted the emigrants from both companies to Utah through more snow and severe weather, and the handcart pioneers continued to suffer death from disease and exposure. When the Willie Company arrived in Great Salt Lake City on November 9, sixty-eight members of the company had lost their lives.[9]

The Martin Company arrived in Great Salt Lake City on November 30; at least 145 members of the company had died. Many of the survivors had to have fingers, toes, or limbs amputated due to severe frostbite.[10]

Who was to blame?

Writer Wallace Stegner described the inadequate planning and imprudent decisions leading to the tragedy in his *Gathering of Zion*:

> In urging the method upon Europe's poor, Brigham and the priesthood would over-reach themselves; in shepherding them from Liverpool to the valley, the ordinarily reliable missionary and emigration organization would break down at several critical points; in accepting the assurances of their leaders and the wishful importunities of their own hope, the emigrants would commit themselves to greater sacrifices than even the Nauvoo refugees; and in rallying from compound fatal error to bring the survivors in, the priesthood and the people of Mormondom would show themselves at their compassionate and efficient best.[11]

Brigham's misbegotten instructions for the emigrants to use handcarts to make their way west resulted in the deaths of more than two hundred men, women, and children.

While the Willie and Martin companies were still making their way to safety, Brigham Young responded to criticism of his own leadership by rebuking his Mormons. In a speech delivered in the Salt Lake Tabernacle on November 2, 1856, we have an example of the angry Brigham berating his critics:

> If any man or woman complains of me or of my Counselors, in regard to the lateness of some of this season's immigration, let the curse of God be on them and blast their substance with mildew and destruction until their names are forgotten from the earth. I never thought of my being accused of advising or having anything to do with so late a start. . . . I do not believe that the biggest fool in this community could entertain the thought that all this loss of life, time and means was through the mismanagement of the First Presidency.[12]

Brigham, as author of the plan, was responsible. The buck had to stop somewhere. Ann Eliza Young, daughter of one of the men in charge of building the carts and later a divorced wife of Brigham Young, described her ex-husband's plan as a "cold-blooded, scheming, blasphemous policy."[13] Angry at Brigham and making money on the lecture circuit, Ann Eliza's motives must be considered.

Howard Christy, professor emeritus and former senior editor of scholarly publications at Brigham Young University, wrote, "It was at once the most ill-advised and tragic, the most heroic, and arguably the proudest single event in the Mormon pioneer experience."[14]

Blaming others would be Brigham's doctrine in 1862 when the dissident Joseph Morris was killed, a man who, with a hundred breakaway followers, would taunt Brigham as a false prophet from their redoubt at the mouth of Weber Canyon. Six died before the dissident rebellion was put down.[15]

Scapegoating would become critical to the Mormon version of the Mountain Meadows Massacre of 1857. The church's inability to squarely face its own history would feed 2013's acts of retribution against the *Salt Lake Tribune.*

Chapter 12

BRIGHAM'S FURY AT THE FEDS AND CARPETBAGGERS

To learn who rules over you simply look to those you cannot criticize.

—Voltaire

Brigham was closer to being an emperor than a governor during the early 1850s. He enjoyed unfettered powers. A theocratic sovereign, he said he could "dictate this community better than any other man."[1] At one point he called for the beheading of a Mormon "thief and swindler" named Ira West.

Hyperbole? No.

The extra-legal proceedings in the West case were a direct outgrowth of calls to cleanse the church, and it was during this time that Brigham expanded on the doctrine of blood atonement.

The idea of atoning in blood had been around since Nauvoo, when a man named Irvine Hodges was murdered by a gang of fellow thieves. Brigham explained that his killers had done a good deed. Since Hodges could do no further evil, it had increased Hodge's chances at redemption.[2] At Winter Quarters Apostle Heber Kimball encouraged adulterers to make confessions and be willing to have their heads cut off.[3] The attempted murder of former Missouri governor Lilburn Boggs was also an act of blood atonement.

At Brigham's call to behead West, Apostle Erastus Snow bluntly said it would have been right for Joseph Smith's faithful followers to have slain those who dissented against his policies in Nauvoo.[4] Brigham vowed not to let disunity reemerge in the Great Basin. He expected his followers to adhere to his every word. When John Pack, a member of the Council of

Fifty, apparently "divulged the secrets of the council," Brigham warned him to leave the valley, intimating his life was in danger.[5] The Destroying Angels were in wait, whetting their blades. Pack begged for forgiveness and offered to have his head cut off as blood atonement if he should ever again break the secrecy of the council.

Writes Turner, "By giving an assembled crowd the license to kill petty criminals like Ira West, Young gave his blessing to what many observers would regard as church-sponsored vigilantism."[6] It also muted dissidents, which was its main purpose.

Brigham "had no intention of separating ecclesiastical from political authority," wrote author John G. Turner.[7] He established a civil government that was in tandem—and indistinguishable—from the hierarchy of the priesthood. In fact, the settlers saw no need for a written constitution. They considered the Quorum of Fifty constitution enough.

In 1848 the Mormons had petitioned Congress to create the Deseret Territory. Brigham and his counselors soon realized with some alarm that if they were granted territorial status, it would give the federal government the power to appoint territorial officials. He wanted nothing less than for the Mormons to run their own affairs.[8]

The church reconsidered the petition and instead held an election calling for the establishment of the state of Deseret in the hopes they could head off federal entry into Mormon country. The Mormons voted unanimously for Deseret's slate of candidates, including Brigham as governor. Deseret State had its own flag, its own currency, and its own army. The General Assembly of Deseret established counties and created courts and laws. They granted special privileges to the church leadership for owning toll roads, ferries, waterways, and canyons. The general assembly also incorporated the Church of Jesus Christ of Latter-day Saints. It empowered them to solemnize marriages, providing legal sanction, at least in the eyes of the state of Deseret, to polygamy.[9]

While Brigham avowed that the US Constitution was divinely inspired, he was quick to follow up with curses for the politicians and the federal government. "Corrupt as hell," he said and predicted the downfall of the US government, which he felt had been unresponsive to Mormon killings and other outrages in Missouri and Illinois.[10]

Washington was aware of the Mormon hegemony in the Great Basin. After a series of negotiations, primarily having to do with compromises on slave states and territories, Congress deemed Utah one of its territories.[11]

To every Mormon's relief, President Millard Fillmore appointed Brigham as governor. In a short time the state of Deseret was dissolved and a new territorial legislature convened to adopt the state of Deseret's laws as its own. God's law had more force than manmade law.[12] However, Brigham's iron grip on the territory's affairs was about to be challenged.

President Fillmore appointed several non-Mormon officials and judges for Utah. Most were nonresidents, and many were incompetent party hacks enjoying patronage.

In Utah Territory, this became a struggle for political supremacy. It would heighten hatreds and renew old fears.

The non-Mormon appointees had no loyalty to the people they governed and quickly fell into conflict with Brigham and the higher minions of the church, in spite of the church's affirmation of its loyalty to the country and the president. The friction was caused in part by the belief that, ultimately, it was the Mormon priesthood that would save America.[13]

The first federal appointees began to arrive in 1851. Broughton Harris, the non-Mormon territorial secretary, arrived in Utah accompanied by Almon W. Babbitt and John Bernhisel, both of whom represented Mormon interests in Washington.[14]

Babbitt was a Mormon who had been in positions of leadership in Kirtland and Nauvoo. He was a lawyer and a polygamist but seemed to rub Mormon authorities the wrong way; he'd been stripped of church privileges four times, each time being restored.[15]

It was clear from the outset that Brigham thought him a poor selection to represent the Mormons in Washington. Brigham believed Babbitt undermined Mormon interests. Babbitt was suspect, in part, because he enjoyed the company of non-Mormons. He was also something of a dandy.

Brigham, in a test of Babbitt shortly after his arrival, demanded Babbitt turn over $20,000, which he had been allotted by the US Treasury, for a courthouse. "Politicians are a stink in my nose," he told Babbitt, and warned, "If you interfere with any of my dictation in the elections it will be the last. . . . You are shitting in my dish and I will lick it out and you too."[16]

A kind of détente was reached. Babbitt actually turned the money over to Brigham for the courthouse, and he signed a proclamation establishing judicial districts. Mormons unanimously elected John Bernhisel to serve their interests in Washington. Babbitt would later be killed on the wagon route east. It would be blamed on either Pawnees or Mormons.[17]

Arriving about this same time was Associate Justice Perry Brocchus of Alabama, another federal appointee. He was sick after the long journey and had lost many of his possessions to raiding Pawnees. He was sicker when he heard Bernhisel would go to Washington. He had wanted the job himself.[18]

Brocchus familiarized himself with the church and attempted to engage in friendly relations with Brigham. He was received at Brigham's office and was granted permission to address the September session of Mormon Conference. He strode to the podium and began by showing he had much knowledge of the Book of Mormon by quoting scripture. So far so good.

Things started going south when he impugned the patriotism of the Saints. Brocchus said the federal government was right not to become involved in the battles of Saints and gentiles in Missouri and Illinois, as it was "a private wrong."[19] The states should redress these grievances. Brocchus absolved the late president Zachary Taylor and the federal government from anti-Mormonism, and then he stood down.

The Saints seethed with anger at what they felt was an insult and let Brocchus know it. Brocchus and three other government appointees fled the territory, taking $24,000 intended to pay for government expenses. Brocchus and the others returned to the East, loudly questioning the loyalty of the Mormon leaders.[20]

Dismayingly, more federally appointed judges came into the territory. The Mormons came to view them as impediments to righteousness. To circumvent the government judges, the territorial legislature expanded the powers of local (Mormon) probate courts, giving them jurisdiction in both civil and criminal matters—not just the wills of the dead. Church authorities brazenly counseled court verdicts from the pulpit. Through the probate courts the church remained in control of Utah justice for twenty years, much to the frustration of the federal judges.[21]

The struggle often resembled "comic opera more than a political battle," wrote Bagley.[22] Further, it was exacerbated by the Mormon belief in "lying for the Lord," which dated back to Joseph.[23] There were laws, and there was righteousness. You could lie for righteousness. It seemed this policy would be carried over by the church in its twenty-first-century attempts to still the voice of the *Salt Lake Tribune*.

Brigham was determined to complete the work of Joseph Smith. This resulted in a "culture of violence," according to Bagley, quoting D. Michael Quinn's *Mormon Hierarchy: Extensions of Power*.[24] It was within the rights of the Saints "to kill antagonistic outsiders, common criminals, LDS apostates, and even faithful Mormons who committed sins 'worthy of death.'"[25]

With the federal government intruding into their sagebrush Eden and the Mormons stirring up vigilantism, ill will smoldered. And then it burst into flame.

On August 29, 1852, Brigham called a special conference of the church. Orson Pratt read a statement that was by then an open secret: the Mormons were practicing polygamy.[26]

This was the official announcement, word of which spread like wildfire to the eastern press and to Europe. Shocking, said the world's newspapers, that in America, in the middle of the Victorian nineteenth century, men would take more than one wife. Brigham was confident now and flexing his political muscles. The world knew the name of Brigham Young.[27]

Brigham's announcement provided more fuel for the anti-Mormon fires, and the federal judges felt frustrated at every turn by Brigham's hold on the system. (Utah today has its active Mormon judges and its "other" judges. A person seeking legal redress will be guided by an attorney as to which judge would be preferable in hearing his or her case. This identification of judges would play a critical role in the twenty-first-century conflict between the *Tribune* and the LDS Church.)

More streams of antagonism were reaching a confluence between the federal government and Brigham's authoritarian rule.

In the beginning, Brigham invited travelers to rest and recuperate. The first emigrants to spend time in Great Salt Lake City en route to California found the Mormons to be hard traders. Sometimes the emigrants were ruthlessly exploited. The outsiders, who were occasionally disrespectful and venomous, represented the hated federal government.[28]

The Mormons harassed emigrants, especially those traveling south toward Los Angeles. The string of Mormon settlements between Great Salt Lake City and San Bernardino had been scratched from rough, largely scrubby desert and scab lands. Their residents were Saints who held bitter grudges against the government. John D. Lee, Mormon leader and by 1856 an Indian agent in southern Utah's Iron County, believed the past suffering of the Saints justified stealing from any gentile passing through the towns where extreme poverty and religious zeal went hand in hand. There was also the issue of grass, for which the animals of both settler and traveler competed.[29]

The government sent more men to try to manage Utah, described by Bagley as "the renowned Botany Bay of worn out politicians."[30] Brigham believed the only reason these men were chosen to go to Utah was because they hated Mormons.

Brigham's disgust and antagonism toward these appointees was in the open. Ever the diplomat, in a draft of an official letter to Congress, he wrote, "Kiss my arse, damn you."[31] The federal government replaced the runaway officials as fast as they fled.

One of the more colorful appointees was William W. Drummond of Illinois. He had abandoned his family and arrived to live in Utah with a prostitute he said was his wife. He had the temerity to challenge local control of the courts. Outraged Mormons learned of his liaison with the prostitute, and Drummond found it best to leave the territory. He headed east with a litany of complaints about the Mormons.[32]

Garland W. Hurt was sent by President Franklin Pierce to become an Indian agent in Utah. He was a physician and a Kentucky state legislator. He tried to establish good relations with the Mormons, but the goodwill evaporated quickly as he worked under Brigham Young.

Hurt warned of the "rude and lawless young men such as might be regarded as a curse to any civilized community."[33] He was speaking to the Indians of the Mormon missionaries, who were suspected of forging alliances with the indigenous people. Many believed the Mormons were behind several attacks on travelers making their way through the territory, including incidents in which white men, painted as Indians, drove off herds of cattle. It is likely that whites in the territory served as fences for stolen goods brought to them by the Indians.[34]

Agent Hurt disagreed with Mormon policy of giving the Indians food and clothing, feeling it made them dependent. He established farms for the Indians and was well liked by the Ute Indians, who called him "the American."[35] Hurt wrote that Brigham Young would "endure all manner of insult rather than be at war with the Indians."[36] Hurt would later play a dramatic role in the Mountain Meadows Massacre.[37]

The battle for control of the territory's legal apparatus continued. Statehood was not total independence, but Brigham would settle for it if it kept control in the hands of the church.

Apostles John Taylor and George A. Smith took a statehood petition to Washington during the winter of 1856–57. They may have given a good accounting of the Mormon side of the story, but they couldn't easily toss off the state's failure to accept federal officials. Whatever sympathy the church had gained after being hounded from Missouri and Nauvoo had been lost in the bombast of Brigham as he exhorted the Saints to polygamy and defied the federal government. The petition never reached Congress.[38]

Religious extremism came to the Mormons in early 1856. It was known as the "Reformation" but might as easily have been called the Inquisition.[39] Brigham felt the Saints had lost their way and had shrugged off their commitment. His network of spies and his bishops and home teachers were encouraged to pry into the most personal matters of the members.

"Now is the time to awake, before the time of burning," he preached.[40]

In this matter, Jedediah Grant, zealot mayor of Great Salt Lake City, became Brigham's Torquemada. He had a list of eighteen questions that winnowed out the sinners. "Have you committed murder or shed (innocent) blood?" "Have you betrayed your brethren?" "Have you ever committed adultery?" "Do you wash your body once a week?"[41] Brigham admitted he'd tried the latter once but said it wasn't for everyone.

Grant traveled from town to town, exhorting atonement and rebaptizing hundreds of Mormons in an orgy of repentance. As Bagley wrote, "Perhaps the most troubling aspect of the Reformation was the Mormon leadership's obsession with blood."[42]

During this time there were several castrations of Mormon men for immoral or criminal conduct, perhaps the most famous being Thomas Lewis, castrated by Bishop Warren S. Snow. Some hold the view that Lewis was interested in a woman whose hand was sought in marriage by an older polygamist. Some apologists said he was on the way to jail for sex crimes anyway. The apologists claim Brigham condemned the act. Turner wrote that Brigham "conveyed to her [his mother] his approval of the punishment."[43]

The Reformation was a time of fire and brimstone and a return to the dark and perplexing doctrine that had begun after Joseph's death: blood atonement.

By 1857, the Mormons were edgy and ready to fight. A cavernous break had opened with the federal government.

The rift had widened when the *Deseret News*, on March 30, 1857, published the resignation letter of Utah Supreme Court justice W. W. Drummond. He charged the church with having men "set apart by special order of the Church, to take both the lives and property of persons who may question the authority of the Church."[44] Drummond was just warming up. The letter accused Brigham of pardoning murderers convicted by the high court and of slandering the nation and its leaders. He then went on to say that Brigham's Destroying Angels, the Danites, had been the ones to order the Indians to kill Gunnison in 1853. There was more: Drummond's predecessor, Leonidas Shaver, "came to his death by drinking poisoned liquors given to him under the orders of the leading men of the Mormon Church in Great Salt Lake City."[45] He accused two of Brigham's closest apostles, Heber C. Kimball and Jedediah Grant, of the murder of the former secretary of state, Almon W. Babbitt, on the plains after he left the Great Basin.[46]

On May 23, 1857, the *Deseret News* printed a refutation of the accusation that Babbitt was murdered by Mormons. It was from the Council Bluffs *Bugle*, and it sounds convincing. Babbitt was in his wagon three hundred miles east of Great Salt Lake City when set upon by Indians. He fired his weapons but was tomahawked in the back of the head. His companions, Frank Rowland and a Mr. Sutherland, were also killed. At Fort Kearny a Major Wharton had possession of Babbitt's papers, including a draft for $8,000 and some of his hair. Babbitt's watch was obtained from the Indians by a Frenchman, according to the dispatch.[47]

+++

A new president, James Buchanan, had taken notice of the Mormons' disregard of federal law. He viewed an action against the Mormons as a way to divert the public's attention from the thorny and raging issue of slavery.

An anti-Mormon crusade began. The president told Congress that Brigham had been collecting weapons for war against the government for years. He avowed that Brigham, superintendent of Indian Affairs in the territory, was inflaming hostile feelings among the Indians against the United States. All but two Indian agents had left the territory on the run, and of course there were the judges and other appointed officials who had fled Utah with the tales of Mormon wantonness, reckless disregard for law, and other excesses.[48]

Meanwhile, Brigham believed what he preached: the Second Coming was imminent. God would usher in the millennium, and the Indians, as predicted in Mormon scripture, would play a necessary role in the Last Days. He blasted the government from the pulpit and warned the people to prepare to repulse the invaders.[49]

+++

The May 20, 1857, issue of the *Deseret News* brought word that stunned the Mormons: Parley P. Pratt, one of the most beloved of the church's apostles, had been killed in Arkansas. Hector H. McLean had done the deed, "presumably in jealousy at the conversion of Mrs. McLean to Mormonism."[50] Convert Eleanor McLean had left her abusive husband and had married Parley Pratt, then attempted to take her children to Utah. Hector tracked Pratt from St. Louis to Arkansas, stabbed Pratt three times, and shot him in the neck.

Brigham praised and eulogized the late Pratt, but in fact he may have been relieved that one of the main voices of conflict with the church president had been stilled. Pratt and Brigham had skirmished for years, and Brigham was wary of Pratt's popularity. He later suggested Pratt deserved his fate, since he had taken a number of additional wives without Brigham's authorization.[51]

Parley Pratt was killed in Arkansas; his place of death would fuel the conflagration that became the Mountain Meadows Massacre.

✚✚✚

About the same time as Parley Pratt was killed in Arkansas, President Buchanan authorized that 2,500 soldiers be sent to Utah to have Brigham replaced with a federally appointed governor. National sentiment was on the side of sending the army. Even Senator Stephen A. Douglas, who had once been favorably disposed toward Utah's Mormons, said it was "the Duty of Congress to apply the knife and cut out this loathsome, disgusting ulcer."[52]

On July 22, 1857, Brigham led 2,500 Mormon faithful up Big Cottonwood Canyon southeast of Great Salt Lake City. They planned to celebrate the tenth anniversary of the pioneers' arrival in the valley while encamped at Silver Lake. The festivities were underway when riders reigned up on sweaty horses. They had news that an army under the command of General William Harney was en route to Utah.[53]

In spite of the high stakes and poor odds, Brigham was determined to fight the US Army. The wounds from Missouri and Nauvoo were still fresh, and he was not about to allow an army to destroy his mountain Zion. This was the prelude to the Last Days, and so be it. He stepped up the anger and added more pepper to his rhetoric. His followers felt the divine vengeance of the coming battle.[54]

Meanwhile, Brigham was laying out a military and political strategy. He would not give himself up to become a martyr. His people needed his leadership. He calculated that the 1,200 miles between Great Salt Lake City and the federal troop staging area in Kansas allowed his people some time to set up defenses. Gathering his counselors, they decided on a guerilla war against the supply trains. They set up harassing units where the incoming soldiers would be most vulnerable. The Nauvoo Legion would defend Great Salt Lake City, and if they failed, Brigham would evacuate and burn the town, he said in a fierce speech in August. "I shall lay my dwelling houses in ashes, I shall lay my mills in ashes, I shall cut every shrub and tree in the valley, every pole, every inch of board, and put it all into ashes."[55]

In August, George A. Smith reviewed the Iron Battalion in southern Utah. For two weeks he watched the troops drill, instilling them with martial zeal and telling settlers that the US Army was preparing a war of extermination. In Parowan, Smith fanned war hysteria toward the oncoming outsiders. "Legend has it Smith advised the people to plant fruit trees on the public square and reminded them that bones make good fertilizer."[56]

The hatred of outsiders, invasion by an army sent by the federal government, the murder of Parley Pratt, and the battle cry of Brigham and his counselors set a stage with horrible consequences.

Chapter 13

THE MASSACRE AT MOUNTAIN MEADOWS

> It is forbidden to kill; therefore all murderers are punished unless they kill in large numbers and to the sound of trumpets.
>
> —Voltaire

"Language fails to picture the scene of blood and carnage," wrote Jacob Hamblin, a devout Mormon and colonizer of southern Utah, when, on September 26, 1857, he came upon the site of the Mountain Meadows Massacre.[1]

The fighting lasted five days and did not end until September 11, fifteen days before Hamblin's stunned view of the battleground. "[Wolves] had disinterred the babies and stripped the bones of their flesh, [and] had left them strewn in every direction. At one place I noticed nineteen wolves pulling out the bodies and eating the flesh. [The scene] was dismal in the extreme. This was one of the gloomiest times I ever passed through."[2]

Mountain Meadows, in the low hills fifty miles southwest of Cedar City, is the site of the worst slaughter of white civilians in the history of the frontier West. "It was violence to achieve political ends," said historian Will Bagley of the bloodbath.[3]

The massacre was planned and conducted by whites—Mormons, disguised as Indians. The Mormons were joined in the slaughter by a band of Paiute Indians with the promise of rich spoils.[4] Mountain Meadows is a valley on the Old Spanish Trail where wagon parties bound for southern California regularly stopped to sip the sweet water from Cane Springs, to graze their cattle, and to rest before pushing on toward the Mojave

Desert. Walking along the six miles of the valley a visitor can imagine the horror of the five-day siege in 1857. The bones of some of the murdered still lie beneath the earth.

From the very beginning, the Church of Jesus Christ of Latter-day Saints tried to deflect responsibility for its involvement in the massacre. Over the years the official position of the church would change and change again. Even today, some apologists for the church refuse to put the blame in Brigham's pocket. Historian John G. Turner wrote, "Young bears significant responsibility for what took place at Mountain Meadows."[5] Bagley goes further, claiming Brigham sent George A. Smith to southern Utah in August 1857 to set in motion the destruction of the Fancher-Baker train.[6]

Already on a war footing, Brigham Young told his Saints not to let a kernel of grain go to waste or to be sold to their enemies. Their enemies were the US government and gentiles.

Into this boiling pot of Mormon fear and emotion came the Fancher-Baker emigrant wagon train, known to history as the Fancher party. Originating in Arkansas, the train reached Great Salt Lake City from the Oregon Trail–Mormon Trail sometime in early August. They camped overlooking Salt Lake Valley some six or seven miles east of Great Salt Lake.[7]

Rumor mutated into fact among the Mormons. In the Fancher party were men said to have killed Apostle Parley P. Pratt three months before in Arkansas. It was also rumored that the Fancher party included militia who had killed the eighteen Mormons in the Missouri massacre at Haun's Mill in 1838. Arkansas was close enough to Missouri that for many Mormons it was true. It was even whispered that some of the Fancher party were in the mob that killed the prophet Joseph Smith. Great Salt Lake City was already braced for war with the US Army, and the people refused to sell supplies to the Fanchers.

Mistrust of the Fanchers grew as they slowly moved south from Salt Lake Valley. Rumors were like wildfire in a wind, fed by Apostle George A. Smith and a band of officials representing Brigham Young. Smith moved south ahead of the Fancher wagons. Every village was alerted. The enemy was advancing. Prepare.[8]

As Bagley put it, "Once the party left Salt Lake, it disappeared into a historical maze built of lies, folklore, popular myth, justification and a few facts." Much of the party's southward trek became hearsay.[9]

Reaching American Fork, thirty miles south of Great Salt Lake City, the wagon train was again refused provisions, even though the local Mormons had plenty of flour, bacon, vegetables, poultry, butter, cheese, and eggs. One woman in southern Utah traded the Fancher party a cheese for a bed quilt. She and her husband would later be cut off from the church.[10]

The Fancher men were said to be very free in their language and committed "little acts of annoyance" for the purpose of provoking the Saints.[11] In a frenzy of rumor, the Fanchers were also accused of having camped at Corn Creek where it was alleged they killed eighteen head of cattle and then poisoned the carcasses and a spring. Two or three or six or ten Indians who had eaten the cattle had died. The story was never told the same way twice, but the edgy Mormons were certain it was true. George A. Smith, like a Mormon Paul Revere, called out the outrages as he continued south, whipping up anti-emigrant sentiment.

The Fancher cattle herd grew in size as rumor blazed ahead of them. Their cattle were said to be heedlessly feeding on land set aside for Mormon herds. "From the moment they left Corn Creek nothing is certain about the Fancher party except that in less than three weeks every member who could have given a reliable account of its fate would be dead," wrote Bagley.[12]

At a meeting in Cedar City, Mormon militia colonel William H. Dame gave Stake President Isaac Chauncey Haight the tacit go-ahead to attack the wagon train and destroy the whole company.[13]

In an inflammatory speech to the gathered militia in Cedar City, Haight recited the list of abuses suffered by the Mormons, blaming it on gentiles whom he compared to the approaching Fancher party. "When we pled for mercy, Haun's Mill [massacre of Mormons] was our answer, and when we asked for bread they gave us a stone. . . . [We went] far into the wilderness where we could worship God according to the dictates of our own conscience without annoyance to our neighbors. We resolved that if they would leave us alone we would never trouble them," announced Haight. Yet the nation had sent an army to exterminate the Mormons, he said, and he pronounced that he would give his "last drop of blood in defense of Zion."[14] It was strong stuff.

John D. Lee sent runners to gather Indians from the surrounding countryside and treated forty or fifty of them to a feast in Harmony, a southern Utah town not far from Mountain Meadows. With a sword in hand and a red sash around his waist, on September 5, 1857, he exhorted to Indians to shout out their support for the attack. He was not happy with their ho-hum response. "Lee called for a better response," said Bagley. "It was not much better."[15] The Paiutes had been promised the spoils of the Fancher party, including its large cattle herd. But they seemed to be losing heart.

With Lee calling for men to take arms against the party, men of conscience resisted the order. As for avenging the death of the prophet Joseph Smith, who could say any of these men had a hand in it? "You only suppose and that will not do for me," said John Hawley.[16] He had listened to Lee inciting the Paiutes to attack. He had heard Captain Harrison Pearce say he wished to "see all the Gentyles strippt naked and lashed on their backs and have the Sun scorch them to death by inches."[17]

A final war council was held in Cedar City, led by Lee, Haight, and John M. Higbee. Lee would lead the attack. He made his way toward the Fancher party, now resting their stock at Mountain Meadows and making ready for the harsh desert trek that lay ahead. With Lee was a large body of Mormon men who stopped in the hills not far from Mountain Meadows. Here the Mormons painted their faces and disguised themselves as Indians. They were joined by an unknown number of local Indians, mostly Paiutes.[18] Lee led his men to hills overlooking the scattered wagons of the Fancher party.

In the morning darkness of September 7, the Fancher party rolled out of their blankets and rekindled their fires. Water was carried from Cane Springs. Faces were splashed. Coffee was set to brew.

The Mormon and Indian raiders—perhaps 150 in all—descended undetected down a ravine cut by Mogotsu Creek and took up positions mere yards from the wagon party. At first light, the Mormons and Indians opened fire. The deadly barrage killed between ten and fifteen. A surviving child would later say his family was just sitting down to a breakfast of quail and cottontail rabbit when the first shots rang out, toppling one of the children.[19]

Coordinated attacks came from the ravine and from a hill to the west, but Arkansas gunfire killed at least one Indian and shattered the knees of two Paiute war chiefs.[20] The return fire broke the surprise and temporarily frightened away the Mormons and Indians.

During the lull that followed, the Arkansans circled their wagons a hundred yards from the bullet-spitting ravine. They shoveled dirt beneath the wagons to form ramparts against the flying lead. They also counterattacked, and Lee watched his irregular army fall back in the face of the unexpectedly strong resistance. Hopes for a quick victory faded, and a siege began. The Fanchers were cut off from Cane Spring by Mormon sharpshooters. The emigrants' cattle were rounded up by the attackers and taken away.[21]

The next day, Lee made another attack. It was a disaster, causing more Indian casualties and demoralizing the Paiutes, who had been told they had been blessed by the Mormons and would be impervious to gunshots. The Paiutes later said that "the emigrants had long guns and were good shots."[22] Lee later recalled, "Now we knew the Indians could not do the work . . . and we were in a sad fix."[23]

For five days the emigrants lay in their rifle pits waiting each assault. The stench of dead animals and human corpses rose in the warm September air. At one point the Fanchers sent William Aden and another man for help. Aden was killed when he approached a Mormon campsite, and his companion was likely also killed.[24]

Early Thursday morning, September 10, Haight rang the Cedar City town bell and ordered the Nauvoo Legion regiment out. He selected only men chosen for their proven loyalty to the LDS Church. According to historian Bagley, each man had probably sworn a temple endowment oath to avenge the blood of the prophets.[25] Another failed assault on Thursday resulted in the deaths and desertion of more Paiutes.

John D. Lee, while crossing the valley to get a better view from a nearby ridge, was spotted by the emigrants. By then it was clear to the Fanchers that white men were among their attackers.[26]

In Great Salt Lake City, Brigham Young welcomed a dusty rider named James Haslam. Haslam had come two hundred miles from Cedar City. It was September 10. Brigham told him to wait and after an interval bade him to return to Cedar City with a letter of instructions that "a company of emigrants then in southern Utah and bound for California were to be protected and assisted on their way."[27]

Haslam reversed his route and rode hell-for-leather to deliver the letter to militia commander William Dame, arriving sometime before September 14 but after the attack on the Fanchers was well underway.[28]

The letter from Brigham said the Mormons "must not meddle with them [the Fancher party]. The Indians we expect will do as they please but you should try and preserve good feelings with them."[29] Bagley says this was Brigham's letter of plausible deniability.[30] The letter arrived too late to halt the massacre but was presented as cover for any allegations against Brigham.

At dawn on Friday, September 11, 1857, fewer than two dozen men of the wagon party were able to defend the wagons. Bagley describes how women and children huddled in the rifle pit to escape sniper fire. Death had claimed a number of wounded. Cut off from water, the survivors had little ammunition left.[31]

Then the sniping stopped. The Mormon leaders at Mountain Meadows had agreed on a plan to draw out the defenders through the ruse of offering help. Lee's orders allegedly came from Colonel William Dame, and it was decided that the only safe course "was the utter destruction of the whole rascally lot."[32]

There were arguments against shedding innocent blood, but the response was that these were not innocents; they were cutthroats, robbers, and assassins. "Had they not boasted of murdering our Patriarchs and Prophets, Joseph and Hyrum?" asked John M. Higbee, a major in the militia.[33] Some Mormon men of conscience "resisted orders to assault civilian Americans," wrote Bagley.[34]

As the sun rose on that Friday, Lee was faced with a double dilemma: he had to convince the defenders to surrender, and he must convince his Mormon militia to murder defenseless women and children who would place themselves in their trust.

Bagley describes how the Mormons devised a plan that would allow the militia to kill the male emigrants easily, and murder the women and children separately. Lee would lead the first party in two wagons containing the wounded and the youngest children, with the women and older children marching behind them, thus isolating the innocent blood from the adult men. The men would follow in single file, each guarded by an armed escort.[35]

Lee said the men ate breakfast and "prepared for the work at hand."[36] To the beleaguered emigrants it was inconceivable that the Mormons could devise such a devious plan to murder them all. Besides, they were parched from lack of water and famished from lack of food.

Lee carried a truce flag toward the camp, promising protection if they surrendered. Rebecca Dunlap, a child survivor of the massacre, recalled that when three wagons approached their camp, the emigrants dressed her eight-year-old sister Mary in white. The child "went out towards them and waved a white handkerchief in a token of peace. The Mormons in the wagons waved one in reply and advanced to the corral."[37]

The two parties met. The Fanchers and the Mormons talked for about a half hour. Lee told the Fanchers that if they gave up their weapons it would show the Indians they no longer wanted to fight. The Mormons promised to take them back to the settlements. Lee recalled that the "men, women and children gathered around me in wild consternation. Some felt that the time of their happy deliverance had come, [but others] all in tears, looked upon me with doubt, distrust and terror."[38]

Lee divided them into three groups and began on the alleged march to safety. Leading the first group of young children in wagons, Lee started away from camp. Daniel McFarlane led the second group, consisting of the women and older children. The men followed fifty yards behind. An armed Mormon soldier fell in beside each of the men.

After half an hour, John Higbee fired a shot and shouted, "Halt! Do your duty!"[39] At the command the escorts turned and shot down the men. The women and children were ridden down by Indians and Mormons painted and dressed as Indians.

Nancy Huff, a member of the Fancher party and four years old at the time, recalled that "[Captain Jack Baker] had me in his arms when he was shot down, and fell dead. I saw my mother shot in the forehead and fall dead. The women and children screamed and clung together. Some of the young women begged the assassins after they had run out on us not to kill them, but they had no mercy on them, clubbing their guns and beating out their brains."[40]

Bloodlust took over. Two girls were shot down as they were pulled from the arms of an Indian shaman trying to save them. A militiaman was ordered to kill a wounded woman recovering consciousness. Another Mormon was alleged to hear militiaman William Stewart boast the he took the "d—d Gentile babies by the heels and cracked their skulls over the wagon tires."[41] Others said this crime was committed by George Adair, who in "his drunken revels . . . would laugh and attempt to imitate the pitiful, crushing sound of the skull bones as they struck the iron bands of the wagon hubs."[42]

A Paiute eyewitness told how the children begged for mercy. William Stewart, catching girls by the hair, would throw them to the ground and place his foot upon their bodies and cut their throats. Witnesses claimed John D. Lee shot down men and women, but Lee later claimed he saved the lives of several children. Throats of men, women, and children were cut in accordance with Mormon custom of blood atonement. Some were scalped.[43]

Mormon elder James Gemmell said that "a few small children were not killed at once, but on consultation it was agreed they could tell too much after they grew up. They were then slain."[44]

Survivor Nancy Huff recalled that in the aftermath there were eighteen children still alive. "[O]ne girl, some ten or twelve years old, they said was too big and could tell, so they killed her, leaving seventeen."[45] Huff said John Willis shot the girl "after we were gathered up." This public execution demonstrated to the surviving children "the consequences of knowing too much," as Bagley wrote in his history of the massacre.[46]

There may have been rape, although in Juanita Brooks's history she doubts this, due to Mormonism's condemnation of sex outside of marriage, further reinforced by the Reformation. But in some accounts rape was an implied part of the massacre. An army report claimed Lee took "a beautiful young lady away to a secluded spot. There she implored him for more than life. She, too, was found dead. Her throat had been cut from ear-to-ear."[47]

Gemmell heard that two pretty little girls survived the slaughter "and the killers told them that if they would strip naked and dance nude upon the green sward they would spare their lives. The little Girls did so, but a little after were put to death."[48] He also claimed he saw "indignities that were perpetrated upon three persons after which they were shot. But they are too shocking to put on paper."[49] Rape cannot be entirely discounted, but there are many lurid and apocryphal stories about every aspect of early Mormonism.

Sorting truth from fiction in the Mountain Meadows incident is a tricky business. On one hand the only survivors of the Fancher party were children. Yet the tales told by the murderers are disingenuous.

Said Bagley, "The standard accounts skillfully distorted the truth to shift blame to the Indians for the most horrible crimes, particularly the murder of the women and children."[50] But participant Nephi Johnson confessed forty years later that "white men did most of the killing."[51]

The final murders were over quickly, perhaps in less than five minutes. Lee reported seeing the corpses of six or seven women, "stripped perfectly naked . . . all of their clothing . . . torn from their bodies," claiming the Indians had taken the clothing from the dead.[52] Fifteen months later, however, Paiutes visited by H. L. Halleck while passing through southern Utah claimed the women came from a nearby settlement and stripped off the clothes.[53]

The corpses of women and children were scattered along the road for some distance. Lee counted ten children ranging from ten to sixteen years old killed close to each other. Higbee looted corpses, picking up a little money and a few watches.[54]

Later, many of the killers would claim they tried to protect the children, seventeen of whom survived, all young enough that they were not considered a threat to the Mormon version of the massacre. Rebecca Dunlap later said that not one was over six years of age.[55]

Christopher "Kit" Carson Fancher said two years after the attack, "My father was killed by Indians; when they washed their faces they were white men."[56]

The day after the massacre, Mormon officials from Cedar City arrived at the site to see more than a hundred corpses. Colonel William Dame was especially shocked by the carnage, men, women, and children who lay in grotesque positions. Dame said he would have to "publish it," according to Lee, who stood next to the shaken colonel.[57]

Remonstrations and denials started flying, with Haight saying to Dame, "You know you counselled it and ordered me to have them used up."[58] Dame looked uneasy and fearful, according to Lee. Haight continued to address Dame: "Nothing has been done except by your orders and it is too late in the day for you to order things done and then go back on it."[59]

When Dame recovered he said, "I thought they were nearly all killed by the Indians. . . . I did not think that there were so many women and children or I would not have had anything to do with it."[60] This infuriated Haight. "You throw the blame of this thing on me and I will be revenged on you, if I have to meet you in hell to get it."[61]

Some accounts say bodies were left unburied for some time. Bagley said the Mormon militia sought a haphazard burial, including dumping some bodies in a wash. The weather and the animals soon uncovered the remains.[62]

After the completion of the grisly business, the Mormon leaders gathered the men, praising God for delivering their enemies. The Indians did it, not the Mormons, and that was part of the oath that every man in the party swore. Stake President Haight led the oath. With right arms raised, the murderers swore to never discuss the killings, even among themselves. It would be treason to the church. And they were not even to tell their wives.[63]

Three men from the Fancher party had escaped. Two were tracked down almost immediately and shot. A third seems to have made it almost a hundred miles to the Muddy River. He was found by Mormons who first assured him of safety, then shot him.[64]

The children were dispersed among southern Utah's Mormon families as alleged victims of the Indians. Two years after the massacre a US Army team arrived to take them back to relatives in Arkansas. Despite their youth, many of the children had nightmarish memories of the slaughter of the parents, sisters, and brothers.[65]

John D. Lee would be the scapegoat for all the Mormons involved in the massacre. He would be executed in 1876 for leading the murders, ostensibly letting Brigham Young and the other Mormon officials off the hook. A small cairn built at the site and in place until about 1930 displayed a plaque that said, in essence, "John D. Lee and 100 Indians Killed a Party of Emigrants Near This Site." Said historian Will Bagley, "It was a calculated act of terrorism."[66]

Salt Lake Tribune editor Jay Shelledy wanted to throw light on the questions that lingered, even after 143 years.

Chapter 14

THE WAR THAT ALMOST WAS

Agreement is the best weapon of defense and the matter
would be buried.

—Franz Kafka

W hile the Mormon militia buried the dead at Mountain
Meadows, the outside world was little concerned with the so-
called Utah War and the Mormons' defiance. The American economy
had crashed. Banks collapsed, bringing down traders, companies,
and manufacturers. Politics went on the back burner, and President
Buchanan heard little in the way of public support for his Utah War.

Nonetheless, two thousand members of the Tenth Regiment left
Fort Leavenworth on July 18, 1857, two months before the Mountain
Meadows Massacre. Colonel Albert Sidney Johnston was in command
of the Utah War and warned his men to expect hardships. Johnston
hurried west, learning his troops were green and his supply system was
spotty at best. His troops were spread along the Oregon Trail from Missouri to South Pass, and they lacked any cavalry to deal with any attacks
in strength. Colonel Johnston's planners devised strategies but worried
they couldn't be implemented before winter came to the high plains.[1]

The Mormons had a defensive plan in place, but its formations were
comprised of ragtag irregulars and amateur volunteers led by officers
with no formal military training. What they lacked in professionalism
they made up for in grit and determination. And the Mormons knew the
geography where fighting might take place.[2]

On September 27, 1857, Commander Daniel Wells of the Nauvoo
Legion left Great Salt Lake City, and his raiders burned Fort Bridger,
115 miles to the east in Wyoming, thus depriving the US troops of comfortable winter quarters.[3]

The ubiquitous Orrin Porter Rockwell sneaked up on an army encampment at South Pass and stampeded the army's mule herd. It turned out to be a fiasco when the mule herd turned back toward the army camp, taking with them the raiders' horses. Rockwell and his men had dismounted after what they thought was a finished action.[4] The Mormons followed the army on foot, and the next night they captured fifteen horses and rode back to the Mormon lines.

The greatest coup by the Mormons came on October 5, 1857, when guerillas led by Lot Smith captured and burned three wagon trains in the Wyoming prairies west of what is now Farson.[5] The Mormon military actions, though celebrated in Mormon legend, were little more than flea bites on the US Army.

By mid-October the Nauvoo Legion had only 1,100 men under arms, although they had seven hundred men in reserve in Great Salt Lake City. On a moment's notice, another three thousand could be called upon to rush to the canyons to take defilading positions against the army.[6]

Johnston marched through winter storms, and after fifteen days his army plodded into the burned-out Fort Bridger. They would spend a cold, wet winter at what they called Camp Scott on Blacks Fork, two miles above Fort Bridger.[7]

As the year drew to a close, Brigham was ensnared in a web of political and military dilemmas. His continued defiance and Mormon military raids had refocused the enmity of Washington. A replacement governor for Brigham Young, Alfred Cumming, was waiting with Johnston at Blacks Fork, ready to take over the territory as soon as Brigham was captured and deposed. The new chief justice of the territory, Delana Eckels, had indicted Brigham and other Mormon leaders after convening a grand jury.[8]

Under direction of the president, Colonel Johnston and his officers relished concluding their conquest of Utah and imposing the strictest possible punishment. There was talk of opening a second front, starting on the Pacific Coast.[9]

The Mormons were now isolated. They received no mail. They had bought out and sent away the gentile merchants. They had lost their political allies in Congress. Only the winter lay between the Mormons and certain disaster.

+++

So much was happening that autumn of 1857.

Within a few days of the massacre at Mountain Meadows, the "authorized fiction," as historian Will Bagley put it, was cemented into place by Brigham and the church leaders.[10]

Mormon Indian agent George W. Armstrong waited to report the massacre until after he could confer with John D. Lee. The report Armstrong filed paraphrased Lee something like this: The emigrants poisoned a cow (not a spring, as in previous versions) that caused the death of four natives and made many more ill. The Indians met and decided to take revenge on the wagon train that poisoned the cow. They followed the wagon train to a place called Mountain Meadows where they attacked the camp and after a desperate fight killed fifty-seven men and nine women.[11]

As Bagley put it, "Thus the first official comment on the subject in federal records blandly passed off the largest act of violence ever to take place on the overland trails—an event that would have triggered immediate retaliation anywhere else in the West—as the fault of the victims."[12]

In the Mormon colonies of the Great Basin, the news spread like wildfire. Mormon apostates said the church was behind the massacre, but who listened to them?[13]

The *Los Angeles Star* reported the disturbing news of the massacre on October 3, 1857, and confessed "our unwillingness to credit such a wholesale massacre."[14] A week later the *Star* confirmed it as "the foulest massacre which has ever been perpetrated on this route."[15] The *Star* blamed it on the Mormons, accepting a general belief that it had been the church's Destroying Angels who had cut throats and shot bullets into skulls. The paper reported that "the blow fell on these emigrants from Arkansas, in retribution of the death of Parley Pratt."[16] Newspapers in Los Angeles and San Francisco called for the annihilation of the Saints but warned that Mormon military power included ten thousand soldiers and fifty thousand Indians.[17]

Rumor was rife, and blood was high on both sides.

Meanwhile, the US Army continued its approach through Wyoming. One can imagine how threatened Brigham and his Saints must have felt. Brigham used his exhortations to draw the Saints closer together to form a defensive circle against the world. During the October conference of the church, many of the faithful wanted a revelation from Brigham on how they were going to get out of this mess.

"God will fight our battles," was his response.[18] Outside observers believed Brigham and the Saints would bolt from Utah and head for Sonora, Mexico, Central America, or even Russian Alaska.[19]

Brigham's official report on January 6, 1858, to James Denver, commissioner of Indian Affairs, reads, "Capt. Fancher & Co. fell victim to the Indians' wrath near Mountain Meadows."[20]

"Lamentable as this case truly is," wrote Brigham, "it is only the natural consequences of that fatal policy which treats the Indians like the wolves or other ferocious beasts."[21] Brigham claimed he had tried for years to persuade emigrants not to follow such a suicidal policy and his people had frequently risked their own safety to help travelers.[22]

He then submitted his financial statements for payment. "In an audacious fraud, Young billed the government twenty-two hundred dollars for charges from Indian Farmer [John D.] Lee that included items obviously looted from the Fancher party, a bold if ill-considered expression of his contempt for the government."[23]

His accounts for the last quarter billed the government nearly $4,000 for goods distributed at Mountain Meadows to the Paiute Indians. "If white men in their boasted enlightenment suffer themselves to act thus unwisely and fiendishly towards the red men, what can they expect?" the prophet asked.[24]

The imminent war with the federal government seemed insoluble. But Brigham and the Mormons still had one ally in Washington: a gentile lawyer and friend to the Mormons, Thomas L. Kane. President Buchanan at first resisted Kane's offer to go to Utah and see if he couldn't make peace with Brigham. Finally winning the president over, Kane took a ship around the horn and made it to Great Salt Lake City on February 25, 1858. Kane brought with him news that he believed the president, under political pressure and strain of the economic collapse, wanted to end the embarrassing and costly Utah campaign.[25]

Kane cleverly wrote the president and described a nonexistent division between Mormon warmongers on one hand and Brigham on the other. Ignoring years of fiery rhetoric, Kane described Brigham as a peacemaker who had prevented his rabid war faction from attacking the army. In turn, Kane asked Brigham to join the charade and extend a palm of peace by offering to send provisions to the army. Kane slyly told Brigham that the president had offered an apology and spoke of a possible pardon. He was taking considerable license with an earlier conversation with the president. Brigham didn't much like it, since it would mean that blue coat soldiers would be garrisoned in Utah.[26]

Kane undertook part II of his diplomacy: an attempt to create a rift between incoming governor Alfred Cumming and the colonel Albert Sidney Johnston. They were together at the encampment on Blacks Fork. Kane's tactics included letters clashing with Johnston at every turn, and letters of conciliation and goodwill toward Cumming. Essentially, he was lying to both men. Kane's tactics didn't work; Johnston announced he expected to move his troops into Great Salt Lake City.[27]

Brigham now publicly announced that he would not fight the army after all. He declared military resistance futile and "not worth a single Mormon life."[28] Instead, the Mormons would retreat from Great Salt Lake City, and, as Brigham had threatened, they would leave Utah towns torched and empty. For Johnston and Cumming there would be nothing left to govern and no way to buy local supplies.

The Mormons began to evacuate Great Salt Lake City on the first of April. Wagons and families headed south, congesting the roads.[29]

About this time the new governor, Cumming, accepted an invitation from Brigham (via Kane) to visit privately with Brigham in Salt Lake. Cumming figured he could save lives on both sides if he reached some kind of détente with Brigham. Escorted by Kane and some of the Nauvoo Legion, Cumming traveled down Echo Canyon, a site where Mormons had constructed a series of defensive defiles.[30]

Arriving in Salt Lake, Brigham and his aides sized up Cumming: "corpulent, alcoholic, and of limited intelligence and morals."[31] While Brigham was most cordial, he had instructed his counselors to treat Cumming frostily. Good cop, bad cop.

Brigham invited Cumming to speak to a congregation of Saints on April 25, 1858. He did little better than the inept Brocchus had done seven years earlier.

Cumming promised not to interfere with the Mormon "social habits" and then offered to help anyone leave the territory who was being held against his or her will. He was appealing to what he assumed must be the many unhappy polygamous wives.[32]

Brigham's wife, Augusta Adams Young, stood up and declared she had "known nothing but liberty since I have been here."[33] In truth and in private, "she had repeatedly demanded freedom from what she considered Young's neglect."[34]

The Saints played Cumming well that day, whipsawing him with threats and placating him with creamy words. Apostle John Taylor was interrupted by Brigham during his harsh remarks to Cumming. Brigham asked the apostle to tone down his rhetoric, "and not be so personal in your remarks."[35] The Saints roared their approval when Taylor insisted that "those troops must be withdrawn before we can have any officers palmed upon us."[36]

Brigham followed with soothing words about "his friend Governor Cumming."[37] Later Brigham told Cumming that had it not been for his influence over the hotheads among the Saints, the people would have destroyed Johnston's army.

That evening they made certain Cumming received a report that Brigham was preparing to move south, to Sonora. Cumming would be a governor without a people.[38] The tactical ruse created by Kane and implemented by Brigham succeeded brilliantly.

"I can do nothing here without your influence," Cumming told Brigham.[39] In a letter to the Speaker of the US House of Representatives, Cumming identified Brigham Young as the head of the peace faction and even speculated that "some Mormons hate him in consequence perhaps of his pacific measures."[40]

Kane, Cumming, and Brigham huddled and forged an understanding. They agreed that Brigham would not impede Johnston's oncoming army as it entered the valley. Cumming in turn promised to shield Brigham from Chief Justice Delana Eckels's grand jury.[41] President Buchanan sought peace roughly along the lines of this understanding, offering "a free and full pardon to all who will submit themselves to the authority of the federal government."[42]

Bearing these terms was a two-man peace commission that arrived in Great Salt Lake City on June 7, 1858, nine months after the Mountain Meadows slaughter. Brigham was reluctant to embrace the offer.

He feared political subordination and likened it to slavery.[43] Finally, however, he accepted the president's offer as long as the federal troops were billeted some distance from the city.

On June 13 Johnston's army resumed their march from Wyoming into Utah and headed down Echo Canyon, prepared to fight. Not a shot was fired. Two weeks later he entered Great Salt Lake City not to cheers and bands but to sullen emptiness. Per the agreement, he marched forty miles southwest of the city and established Camp Floyd, named for the secretary of war, near what is now the town of Fairfield, an old Pony Express stop. At the time it became the nation's largest military garrison.[44]

Brigham refused to acknowledge the arrival of Johnston's army as a defeat. In fact, as the soldiers marched through the city, Brigham considered it a victory.[45]

In a contrary view, Secretary of War John B. Floyd wrote in his annual report of 1858 that "[the Mormons'] bluster and bravado sank into whispers of terror and submission."[46] Brigham locked himself into his compound and set guards at the gates, perhaps fearing lynching at the hands of the soldiers. Whether depressed or fearful, he did not reemerge for several months. Many Mormons, disaffected by three years of poor harvests and perhaps feeling they'd been dealt with too harshly under the Reformation, took this time as an opportunity to leave the Great Basin.[47]

The federal government strained to establish a judiciary independent of the LDS Church.

Judge John Cradlebaugh, brought in with Johnston's army, was about to become Mormondom's new pain in the neck. Cradlebaugh, with his one good eye, perceived unpunished injustice as he set up at Camp Floyd. Some apostate Mormons in southern Utah were talking about what happened in the year before at Mountain Meadows. Cradlebaugh wanted to investigate the Mountain Meadows Massacre. He didn't believe the Mormon leader's cover story. Escorted by a military detachment he left Camp Floyd on March 7, 1859, and made his way to the massacre site. The party observed "human skulls, bones, and hair scattered about, and scraps of clothing of men, women and children."[48]

The sworn silence of the Mormon perpetrators had not held up.

Whispered names flew among the brethren, especially from the apostates, and found their way under cover of dark to the judge as he waited in Cedar City. Cradlebaugh issued warrants for forty alleged Mormon perpetrators. Abruptly, in response from Cumming, who was now basically Brigham's lackey, President Buchanan ordered that only the territorial governor could request army escorts for judicial investigations. It was justice diverted for Cradlebaugh and a win for Brigham's Cumming.[49]

However, Brevet Major James H. Carleton and the First Dragoons from Fort Tejon, California, had been dispatched to escort Camp Floyd's payroll, a $150,000 in gold, to the Utah military post and to investigate the Mountain Meadows Massacre along the way.[50]

Surgeon Charles Brewer "found mases of women's hair, children's bonnets, such as are generally used upon the plains, and pieces of lace, muslin, calicoes and other material, part of women's and children's apparel." He reported that many of the skulls "bore marks of violence, being pierced with bullet holes, or shattered by heavy blows, or cleft with some sharp-edged instrument."[51]

Carleton reported seeing several bones of what must have been very small children. He and his officers concluded the Paiutes were incapable of executing the massacre. They thought the Indians "a miserable set of root diggers." Major Carleton argued that the entire massacre was done with skill, patience, and tenacity, which "only the Mormon settlers possessed."[52]

Carleton's men measured the site and marked it. They buried some bones between 2,500 and 2,900 yards from the spring. They identified one cluster as women, the other as men, presumably from the clothes still clinging to the remains. Later, Jacob Hamblin appeared on the scene, coming from his ranch a few miles away. He showed Carleton a place in the sage where he said he had buried some bones. Carleton's men gathered the skeletons of thirty-four persons and interred them on the north side of the emigrant's rifle pit.[53]

Army surgeon Brewer wrote about what he saw, and *Harper's Weekly* published his account of the massacre, including a grisly illustration of wolves gnawing on bones. Now the world knew the name of Mountain Meadows.[54]

The soldiers built a conical monument fifty feet in circumference and topped it with a cedar cross bearing an inscription, "Vengeance is mine: I will repay, saith the Lord." The soldiers erected a slab of granite and chiseled into it, "Here 120 men, women and children were massacred in cold blood in early September, 1857. They were from Arkansas."[55]

Carleton's fury surfaced in the report he made on the massacre at Mountain Meadows. "Who composed the jury to find the indictment? The brethren. Who are generally the witnesses before that jury? The brethren. Who are the officers and jailers who have custody of the prisoner before and after the trial? The brethren. Who are the members of the jury before whom the trial takes place? Still the brethren. Who are the witnesses for the prosecution, and, more particularly, who are those for the defense? The brethren." He further complained that if a criminal should be found guilty, there was still the power of the pardon. And that came from the brethren—Brigham's lackey, Governor Cumming.[56]

Nothing had been settled between the government and the rebellious Mormons. Rifts remained. No one had been indicted for the Mountain Meadows Massacre. There would be continuing imbroglios with the army and the courts, but the church leaders managed to dance away from attempts to either prosecute or muzzle them.

Polygamy, equated by some with slavery, was still unresolved. Three years later Colonel Albert Sidney Johnston, now Brevet Brigadier General Johnston, would leave Camp Floyd to join the Southern cause in the Civil War, where he would be killed at Shiloh.[57] The camp was shut down in 1861, and the three thousand soldiers still stationed there scattered to choose sides in the War Between the States.

Governor Cumming was in the thrall of Brigham and would do little to upset the status quo. Besides, Brigham had promised to deliver the miscreants at Mountain Meadows for trial. Cumming wanted to believe it and waited patiently.[58] The Mormons were busy as ever concocting cover stories and tightening loose lips. Trouble was the recounting of events kept shifting, like shadows from a candle.

The erosion of Brigham's autocratic reign had begun, but Utah as a theocracy would continue to thrive until this very day, in spite of the *Salt Lake Tribune*'s attempts to curb it.

Chapter 15

"FANATICS AND WHORES"

> In every gold rush . . . the suppliers and service industries will
> gather up the dust while ninety-nine percent of the minors
> go home with empty pokes.
>
> —John McPhee

While Mountain Meadows simmered on the back burner, Brigham returned to consolidating his power and to bringing more converts to the Great Basin.

In the late 1850s and early 1860s, Brigham sought to make his Mormons more self-reliant. He tried growing cotton, which for a time seemed promising, especially in light of the blockade of the South during the Civil War. While Brigham had quit using tobacco in 1860, he nevertheless calculated that by home growing tobacco he could keep $60,000 a year out of the hands of non-Mormon merchants.[1]

With initial reservation, Brigham had allowed the brethren to conduct limited trade with Johnston's soldiers at Camp Floyd. When it became apparent the army was a very good market, he went full out, selling timber and food. The result was an influx of cash to the economy.[2]

When the army abandoned the fort at the start of the Civil War, Brigham—through several intermediaries—bought the army's flour, iron, machinery, and many wagons and horses at a fraction of its real price. He attempted to create self-sufficiency while at the same time encouraging the government to build a transcontinental railroad that would go through Utah. It would make the process of settling converted Mormons in Utah faster and cheaper, and it might create trade favorable to the church.

Brigham continued to be staunchly anti-mining. He wanted the church to benefit from any mining strikes but was worried that if gold was discovered, it would bring an overwhelming number of non-Mormons into the state. He had watched Mormons lose power in western Nevada when the Comstock Lode brought thousands of miners into what had been Mormon turf. The miners soon consolidated political power. Congress created the Nevada Territory in 1861 as a result. Mining would "weld upon our necks chains of slavery, groveling dependence and utter overthrow," Brigham complained.[3]

Brigham himself was hardly impoverished. He told journalist Horace Greeley in 1859 he was worth a quarter of a million dollars. This didn't include most of the assets of the church, which were held in trust by Brigham or in his name. He sometimes mixed his personal funds with church funds. Brigham lived in spacious houses and drove a fine carriage. He'd grown up poor; now he was rich and not afraid to display his wealth, in spite of the poverty of many Utahns. "God heaps property on me, and I am duty bound to take care of it," he said.[4]

The Civil War brought this comment from Brigham: "I earnestly prayed for the success of both North & South."[5]

President Buchanan had been replaced by Abraham Lincoln. General Johnston had left Camp Floyd to join the rebels. Governor Cumming, a Southerner, also left the state. Western territories and states, including California and Oregon, had many Confederate sympathizers, but Brigham had made clear that Utah wanted entry to the Union as a free state. He was firmly pro-Constitution, firmly anti-government, and said so in the first telegraph transmission that went from Utah in 1861.[6]

Wars have always kindled Mormon hopes for the millennium, and the Civil War seemed to bring the Last Days even closer. Joseph Smith purportedly prophesied that Mormons would step in and save the Constitution. The future spread of their kingdom was linked to God's destruction of the US government.[7]

Governor Cumming's replacement was on the way, and he was rumored to be Broughton Harris. Harris had been one of the original 1851 appointees and had fled the state in fear of Brigham's hammer, and Brigham expressed his hope that "if Harris did come the boys & dogs would piss on him."[8] Harris did not come and dogs waited.

Instead, the new Utah governor was John Dawson. Dawson blocked Brigham's renewed attempt to gain statehood and thus frustrated Brigham's desire to be elected governor. Dawson's tenure was the shortest of any territorial governor's, and it was because of a sex scandal. Mormon Albina Williams, the subject of Dawson's unwanted advances, ostensibly drove Governor Dawson off with a shovel and then presented the attempted seduction in an affidavit to Brigham.[9]

Dawson threatened to shoot the editor of the *Deseret News*, Thomas Stenhouse, if he published anything about Dawson's alleged desire to "sleep with Tom Williams['s] widow."[10] Dawson left Great Salt Lake City on New Year's Eve 1861. Stopping at Ephraim a hundred miles south of Salt Lake, he was badly beaten; some rumored that he was castrated.[11]

Editor Stenhouse would be excommunicated from Mormonism in 1871, and in a retaliatory exposé, he would claim Dawson had been entrapped by church leaders "in an offense."[12]

Dawson was replaced by Stephen Harding, whose initial sympathies for the Mormons "evaporated within weeks." He called the Mormons' predictions of the downfall of the government "disloyal."[13]

Utah impatiently waited for statehood. Congress rejected its petitions, based on polygamy and lingering questions about the Mountain Meadows episode.

Utah was strategically placed on the Overland Trail, and Brigham was ordered by President Lincoln to provide one hundred men to protect the mail route. Lot Smith, who had destroyed the army wagons in Wyoming in the Utah War of 1857, was named to lead the unit.[14]

However, in August 1862 Brigham received the unhappy word that a new detachment of federal troops from California would be sent to Utah. In anger and defensiveness, he withdrew Smith's services. Thus ended Utah's only contribution to the Civil War.[15]

In 1863, Colonel Patrick Edward Connor arrived in Great Salt Lake City with five hundred men of the Third Regiment, California Volunteer Infantry. His stated mission was to protect the route to California through the Utah Territory from Indian depredations. He was also in

Utah to quell any possible Mormon "uprising." Connor established Camp Douglas, named for Stephen A. Douglas, on a hill overlooking Great Salt Lake City. Connor, an outspoken Irishman, would become a hated Catholic symbol of authority over the Mormons.[16] It may be apocryphal, but it was said that one of his first acts was to install a cannon aimed at Brigham Young's Beehive House three miles away.

Connor was among "the nation's foremost haters of Indians and Mormons."[17] He warned the Mormons that their treasonable sentiments would be harshly punished. On a foray into Great Salt Lake City he declared it "a community of traitors, murderers, fanatics and whores." He called Brigham a despot and declared that he ordered the execution of "those disobedient to his will." Connor said federal appointees were entirely powerless and lived in fear of Brigham's spies. He warned Washington of a Mormon attack and said if it should come, he would strike at the leaders of the church.[18]

On two occasions, believing Connor was about to arrest Brigham, signal flags were raised on the Beehive House. They summoned hundreds of armed Mormons who vastly outnumbered Connor's contingent.[19]

During the rest of the Civil War, Fort Douglas served as the headquarters of the District of Utah in the Department of the Pacific. Connor sent soldiers into the nearby hills seeking gold, silver, and other minerals, and also founded the first non-Mormon newspaper, the *Union Vedette*.

The *Vedette* was published from 1863 to 1867 and was an anti-Mormon voice.[20]

Said the *Territorial Enterprise*, published in Virginia City, Nevada, "The *Vedette* is the Wooden Horse entered into the Troy of Polygamy. . . . The *Union Vedette* of Salt Lake is a thorn in the side of Mormonism. It is a Daily journal, published under the guns of Camp Douglas, and the 'Destroying Angels' are not disposed to molest the audacious little sheet. It is the enemy of polygamy and the effects of its broadsides are beginning to be seen and felt. Were the Federal Troops to be withdrawn from Salt Lake City, the *Vedette* would not long be permitted to assault the sacred symbols of Mormonism."[21]

Connor was looking for a fight, and Brigham roared his readiness to take up the challenge. However, cooler heads prevailed. Brigham was a fox as much as a lion.[22] Accommodations were reluctantly made by both sides.

Lincoln's second inauguration brought a troop of Connor's soldiers and members of the Nauvoo Legion together in a march through the streets of Great Salt Lake City. A month later Brigham lowered the flags to half-mast following the assassination of the president, whom just two years before he had labeled "as wicked a man as ever lived."[23]

Indian problems continued to beset the settlers, and in the natives Connor saw a foe he could fight with bullets and powder.

In January 1863, a Mormon scout led Connor's soldiers toward a Shoshoni village on the Little Bear River near the Utah-Idaho border. They attacked the sleeping village at dawn and in the end killed 235 men, women, and children. Connor declared a great victory, and even the *Deseret News* was supportive. In fact, it was a slaughter of innocents based on the report of a stolen cow.[24]

Today at the Fort Douglas Military Museum (the fort has largely been subsumed by the University of Utah), a tasteless paean to General Connor's massacre of Native Americans on the Little Bear is inscribed on a plaque: "In May, 1863, following his impressive victory at the Battle of the Bear River, Connor was appointed to Brigadier General."[25]

At the museum Connor is described as the "Father of Utah Mining," certainly accurate, but he is also described as "First Gentile of Utah." The latter is accurate in a weakly symbolic sense. In 1854, seven years before Connor came to Utah, Julius and Fannie Brooks became one of Utah's early gentile families. They were Jewish.[26]

Connor encouraged the development of mining, and many of his California volunteers had experience in the gold fields. By 1863 the first claims had been filed in Bingham Canyon in the southwest corner of Great Salt Lake Valley.[27] More claims would be staked in adjacent Tooele County and at Alta in Little Cottonwood Canyon, just twenty-nine miles from the Beehive and Lion Houses. Shortly thereafter, mines were opened in the Tintic District, eighty miles to the south, and Park City, thirty-three miles east.[28] By 1864 non-Mormons were pouring into Utah to pry precious metals from Brigham's Great Basin Kingdom.[29]

In 1866, Utah again heard threats of a possible invasion by the federal government—this time over a case of adultery. In March, Newton Brassfield was shot after he married Mary Emma Hill, who was already married to a polygamous Mormon, Archibald M. Hill, then absent on a church mission. Since the Morrill Anti-Bigamy Act had been passed by Congress in 1862, US judge Solomon McCurdy had told Mrs. Hill that her plural marriage's illegality rendered a divorce unnecessary.[30]

Brassfield, a gentile from Nevada, had been arrested and released following an attempt by him and Mary Emma to remove household items from the Hill residence. Mr. Hill's Mormon friends threatened them. Brassfield threatened back. He was arrested, placed in jail, then released on bail. When Brassfield was about to enter his hotel with US marshal J. K. Hosmer, a gunmen stepped out of the shadows and shot Brassfield. The assailant was pursued by police but escaped. Brassfield died forty-five minutes later.[31]

Brigham denied any involvement by the church, but at an April conference he condoned the murder. If he were absent from his home, he would "rejoice to know that I had friends there to protect and guard the virtue of my household."[32]

This statement stung the angry anti-Brighamites.

General Connor's California Volunteers had been scheduled to leave Camp Douglas. Judge McCurdy wired military authorities of the rising conflict in the Brassfield affair. General Ulysses S. Grant instructed General William T. Sherman in St. Louis to keep the volunteers from Utah.[33]

Sherman sent Brigham a scorching telegram: "Our country is now full of tried and experienced soldiers who would be pleased, at fair opportunity, to avenge any wrongs you may commit against our citizens."[34] Brigham claimed he knew nothing of the murder but said any man had the right to take vengeance on a seducer of his wife.

Six months later Dr. John Robinson was killed after he attempted to file a claim for land within the expansive Great Salt Lake City limits. He built a shack on his claim, and the police tore it down. Robinson went to court to challenge the city's charter. On October 22, 1866, someone knocked on Robinson's door claiming his brother needed medical help. He stepped from his house and was shot. Colonel Connor, named a brevet major general after the end of the Civil War, immediately said Brigham's Destroying Angels had killed Dr. Robinson.[35]

Brigham once again said he had no knowledge of who might commit such a dastardly deed, but in his usual fashion added, "If they jump my claims here, I shall be very apt to give them a preemption right that will last them to the last resurrection."[36]

"Young's blunt talk increased suspicion that the church hierarchy sanctioned anti-gentile violence."[37] As an example of such talk, Brigham had a proposition for certain senators and congressmen who were particularly anti-Mormon. He wrote to William Hooper, Utah's congressional delegate, "I have a proposition to make to the [senators] . . . when my old niger has been dead one year, if they will wash their faces clean they may kiss his ass."[38]

Non-Mormons hoped that the coming of the railroad would dilute Brigham's power as more gentiles poured in to work the mines and settle the territory. Yet Brigham welcomed the transcontinental railroad in spite of fears that it would bring more non-Mormons. He obtained contracts for the brethren to dig grades for both the Union Pacific and the Central Pacific. He liked the money, and he saw it as a way of keeping out the rascals he expected to comprise the construction crews. It would help shore up the economy, since Brigham and the church were having financial difficulties. (Brigham was habitually late in paying his bills.) Better yet, the railroad would bring more Mormon converts and they would be able to come to Utah more cheaply.[39]

Chapter 16

THE *TRIBUNE* AND ZCMI ARE BORN

The beginning is the most important part of the work.

—Plato

T he *Union Vedette* ceased printing in 1867, much to the relief of the church. Gone were the advertisements for liquor and burlesque and bear meat dinners at Wilton and Taylor's Saloon. Gone was the blatant Brigham bashing and constant harping on polygamy, since one of the two relics of barbarism, slavery, had been resolved. The second relic, polygamy, remained alive and flopping on the table.[1]

Orvin Nebeker "O. N." Malmquist (1899–1985), the *Salt Lake Tribune*'s political editor for nearly fifty years, would author a history of Utah's biggest newspaper.[2] Known as "Quist," he wrote, "There is abundant evidence to show that it was the economic issue more than anything else which led to the establishment of the *Tribune*. And if there was one facet of church economic policy which triggered the launching of the newspaper it was the organization of Zions Cooperative Mercantile Institution."[3]

Brigham's dictatorial methods had failed to eliminate the gentile merchants who, he believed, sucked money from the Mormon economy and sent it out of state. Nor had he been able to curb what he considered were the high prices set by many Mormon merchants.[4]

In 1868 he hit upon a church-controlled, cooperative economic system, which soon became known by its initials, ZCMI, or just as "ZC." By 1869, ZCMI retail stores began dotting the territory, swallowing up independent merchants by buying their stock.[5] Brigham wanted it known that it was a holy business and essential for every Mormon to buy from ZCMI.

Merchants who were investor members of the cooperative displayed a sign with the ZCMI logo with a depiction of an all-seeing eye and the tagline, "Holiness to the Lord."[6]

How could the faithful now shop elsewhere?

There was great risk and significant capital required for ZCMI. There was also controversy, especially from the economic elite of Mormon society.[7] Cooperatives elsewhere had failed as city wholesalers undercut their prices.

Halt the cooperative?

No. Brigham Young was as steely as he was intrepid. He was unmoved by the counsel of many of his brethren. A prosperous Mormon, William Godbe, was among those who felt Brigham's dictatorial powers regarding ZCMI had overstepped the bounds of competitive capitalism. Mormon Elias Harrison shared Godbe's views. They also believed Brigham had lost sight of Joseph's spiritual piety, consumed as he was with what would today be called job creation. Godbe and Harrison were, however, in favor of keeping polygamy.[8]

In the spirit of the visions of Joseph Smith, Godbe and Harrison traveled to New York City and visited a spiritual medium named Charles Foster. Through him they received messages from such diverse persons as the German naturalist Alexander Humboldt, the late Mormon apostle Heber C. Kimball, and Jesus Christ. The spirits summoned by Foster were said to have written their names in blood on his hand or arm.[9]

Godbe and Harrison came away believing they had been chosen to reform the LDS Church by casting off the yoke of Brigham Young. Now it was time to spread the word.

In January 1868, the *Utah Magazine* appeared on the scene. Its publishers were Harrison and Godbe, and it was edited by Harrison, Edward W. Tullidge, and John Tullidge. At first it was condoned by the church with the *Deseret News* greeting it as an "enterprise worthy of commendation and support."[10]

The church powers were unaware that Godbe and Harrison had some ideas of their own about how Utah's economy and ecclesiastical matters should be run. The two men quietly gathered a following of fellow dissenters who would soon be called New Movement Mormons, or Godbeites.[11]

Brigham was completely in the dark about this new threat. He presided over the plural marriage of Godbe to Charlotte Cobb, Brigham's stepdaughter by Augusta Adams, as late as the spring of 1869.[12]

By autumn of 1869 the *Utah Magazine* began to express the views of its owners more openly. "Think freely and think forever," wrote Harrison, saying Utahns were letting the Mormon priesthood do their thinking for them.[13] Harrison wrote an editorial:

> Common sense would seem to say, develop that first which will bring money from other Territories and States, and then these factories and home industries which will supply ourselves will have something to lean upon . . . we live in a country destitute of the rich advantages of other lands—a country with few natural facilities beyond the great mass of minerals in its bowels. These are our main financial hopes. To this our future factories must look for their life, our farmers, our stock, wool and cotton raisers for their sale, and our mechanics for suitable wages. Let these resources be developed and we have a future before us as bright as any country beneath the sun.[14]

The magazine also editorialized about Brigham's cottage industries, saying that only the vigorous development of mining could provide Utah's citizens with the currency they had long needed.

This would not do. The new publication found itself in collision with Brigham Young's wishes. The *Deseret News* reversed its positive opinion about *Utah Magazine* and ran an editorial on October 26, 1869, signed by Brigham, George A. Smith, Daniel H. Wells, Orson Pratt, Wilford Woodruff, George Q. Cannon, and Joseph F. Smith—the biggest guns in Mormonism and the leaders of the church:

> The *Utah Magazine* is a periodical that in its spirit and teachings is directly opposed to the work of God. Instead of building up Zion and uniting the people, its teachings, if carried out, would destroy Zion, divide the people asunder and drive their Holy Priesthood from the earth. Therefore, we say to our Brethren and Sisters in Every place, the *Utah Magazine* is not a periodical suitable for circulation among or perusal by them and should not be sustained by Latter-day Saints. We hope this will be sufficient, without ever having to refer to it again.[15]

Brigham simmered, then unexpectedly invited Godbe and Harrison to explain themselves. He heard Godbe and Harrison before an ecclesiastical court. He listened to their opposition to his economic plans for the territory. His response was that he did not want his pastoral settlers distracted by mining, nor did he want an influx of outsiders who might tip the political and cultural scales. Brigham also perceived a threat in the spiritualism Godbe and Harrison had used as guidance on their New York trip: spiritualism was *not* revelation. Only Brigham was a revelator.[16]

The two men were a threat to his leadership.

The founders of the *Utah Magazine* were excommunicated for their deviation from Brigham's word. In a last hurrah, the editors and publishers announced,

> The present volume of this magazine was commenced by the publishers with the express purpose of presenting before the people of Utah some of the broad and grand conceptions of God and humanity which they felt themselves called upon to present. . . . In the face of special prohibition by the absolute ecclesiastical authority which has prevailed in this territory, it has run its course, a silent preacher of advanced thoughts . . . and a steady opponent of absolutism in Church and State. It is now withdrawn to make way for a more prominent advocate of the same great principle.[17]

Undaunted by their banishment from the church, Godbe and Harrison founded the New Movement and attracted a small band of adherents, including some of the more well-to-do artistic and intellectual Mormons, quite unlike the dissident, murdered Morrisites of 1862.[18]

The New Movement founders of the *Utah Magazine* were already thinking about a new publication. New Movement Mormons saw ZCMI as the consummate act to enclose the Mormon economic system. To gentile businessmen it was a threat to their very existence. To the noncooperating Mormon merchants it was an ultimatum to join or leave the territory.

Brigham told the noncooperators, "[W]e shall leave them out in the cold, the same as the gentiles, and their goods shall rot upon their shelves."[19]

+++

The weekly *Mormon Tribune* made its first appearance on New Year's Day 1870. Its publishers were Godbe and Harrison. Managing editor was a newcomer to the territory, Oscar G. Sawyer. Associate editors were Edward Tullidge and George W. Crouch.[20]

It followed the same spiritual and economic philosophies of its *Utah Magazine* predecessor. By now, the mining camps were burgeoning in the canyons of the territory, and to the displeasure of Brigham, the *Mormon Tribune* followed the news of the mines. Editorials emphasized the need for cooperation between Mormons and non-Mormons and argued for freeing politics of control by the church. In spite of woeful finances and internal schisms, readership grew. The *Tribune* became a daily newspaper on April 15, 1871. It dropped the word "Mormon" from its masthead when it realized it might limit its readership.[21]

And what happened to the territorial economy after ZCMI was founded? The business of gentile merchants at first went into decline. Some left the territory. The Walker brothers, merchants who had earlier left the church over Brigham's tithing demands, claimed sales dropped from $60,000 in one month to $5,000. The Auerbach brothers claimed a similar drop. Tax records for the era indicate no such drop. It is possible that at least these two merchants may have benefited from other non-Mormon merchants leaving the territory.[22]

Both firms told Western historian H. H. Bancroft that they offered to sell to the church at fifty cents on the dollar and leave the territory, but that the offer was declined. By the time the 1869 LDS Semi-Annual Conference rolled around the non-Mormon stores were once again packed by Mormons.[23]

Chapter 17

THE GREAT DIVIDE AND THE BORDER RUFFIANS

The world is not ready for some people when they show up, but that shouldn't stop anyone.

—Ashly Lorenzana

The new daily *Salt Lake Tribune* became "pungently anti-Mormon" under editor Oscar G. Sawyer, an experienced journalist trained in sensationalism by James Gordon Bennett's *New York Herald Tribune*.[1]

Harrison resigned as publisher, and Tullidge later wrote that "a Utah journalist ought to have perceived the unfitness of the *New York Herald* Bohemian to take the editor-in-chiefship of the *Mormon Tribune*."[2]

Sawyer's editorship created schisms within schisms among the Mormons who had founded the paper and the gentiles who cooperated with the New Movement Mormons to effect economic change in the territory. There was a clash of philosophy. The excommunicated Mormon publishers did not consider themselves anti-Mormon. They just wanted things to change.

The non-Mormons and editor Sawyer believed the aim of the paper was to crush Brigham Young's economic and political grip on his people—nothing less. And the way they believed that could be done was by bringing to bear the power of the federal government.[3]

Sawyer and his adherents gained the upper hand in the editorial practices of the *Tribune*. Since sex provides sensational reading and was sure to draw public attention from the rest of the country, Sawyer lobbed plenty of sensational polygamy stories to the paper's readers. When referring to the "Utah problem" in Congress, it was understood this was polygamy. It was polygamy as much as politics that brought successive threats of invasion by government troops.[4]

Meanwhile Judge Dennis J. Toohy, a shareholder in the *Tribune*, added fuel to the fire of conflict. He gave a speech to a political party meeting, saying, "Here in Utah . . . sensuality and crime have found a congenial home; here immorality has been lifted up where virtue ought to reign. If I had time I could prove the leaders, not the people, were to blame for this."[5]

Meanwhile, editor Sawyer, to the alarm of the founding publishers, was using plural marriage to inflame opposition to the Mormons on all levels.[6] A powder keg sat within the staff of the *Tribune*. Editorials were erratic, depending on whether the bombastic Sawyer wrote them or whether one of the founders wrote them. It was a tussle in typography and must have left readers confused.

The keg blew when it was learned that Sawyer had allowed Chief Justice James B. McKean to write editorials in the *Tribune* sustaining his own decisions. McKean was hated by both the conventional Mormons and the New Mormons.[7] The New Mormon founders called a meeting.

Harrison accused Sawyer of having given short shrift to maintaining the cause of freedom and the rights of all classes, without distinction of Mormon or gentile. He said Sawyer had been brought to Salt Lake City (the "Great" was dropped from its name in 1868) by Godbe with the

> expectation that he would carry out the design of its founders; that he, Harrison, had resigned the editorship, and control of the paper, to give himself a temporary rest, with the said understanding that Mr. Sawyer, having obtained control, had turned the *Salt Lake Tribune* in a new direction and given it other aims and purposes from those for which it was established; but above all he impeached the managing editor on the specific charge of having permitted Judge McKean to write editorials sustaining his own decisions.[8]

Sawyer told the directors they were mere merchants and knew nothing about journalism. Maybe so, but they knew how to terminate an employee. Facing this, Sawyer resigned, citing journalistic incompatibility between himself and the directors.[9] The other directors of the *Salt Lake Tribune*, some of them non-Mormon, felt it was hopeless to attack some policies of the church and defend others.

Financial support withered.

The intelligent, artistic New Movement Mormons who had started

Utah Weekly, later the *Mormon Tribune*, and finally the *Salt Lake Tribune* had underestimated Brigham Young. The prophet and president of the church was tough and pragmatic. He was beloved by devout Mormons, admired by many non-Mormons in the territory, and grudgingly respected by many who hated him.[10]

The New Mormons may have failed financially, but they were visionary when it came to seeing a time when Utah would enjoy a more open economic policy and a compromise by the church over polygamy.

In 1873, the original excommunicated founders sold the economically stressed *Tribune* to three men from Kansas: Fred Lockley, George F. Prescott, and A. M. Hamilton. The general manager was Fred T. Perris. They were dubbed the "Border Ruffians" by the Mormons, an insult to three Union veterans of the Civil War.[11]

The church ordered its readers not to subscribe. They did, anyway. They could read what the church was saying about itself in the church-published *Deseret News*. What they wanted to know was what the world was saying about the church, and only the *Tribune* provided that.

During the ensuing years the *Tribune* would frequently call for a full investigation into the shadowy Mormon explanations of the Mountain Meadows Massacre, suspecting that there was a dark underbelly to the story. Mormons clung to their chimera that the greatest single massacre of an overland wagon train in Western history was caused by Paiute Indians, incited to violence by the Fancher party.[12]

Brigham Young played a clever game, blaming the weak federal governor for not fully investigating the massacre, while continuing to cover it up with deception and outright lies about Mormon involvement.[13]

On September 10, 1873, the new owners of the *Tribune* issued their declaration of a no-holds-barred conflict with the church.[14]

To make the debt-ridden *Tribune* profitable they would have to break the political and economic control of the church in the community.[15] The first volley fired in the paper's new offensive against the Mormons involved a *Tribune* reporter.

The Mormon city council had become enraged at coverage of its meetings by the *Tribune* and ejected the reporter and closed their meetings to representatives of the newspaper. The new owners responded in print:

> Several long-time residents have suggested to us that we were pursuing an unwise course. "You never can disarm the hostility of the Mormons . . . your truckling to their abuses will never aid you. The first moment you assume the right of free speech they will come at you with their old time rancor. You must lend your hand to brush them aside, for you never can live peaceably with them."[16]

The *Tribune* was the voice of those who wanted federal intervention in Utah, a territory long considered a runaway by most of Congress.[17] The *Tribune* attacked Brigham personally, calling him the "Mormon Profit" and "Fat Briggy."[18] They didn't spare his family, either. Reporting on a speech by Brigham Young's son, the *Tribune* wrote,

> Young Brig then made his appearance and after sundry coughs, barks, growls and scowls, proceeded to stammer forth how glad he was to meet the brothers and sisters in their new and commodious building. Brig was exceeding troubled in consequence of a belief dominant in his mind that all did not pan out as well as they ought to. He said he was "mighty liberal" himself and his personal friends and acquaintances, he knew contributed largely also. "But did every person do that?" After repeating this query about fifty times he gave his pantaloons a hitch upward, grunted and took his seat.[19]

But the new *Tribune* owners were up against a tough adversary in Brigham Young. He had organized his people, put down schisms, and had led his band through the wilderness. He held his Mormons firm against the mining that was now surrounding them. He had made the desert blossom. Although arrested and charged with murder and sundry other crimes, he thwarted unfriendly judges at every turn, using his own Mormon courts.[20]

Still, the church's hold in the territory was slipping. More gentiles were coming into the territory. Dissident members of the church may have been growing in number. The Mormons had fewer friends in Wash-

ington. The US Army was firmly ensconced. Indian depredations continued in some of the more isolated villages.

Brigham, now old, gray, and in failing health, began a charm offensive, softening his language and his rigidity. In his heart he believed that
someday the Mormons would return to their Heaven on Earth in Jackson
County, Missouri, in accord with the prophesies of Joseph Smith. Realis-
tically, they were in Utah for the foreseeable future.[21]

The church was not without its defenders. President Ulysses S. Grant
visited Utah Territory in 1875 to see for himself why "Mormon tyranny"
had forced him to send tough federal judges and officials to Utah. He
conferred with Brigham and observed a welcoming demonstration by
hundreds of Mormon children. He turned to his federal appointee,
Governor George W. Emery, and muttered, "I have been deceived."[22]

Charles Dickens, visiting a ship of converts to Mormonism about
to depart for the United States, called them the "pick and flower" of
England.[23] This helped spike the mutterings that only the dregs of
Europe were converting.

To blunt attacks equating polygamous wives to slaves in the South,
the Mormons had given suffrage to Utah women in 1870. *Tribune* biographer O. N. Malmquist called it "a public relations victory."[24]

The *Tribune* was unrelenting, loathing both polygamy and the
Mormon tithing rate of 10 percent, claiming it was economically unsound
for the community. But it was the divorce suit of Ann Eliza Young against
Brigham Young in which the *Salt Lake Tribune* took its greatest glee.[25]

Ann Eliza Webb, age twenty-three and married to James Dee, was
granted a divorce at Brigham's behest. The grounds were abusive treatment. Her father, Chauncey Webb, had interceded on the young woman's
behalf. After the divorce, the attractive Ann Eliza, who had appeared
in a number of theatrical productions (Brigham loved the theater and
attended often), moved back into the home of her parents with her two
young children. She soon had new suitors. When Brigham, then age
sixty-seven, was informed of the interest by one of them, he took Ann
Eliza for a walk and announced his own matrimonial intentions.[26]

Ann Eliza knew the Young family quite well. She was friendly with
some of Brigham's daughters and wives through her visits to the Lion
and Beehive Houses. Good enough. She was married to the church president in April 1868.

Ann Eliza refused to move into the Lion House (where he kept many of his wives), so Brigham built her a cottage nearby. She moved into it with her mother.[27]

Brigham spent far more time with his counselors and friends than he did with any of his wives, and Ann Eliza filed for divorce on July 28, 1873, her grounds being that Brigham treated her with emotional, physical, and financial neglect. She asked $1,000 a month alimony, $20,000 in legal fees, and $200,000 from Brigham's estate. Her bill of divorce claimed that her husband had property worth $8 million and an income exceeding $40,000 a month. Brigham countered that he owned less than $600,000 in property and that his income was less than $6,000 per month.[28] He claimed that since polygamy was illegal, his marriage had no legal basis and neither did the claims of Ann Eliza. He also saw to her excommunication on October 10, 1874.

Ann Eliza stepped onto the front pages of the *Salt Lake Tribune* and into the international limelight. Newspapers all over the country followed the story.

The divorce stuttered along. A federal judge twice quashed the suit on procedural grounds. Backdoor negotiations were conducted with Ann Eliza by Brigham's brother-in-law, Hiram Clawson. His offer was a divorce and $15,000—and that she leave the territory.[29]

She responded in a letter to Clawson in September agreeing to those terms as long as Brigham met them within twenty-four hours. She warned that she had "stronger inducements" to "go before the Eastern public and in person acquaint them with my wrongs."[30]

Apparently Brigham didn't deliver, and the "insubordinate rib of the Prophet," as the *Salt Lake Tribune* called her, carried out her threat.[31]

Ann Eliza had an offer from P. T. Barnum. However, her manager, James Pond, suggested that James Redpath's Lyceum would be a better choice.[32]

With a public endorsement from an anti-Mormon judge in her purse, she trained east, stopping in Laramie, Cheyenne, and Denver. She told audiences about the secret temple endowment ceremony, provided a list of Brigham's wives, and denounced her husband's miserliness.[33]

"The things which I suffered opened my eyes to the hollowness of Brigham Young's pretensions to sanctity and character, and unveiled the system of which he was head and I one of many victims," she told her Denver audience.[34] She was an overnight celebrity, filling lecture halls and earning generous fees. The newspapers loved her.

In the spring of 1874 she arrived in Washington. George Q. Cannon, editor of the *Deseret News* and a church apostle, informed Brigham that Ann Eliza lobbied at the capitol every day. She mingled with congressmen. Cannon wrote, "When a drunkard and a whore unite, the product should be filthy."[35]

As a result of Ann Eliza's story, newspapers pressed Congress to pass the Poland Act.[36] It would curtail the Mormon-controlled probate courts and create a process for the selection of a balance of Mormon and non-Mormon juries. It was passed and set the stage for several court battles, including one over Ann Eliza's divorce.

Federal judge James McKean, who had long been a thorn in the side of the Mormons, decided Brigham should pay Ann Eliza $500 a month alimony. Brigham refused to pay. McKean held him in contempt and imprisoned him for one night. The church president's nephew said his uncle had a good night's rest.[37]

McKean was removed from office by President Grant, the Mormons claiming it was because of the unjust imprisonment of Brigham, while later writers said it was a political disagreement.[38] Ann Eliza's case continued under a new federal judge, Jacob Boreman, who ordered Brigham's house arrest until he paid back alimony. Another justice reversed Boreman, and yet a third justice reduced the alimony but ordered seizure of some of Brigham's property for its payment.

Mule stubborn, Brigham said, "I will spend the remainder of my days in prison before I will pay them one cent."[39]

The case finally went to trial in April 1877. Chief Justice Michael Shaeffer accepted Brigham's argument that his marriage to Ann Eliza was illegal and dismissed her suit.[40] "The fact that Young won the case on the basis of the marriage's illegality, however, augured poorly for the future of Mormon polygamy," wrote historian John G. Turner.[41] With the passage of the Poland Act the church had been stripped of much of its influence over the territory's courts. Federal prosecutors readily pushed ahead to prosecute polygamy.

Ann Eliza would go on to marry a Michigan lumberman and banker. She would divorce him, too. In 1875 Ann Eliza published her autobiography, *Wife No. 19*. In it she would write about life with Brigham and her escape from Mormonism. She would also write about the Mountain Meadows Massacre.[42]

Chapter 18

MOUNTAIN MEADOWS: BRIGHAM YOUNG'S SCAPEGOAT

I have been sent down here by the old Boss, Brigham Young.
—John Doyle Lee

By the early 1870s more than fifteen years had passed since the Mountain Meadows Massacre and no one had been brought to trial. While accolades were common for whites who killed Indians during this period, and even for whites who killed blacks (the Colfax, Louisiana, slaughter of 1873), it is a tribute to Brigham's hold on his flock, the territory's politics, and his scapegoating that "a reviled religious minority who killed one hundred and twenty white, Protestant emigrants eluded prosecution for nearly two decades," wrote John G. Turner, Brigham's biographer.[1]

Now Mormons were speaking up, asking embarrassing questions.

Historian Will Bagley believes that perhaps no one did more to expose the lies surrounding Mountain Meadows than Charles W. Wandell, who wrote under the name "Argus."[2] Converted to Mormonism in 1837, he had worked in the historian's office in Nauvoo and had served a church mission to Australia. On his way from California to Utah in 1857, he had heard rumors that white men, not Indians, had done the killing at Mountain Meadows. Rumor was the killers had been led by prominent Mormons. He saw the scattered bones at Mountain Meadows. His faith began eroding.

Wandell was disfellowshipped from the LDS Church in 1864 for mining. (Disfellowshipment is a temporary suspension of LDS Church membership privileges, while an excommunication expels a person from the church altogether.)[3]

After being disfellowshipped, Wandell moved to Nevada where Mormons circulated the story that Wandell had been at Mountain Meadows at the time of the massacre.[4] To exonerate himself from the innuendo and gossip, he picked up a pen. Using the name "Argus," in 1870–71, Wandell wrote a series of articles for the *Corinne Reporter*, a gentile newspaper coming out of the rough-and-tumble railroad town of Corinne. The town was established at the north end of Great Salt Lake not far from the point where the golden spike was driven to complete the railroad in 1869.

Wandell's open letters to Brigham Young asked uncomfortable questions about the massacre. He claimed that even while camped in Salt Lake City the Fancher party was weary and footsore, and that Brigham ordered the emigrants "to leave their camp at the Jordan [River] with almost empty wagons."[5] He claimed that Eleanor McLean Pratt, widow of Parley Pratt, identified one or more members of the Fancher party and charged they had been present at Parley's murder as he ran from her irate husband, Hector.[6] Wandell blamed Brigham Young's hostility toward outsiders' wagon trains as the reason that Brigham, as territorial governor, failed to protect them.

The Arkansans "were ordered to break up their camp and move on and it is said that written instructions were sent on before them, directing the people in the settlements to have nothing to do with them."[7] By the time they got to Mountain Meadows they had only forty days' rations for the seventy-day journey across the desert of southern Nevada until they could resupply at San Bernardino. Wandell said that as a result they faced certain death.[8]

In full dudgeon now, Wandell gave a series of lectures, including one in Salt Lake City in January 1871, to some three hundred people. The faithful Mormons in the audience did not want to believe Brigham could be responsible for such a heinous crime. Wandell refused to relent, although his articles and speeches were "a strange mix of truth and fiction, and some of his stories appear to be based on intentional falsehoods fed to him by Mormon authorities," according to Bagley.[9]

Wandell kept at it. He insistently raised questions that were stonewalled by Brigham, yet he must have touched the guilt that lay in the breasts of many of the massacre participants. The first confession by a participant was about to crack Mormondom.[10]

The church was being challenged. How to meet the challenge? It would change its position, again and again. It was called "lying for the Lord."[11] When accused of complicity, Brigham repeatedly promised to support an impartial investigation. Such an investigation never came to be.

In spite of oaths of silence among the perpetrators, rumors were seeping out. Questions were being asked. It was not outside pressure so much as devout Mormons themselves who had come to question the official story.

Brigham Young's version said that Paiute Indians had committed a heinous attack on a wagon train, killing a hundred emigrants. That was the story the church was sticking to. As late as 1869, Brigham Young Jr. defended the original church position—it was all done by Paiute Indians. That same year, George Q. Cannon, editor of the *Deseret News*, who'd known the truth of the matter for at least ten years, repeated the lie in an article in December: the Arkansas company was hostile to the Indians; they poisoned an ox and the spring at Corn Creek, and ten Indians died. The Indians took revenge at Mountain Meadows. Cannon claimed that the Mormon leaders of Cedar City had heard of the massacre but arrived too late to help. Brigham and the Mormon people had always "been ready to give every aid in their power to have this occurrence rigidly examined."[12]

Brigham, equally vociferous in his defense, claimed the church would "sift the matter to its uttermost, and discover the guilty ones."[13]

By1870, most Mormons in the territory knew the truth. One convert wrote his family in Scotland saying not to believe the stories in the official church publications: "[T]here has been & is Lies told in the Millennial Star [a widely read church publication] . . . we was told in the Millennial Star that the Mountain Meadows Massacre was Committed by Indians but It is known by Everybody here to have been done by Mormons." Brigham Young, he wrote, termed it "a heartless butchery but harbers [sic] the very Men that did it and there is One if Not More of them Bishops."[14]

Internal dissenters—like the Godbeites at the *Salt Lake Tribune*—were the ones who were kicking up a fuss; Brigham could hold the outside world at bay with disingenuous denials. He could claim that the federal government was dragging its heels in investigating the massacre.

More information came to light through the whispers of Mormon men and women of conscience.

As early as 1868 Mormon settler George Hicks of Harmony, a settlement not far from Mountain Meadows, wrote Brigham that while he once took comfort from Brigham's denunciation of the massacre's perpetrators, he now wondered if the church had sanctioned the murders. Hicks wrote, "Can it be possible that the Church . . . fellowships a Company of men whose hands have been Stained with the blood of innocent women and children?"[15]

Brigham read the letter and replied, furiously suggesting that perhaps Hicks himself had participated "in the horrible deed." In such case, Brigham said that "if you want a remedy, rope round the neck taken with a jerk would be very salutary." In this note he told Hicks that the massacre "does not concern uninvolved Latter-day Saints."[16] This suggests that Brigham was coming around to a new defensive strategy that would perhaps lay the blame on a few of the brethren.[17] Hicks continued to speak out and lost his church membership.[18]

The church was feeling the heat of condemnation and began to alter its position in response to the critics questioning the Mormons' role in the Mountain Meadows Massacre.

Then came the rumor of the mysterious 1857 letter in which it was alleged that Brigham gave orders for the massacre. Charles Wandell claimed John D. Lee could produce written proof that he had simply executed orders from Brigham. Wandell also claimed Lee had been offered $5,000 by Brigham for the letter. The faithful insisted it was a forgery created by Lee to blackmail the Mormon president.[19]

Now the church leadership cannily shifted the public relations spotlight—once shone on the entire church—to renegade southern Utah Mormons. Brigham was distancing himself and the church and focusing on scapegoats in a damage control effort.

The *Salt Lake Tribune* noted the policy change in 1875: "For twelve years their voice was one of indignant denial that any Mormons were engaged in the affair. . . . [T]he Whole Mormon people changed front as suddenly as a well-drilled regiment."[20]

Brigham Young had four scapegoats to point his finger at. First was Isaac Haight, Mormon stake president, territorial legislator, and mayor of Cedar City. Haight had led the planning of the massacre. Then there was John M. Higbee, first counselor to Haight and a major in the Iron County Militia. He was the man who ordered the killing to begin. There was John Dame, the colonel and commander of the Tenth Regiment and bishop of the Parowan Ward. Dame was administratively responsible for the actions of officers and soldiers under his command. Though Dame was under the ecclesiastical direction of Haight, his religious superior was actually his military inferior, thus giving Dame more accountability and responsibility in the matters of the massacre.[21]

Finally, there was John D. Lee, Brigham's adopted son, sealed to him in temple rituals, the same man who sometimes signed himself as J. D. L. Young. An early convert to the Mormon Church, Lee was a friend of the founder, Joseph Smith Jr. He was committed to Brigham and to the church. He married nineteen wives during his lifetime and fathered more than sixty children. In 1856, as the Indian agent in southern Utah, he helped the Paiutes establish farms. He knew their language and their leaders. Lee had encouraged the Indians to join the Mormons in the attack against the wagon train. Brigham's sights came to rest on Lee.

Brigham called Haight, Lee, and Dame to a meeting in St. George in 1870 "for a full hearing and investigation to find out who was the person that led and brought about the fearful tragedy."[22] Josiah Rogerson would vaguely claim that Lee "was heard in his own behalf to the fullest extent, and it was then and there found to be the one most guilty."[23] Lee, an active diarist, wrote nothing of this period, so the truth is diffused by the passage of time. Historian Bagley believes Brigham may have signaled to Lee that he was to take the fall for the massacre. He urged Lee to move south. There are indications that Brigham promised Lee safety and protection from the federal authorities.

In his diary two months after the meeting, Lee expressed shock upon learning that he had been excommunicated by his adoptive father, Brigham Young. The Council of Twelve Apostles, on October 8, 1870, had excommunicated Lee and Isaac Haight, attempting, it would seem, to get at the root and branch of "the problem" and isolate those who took an active role. For committing "a Great Sin . . . they were not to have the Privilege of Returning to the Church again in this life." It was reported that Brigham picked Lee to stand trial for the massacre "because he knew Lee would do whatever he told him to."[24]

Official church records at the time showed no mention of the excommunications, and Mormon historian Juanita Brooks concluded there was an agreement not to mention the massacre in any official church records.[25]

As a sidebar to this story, in 1961 Lee would posthumously be reinstated to full church membership after concerted pressure from his descendants. The Lee family was instructed by church officials to give information only to the family to avoid "undue publicity." When Juanita Brooks decided to write of his reinstatement in her Lee biography, church president David O. McKay threatened to rescind Lee's reinstatement if she wrote about it. Brooks herself feared she might be excommunicated. She wrote about it anyway in *John Doyle Lee: Zealot, Pioneer Builder, Scapegoat.* There were no repercussions from the LDS Church.[26]

One of Lee's wives went to Brigham to see if the excommunication was true. Brigham said it was and told her to leave Lee, for the Lord had commenced to "work out righteousness."[27] To distance himself from the distasteful questions that were growing, Brigham was cutting off his adoptive son.

Mormon James Andrus claimed he saw Brigham and Lee meeting at Shirt's Creek. The prophet's "arraignment and censure of John D. Lee was so direct and pertinent" that he could not forget it. Lee begged for forgiveness, but Brigham said as far as he knew there was none for him in this life.[28]

Lee drove to St. George in December 1870 and sought out Brigham. Lee asked how thirteen years after the massacre, "all of a sudden [he] must be cut off from this church. If it was wrong now, it certainly was wrong then."[29]

Brigham told Lee there was an official new way of looking at the massacre. Yes, there were Indians, but they were led by a few Mormons, including Lee. Brigham claimed he had only recently learned the particulars.[30]

Said Lee, "What we done was by the mutual consent & council of the high counsellors, Presidents, Bishops & Leading Men who Prayed over the Matter & diligently Sought the Mind & will of the Spirit of Truth to direct the affair."[31]

Brigham told him to be "a man, & not a Baby."[32]

A few days later Lee received an unsigned letter from Erastus Snow, the apostle in charge of the southern Utah colonies: "Make yourself scarce & keep out of the way."[33]

Lee had a subtle strategy for fighting back. He began a defense of Brigham Young regarding Mountain Meadows. Brigham had no prior knowledge of it, Lee told Daniel Page, the postmaster at Parowan. The postmaster would reply, "I always understood that that B. Young counselled that Matter to be done."[34]

Many of the Lee family were convinced that Brigham "selected John D. Lee as 'the goat' because he was well aware that Lee would never refuse to do anything he was called on to do by the authorities."[35]

Lee started south, moving his families from their homes to the beautiful but desolate country where the Pariah River meets the Colorado River, just above Grand Canyon. It would become known as Lee's Ferry. A tale was floated to help Lee disappear.

"Argus" Wandell announced that John D. Lee was dead. He claimed he'd been killed under orders from Brigham and that his body had been found at Grapevine Springs. As Bagley pointed out, Charles Wandell was occasionally a conduit for misinformation from what he believed were well-placed Mormons.[36]

On April 10, 1871, one of the participants in the massacre finally went public. Phillip Klingensmith appeared before the clerk of the Seventh Judicial District Court of Nevada and swore out an account of what happened to the Fancher party at Mountain Meadows in 1857. He'd been there, part of the Mormon regiment.[37]

A blacksmith and a bishop in Cedar City, he was the only official involved in the massacre who voluntarily left the LDS Church. In 1858 he'd been kicked in the head by a horse and wandered the settlements of southern Utah and southern Nevada, hiding in the mountains with Lee, building a road with Jacob Hamblin. By 1870 he'd settled near Bullionville, Nevada.[38] As the *Salt Lake Tribune* would later say, Klingensmith may have made his confession out of self-protection. It could also have been made out of guilt.

Klingensmith, while a bishop in ecclesiastical matters, was a mere private in the militia. His confession described the massacre as a military operation. The local militia had been mustered "for the purpose of committing acts of hostility against" a party of emigrants.[39] Haight, Higbee, Dame, and Lee ordered the regiment forward, with Haight initially hoping to let the company go in peace, "but afterward he told me that he had orders from headquarters to kill all of said company of emigrants except the little children."[40]

Klingensmith claimed he participated only as "a matter of life or death to me." He avowed that Lee persuaded the men to carry out their orders and then negotiated the surrender of the emigrants. Klingensmith confessed to firing his gun in the first volley but said he did not fire again and set about saving the children. Lee told Klingensmith he had related the facts to the commander in chief, Brigham Young.[41]

Klingensmith said he was making his statement to the court because "I would be assassinated should I attempt to make the same before any court in the Territory of Utah."[42]

Bagley wrote, "Wandell's charges had been explosive, but Klingensmith's confession cracked the case."[43]

The *Tribune* was delirious with Klingensmith's confession. It quoted John D. Lee as saying that news reports accusing Brigham Young of masterminding the murders had "the saddle on the right horse."[44] Lee, stolidly defending Brigham, told his diary he was furious at this report. He would defend Brigham, saying he knew nothing of Mountain Meadows. It is almost certain that Lee expected Brigham to defend him in return. When he picked his goat in Lee, Brigham had indeed picked the right billy.

Writs of arrest went out for Lee, Haight, Higbee, and Daniel McFarlane, all of whom met with Lee to coordinate their stories. Then they scattered. Lee followed Brigham's directive that polygamous husbands should deed their property over to their wives, and then left for his Pariah River hideaway. He named his homestead there Lonely Dell and took two wives with him. He constructed a ferry to cross the broad and often rambunctious Colorado River and started calling himself Major Doyle.[45]

It may have been Lonely Dell, but this gateway to the Arizona Territory was also a cross road for visitors. They included John Wesley Powell's second expedition of 1872. Lee gave Powell his own version of the massacre, claiming he had tried to stop it "and when he could not do so he went to his house and cried."[46]

Francis Marion Bishop met Lee and said Lee claimed to have been opposed to the whole affair and "was not on the ground at the time."[47] Lee continued to hold Brigham blameless, as he was sure Brigham would save him in spite of the price that was now on his head. He believed Brigham confirmed it in a letter sent to Lee in June 1872, according to Juanita Brooks.[48]

Mormon hater and journalist John H. Beadle was ferried across the river by Lee and felt sorry for him. "He is shunned and hated by his

Mormon neighbors. . . . His mind is distracted by an unceasing dread of vengeance."[49] Lee wrote that he told Beadle that he "did not consent to it & was not present when it was done, although I am accused of it. Neither had Brigham Young any knowledge of it until it was all over."[50]

In public Brigham denounced the murderers; in private he protected them. He sent a number of letters to Lee via Jacob Hamblin. There is evidence that Brigham offered protection in return for silence.[51]

The *Tribune*'s "Border Ruffians" wanted a full explanation of the massacre of a wagon train at Mountain Meadows, located two hundred miles south of Salt Lake City. The paper was printing stories contrary to the church-approved tale.

The passage of the Poland Act, which gave US district courts exclusive jurisdiction over criminal and civil cases in Utah, was a blow to the ecclesiastical system of probate courts that had protected the Mormons for so long. Thus, in 1874, a federal grand jury was able to indict Lee, Haight, Dame, Higbee, Klingensmith, and several others for murder.[52]

Lawmen began searching for the men.

Lee was found by a deputy US marshal hiding in an animal pen near his house in Panguitch, 135 miles north of Lee's Ferry. Brigham knew where Lee was hiding and could have warned him, but did not—clearly he had decided that Lee would take the fall.[53]

Brigham Young happened to be visiting Parowan, fifty miles from where Lee had been captured. When they heard the news of Lee's arrest, Brigham called together his advisors. "Brethren, now what shall we do? Be free but quick. Have any of you any suggestions?" Silence ensued. "If you will not talk, I will," Brigham said finally, "but it is all right. The time has come when they will try John D. Lee and not the Mormon Church, and that is all we have ever wanted. Go to bed and sleep, for it is all right."[54]

The *Tribune* would report in sensational detail the arrest of Lee and, subsequently, of Dame. While the young newspaper had been struggling, the vivid reporting by Frederick Lockley revived it and put it on the map. Reporters came from across the United States. Bagley has compared the sensationalism of that to the Lindbergh kidnapping and the O. J. Simpson trial.[55] With the preliminary hearing before Judge Jacob Boreman, rumors flew that Lee would turn state's evidence on Brigham Young. Mormon leaders held their breath.

Dame's attorneys wanted him tried first, fearful of what Lee might say. Apostle George A. Smith allegedly told a church meeting in February 1875 that if Lee were found guilty "it was only right that he should be punished." Then he asked that everyone pray for Brother Dame.[56] The *Tribune*'s Lockley reported that Lee considered this "sanctimonious treachery."[57]

Lee now said he wanted to come clean and dictated a statement blaming Haight and Higbee but failed to acknowledge the complicity of Dame or any higher authorities.[58] This was not what prosecutors wanted. They were after Brigham.

Relieved that Lee seemed to be holding fast in protecting the church president and other leaders, Brigham bankrolled Lee's legal defense. Brigham believed he could control the proceedings of the trial.[59] It was a miscalculation.

Lee was arraigned and pled not guilty. The trial began the next day in the southern Utah town of Beaver, with a jury of three non-Mormons, one former Mormon, and eight active Mormons. The crowds grew so large that it had to be moved from the upper floor of the Beaver City Cooperative to a nearby saloon.[60]

The trial was chaotic. Attorneys hired by Brigham to defend Lee had two loyalties, one to Brigham and one to Lee.[61] Wrote Lockley for the *Tribune*, the prosecution was "less desirous to convict and punish the prisoner than to get at the long concealed facts of the case."[62]

Klingensmith turned out to be the star witness, saying that he had met with Brigham Young a month after the massacre. He said Brigham's orders were, "What you know about this affair do not tell to anybody; do not even talk about it among yourselves."[63] His detailed retelling of the massacre left America in horror. Klingensmith would later tell the *Salt Lake Tribune* that he fully expected to be killed for his testimony.[64] (Reports came from Mexico in 1881 that he was killed there by a vengeful Mormon. His son believed he was killed and buried in a wash near his Caliente, Nevada, ranch. Others claimed he hid among the Indians on the Colorado River and died about 1902.)[65]

While Lee was locked up, the *Tribune* reported that his wife, Emma, pelted Lee's jailer with stones, raised her fists, and challenged the deputy "to come on."[66] Meanwhile, attorneys for the defense produced a telegram from a doctor stating that two defense witnesses, Brigham Young and George A. Smith, were too feeble to come to Beaver.

As the trial continued, Lee's defense was that the Indians had coerced the whites into taking part in the massacre. "The Indians made us do it," was Lee's position.[67]

And were the Paiutes ever called to testify? No. The prejudices of the time prevented that. However, one correspondent did track down Beaverite, nephew of Chief Kanosh, who told him that the story of the poisoned spring and of the poisoned ox was not true. No Corn Creeks, Pahvants, or Beaver Indians ever went to Mountain Meadows. He said Lee led the Paiutes under his old friend Moquetus in the fight. Lee became scared "and says the Indians did it." Beaverite denounced the cowards who "tried to throw all the blame on the Indians."[68]

The case went to the jury on August 5, 1875, with all of Utah betting on Lee's acquittal. The prevailing theory was that the LDS Church would manipulate the outcome. In fact and in secret, the church had decided that Lee must be convicted. He was, after all, the goat. However, the signals for conviction were apparently misread. The jury became deadlocked. All the Mormons and the former Mormon voted to acquit; the three non-Mormons voted for conviction.[69]

The press across America was rabid with anti-Mormonism after the testimony and the deadlock. One paper wanted Brigham arrested before he could flee the country; another wanted Salt Lake City's streets to be ornamented with the heads of Mormon leaders on pikes. The *Sacramento Record* called the crimes the acts of "priestly demons."[70]

"There can be little doubt that Brigham Young is the arch-fiend who planned and directed the atrocity," wrote the Indianapolis *Herald*. Every Mormon involved, from highest to lowest, should be hanged, it opined.[71]

Lee was held for a second trial at Fort Cameron (at Beaver), receiving Mormon officials, including George A. Smith, whose fiery preaching had inflamed the region against the emigrants in 1857. Besides Apostle Smith, he was visited by Apostles Orson Hyde, Erastus Snow, and other church leaders.[72]

Federal investigators suspected George A. Smith of carrying out Brigham's orders to wipe out the wagon train at the military council in Parowan attended by Haight, Dame, and Lee. Smith would die a few days later, with his doctor attributing death to "fright." So many had been involved; they feared Lee would break as had Klingensmith.[73]

Lee wrote, "They each and all told me to stand to my integrity, and all would come out all right in the end."[74]

But the fix was now in. Lee was moved to the territorial penitentiary in Salt Lake City. Federal prosecutors offered to free him if he would implicate the other leaders, including Brigham Young. Lee wouldn't budge. Dame, still under arrest, was also moved to Salt Lake City. The two conspired in the cells, and Dame told Lee to keep quiet and be patient. Others who could testify against them would soon leave the territory, and they would be safe. Dame was transferred back to Beaver.[75]

The federal agents doubled their efforts in an attempt to find Haight and Higbee. Lee, meanwhile, stood firm, confident that Brigham would save him. "I had his solemn word that I would not suffer," Lee wrote.[76]

A new US attorney for Utah, Sumner Howard, was named in April 1876. The national pressure to produce a conviction was up against the formidable local pressure of the foxy Brigham and his Mormons. No one felt a conviction could be obtained in Utah, where juries would consist largely of Mormons. But attorneys make deals, and Howard began working on Brigham, who needed a deal to distance the church and himself from the hounds of investigation. It was brokered behind the scenes, and the exact terms are not known. However, Robert N. Baskin, an aggressive non-Mormon attorney, former mayor of Salt Lake City, and an assistant US attorney had no doubt that Howard agreed to impanel a Mormon jury on the condition that Brigham would place in evidence affidavits that exonerated Mormon authorities of complicity in the massacre. Brigham would deliver witnesses and documents guaranteeing conviction of John D. Lee. Howard also negotiated an agreement to drop the prosecution of others in custody, including William Dame.[77]

A deal was struck. Brigham withdrew whatever support he had promised Lee.

The second trial began on September 11, 1876, in Beaver, again under Judge Boreman. Lee had been free on $15,000 bond and had roamed southern Utah visiting family and presciently saying his good-byes to his wives and children. He was stunned when the bond, posted by William Hooper, was withdrawn. By now Lee must have sensed that he'd been betrayed, especially when he saw that the indictment against Dame was quashed, allowing Dame to go free.[78] However, he was not to be deterred from his defense of the church and Brigham. "I ain't going on the witness stand to save my scalp," he said. "Cowards and traitors only do that."[79] Bagley reported that an uneasy Lee constantly talked about being true to his friends, even if he hanged for it.

Daniel Wells, Brigham's second counselor, arrived in Beaver. He preached a scorching sermon on duty and then schemed to make certain that the selected Mormon jurors would vote for conviction. Any gentiles were challenged.[80] US Attorney Howard, in his opening statement, surprised the court when he said they were there to try John D. Lee and only Lee, not Brigham and the LDS Church.

Then Daniel Wells provided testimony, a signal that the church supported a guilty verdict. William Bishop, the attorney defending Lee, was stunned when it became apparent that the church was aiding the prosecution, especially in light of the fact that he had earlier been told by church authorities that his client would not be convicted.[81]

An affidavit from Brigham claimed that Lee had tried to give him a detailed account of the massacre but Brigham told him to stop, as he "did not wish [his] feelings harrowed up with a recital of the details."[82]

New Mormon witnesses came forward, saying that at Mountain Meadows they had seen Lee club a woman to death, shoot another woman, as well as two or three of the wounded. Witness Nephi Johnson said he'd watched from a nearby hill and swore that Klingensmith and Lee "seemed to be engineering the whole thing." In fact Johnson, a leader of the Nauvoo Legion, had ordered the assault on the women and children.[83]

Jacob Hamblin took the stand, and his testimony hinted at rape prior to Lee killing two girls. Hamblin and Johnson knew plenty more, but the plan was to convict Lee without involving anyone else.[84]

Lee now realized that "those low, deceitful, treacherous, cowardly, dastardly sycophants and serfs had combined to fasten the rope around [his] neck."[85] He had been betrayed by his adoptive father, by his southern Utah friends, and by his partners in murder. Lee refused any defense, and Howard used his closing argument to say that the Mormon authorities knew nothing of the butchery until after the fact.[86]

The case went to the jury at 11:45 a.m. on September 20. By 3:30 p.m. Lee had been convicted of first-degree murder. He was convinced that some men would "swear that black is white if the good Brethren only say so." He still believed he would be saved, but the line had been crossed.[87]

Judge Boreman sentenced Lee to die on October 10, 1876. Utah law gave him the choice of being hanged, shot, or beheaded, the latter being the preferred method of Mormonism's blood atonement. Lee chose to be shot.[88]

While US Attorney Howard won the agreed upon conviction, Judge Boreman was not happy with the outcome of the trial. At the sentencing Boreman said the trials revealed that high LDS Church authorities had "inaugurated and decided upon the wholesale slaughter of the emigrants."[89]

The *Salt Lake Tribune* wrote that Howard's deal with Brigham had cost him "the confidence of every honest man in Utah in his integrity."[90] Meanwhile, hundreds of southern Utahns wrote letters appealing for clemency for Lee.

On the afternoon of March 21, 1877, Marshal William Nelson and US Attorney Sumner Howard loaded John D. Lee into a closed carriage and headed for Mountain Meadows.[91] It was supposed that execution at the site might cause him to give a fuller confession. He'd refused implicating Brigham and other officials even though he seethed with anger at their perfidy.

In the passage of twenty years the Meadows had changed; the springs had dried up, and the verdant grass was gone. A few scrubby bushes remained. On the morning of March 23 the assembled military drew three wagons in a kind of semicircle a hundred yards east of the ruin of Carleton's cairn, which was now a mass of scattered rocks. About seventy-five persons were gathered at the site, many of them onlookers who had found out the time and place of the execution in spite of attempts to conceal it.[92]

Officials cobbled together a coffin of rough pine boards and then raised a blanket to screen the identity of the firing squad. It is believed that his firing squad consisted of Mormons, since traditionally the military did not take part in civil executions. Lee had a hearty breakfast and coffee. He was dressed in a red flannel shirt and a sack coat. He said, "I did all in my power to save those people. . . . I consider myself sacrificed."[93]

The *San Francisco Bulletin* described the scene as "weird beyond description."[94]

Lee wrote his will and was led to the coffin. He discarded his coat and sat down. He spoke to the assembly, again proclaiming his inno-cence. He denounced Brigham's betrayal: "I studied to make this man's will my pleasure for thirty years. See, now, what I have come to this day! I have been sacrificed in a cowardly, dastardly manner."[95]

The reverend George Stokes, a Methodist minister from Beaver, knelt with Lee and offered a prayer. Lee was blindfolded, but at his request his arms were left untied. He sat upright on the coffin and raised his hands over his head. "Center my heart, boys!" he said to the firing squad. The order was given: "Ready, aim, fire!"[96]

John D. Lee tumbled into his coffin, his feet resting on the ground. Reported the *Salt Lake Tribune*, "The old man never flinched. It made death seem easy, the way he went off."[97]

Historian Bagley summarizes Lee in this way: "In the final analysis any reasonable accounting must reckon Lee as a profoundly tormented and evil man, but at the end he faced the consequences of his acts with simple courage while others buried their guilt under an avalanche of perjury and evasion."[98]

Lee is buried in Panguitch, Utah, beneath what is known as the William Prince Inn.[99] Charges against both Dame and Higbee were dropped, with Dame dying in 1884 and keeping his secrets.[100] Higbee died in 1904, leaving behind myriad conflicting tales.[101] Haight, still a fugitive, lived as an active Mormon in Mexico until his death in Arizona in 1886.[102]

The legend of John D. Lee would live on. He left in book form what purported to be one of his confessions, *Mormonism Unveiled*. It would become a best seller.[103] His family would defend him into modern times, citing Lee's last prophecy: "If I am guilty of the crime for which I am convicted I will go down and out and never be heard of again. If I am not guilty, Brigham Young will die within one year! Yes, within six months."[104]

Brigham Young did die (probably of appendicitis) five months after Lee, on August 29, 1877, still blaming the *Tribune* and others for trying to implicate him in the Mountain Meadows Massacre. He also left behind a remarkable legacy of leadership, colonization, and political savvy, but non-Mormons mostly painted him as tyrannical and crude.[105]

The *Tribune* on August 30, 1877, wrote on the death of Young, "Yet we believe that the most graceful act of his life has been his death . . . if the death of Brigham Young shall be supplemented this fall by an act of

Congress giving the people of Utah a free ballot and an amended jury law, the extirpation of the priestly tyranny will be complete and Utah will be Americanized and politically and socially redeemed."[106] It went on, predicting "the whole decaying structure [of Mormonism] will rapidly fall to pieces."[107] The *Tribune* forecast that John W. Young, a son, would succeed Brigham as president and prophet.

The *New York Post* editorialized of Brigham, "In one respect he was a vulgar cheat, of course. In his character he was essentially coarse and brutal, without refinement, without culture, without the finer instincts of men. He gave free rein to the worst passions of his own nature, and made the worst passions of other men his tools. Yet he was a man of almost unbelievable force of character of a certain kind."[108]

As John G. Turner summarized the life of Brigham Young, "He preserved a church and created a people, but that success damaged and even destroyed some lives."[109]

The church became sensitized to the very words "Mountain Meadows." Its missionaries had them flung in their faces. As early as the 1880s it began an ongoing public relations campaign to protect the reputation of the Mormon people and of Brigham Young. Prophets can never be wrong, since God speaks through them. In the process the church doctored evidence. It ignored records. It stonewalled. The church's position would shift, and shift again, as new facts about the massacre came to light. Well into the twenty-first century the public image of the Church of Jesus Christ of Latter-day Saints would be tarnished by evasive statements about Mountain Meadows.[110]

Chapter 19

THE DEVIL IN THE FORM OF C. C. GOODWIN

> Should we still be friends when it could be more profitable if otherwise?
>
> —Toba Beta

By 1880, Lockley and his Border Ruffians continued pounding on the departed Brigham Young, on polygamy, and on the new president of the LDS Church, John Taylor. They constantly called for more federal laws to curb plural marriage.

However, "there began creeping into the newspaper signs that the 'Border Ruffians' were tiring or running short of money," wrote O. N. Malmquist, the *Tribune*'s selective biographer. During the ten years since they had taken over the paper from the schismatic Godbe and others, "[Business] minutes as are still available show clearly that there was more exuberance in the editorial office than in the business office."[1]

More than half the businesses in the territory were Mormon owned, and they would not risk censure from fellow Mormons or church authorities by advertising in the *Tribune*. Lockley believed that profitability was in sight, but, ragged and worn by cranking out thousands of words each day, he needed help. An editorial writer was brought in.

The new man was Charles Carroll Goodwin, former editor of the *Territorial Enterprise*, the rambunctious newspaper of Virginia City, Nevada, where Mark Twain had once labored. For Goodwin, roughhouse journalism was a way of life. Lockley introduced to readers a tough fire-breathing writer who would bring to Mormondom a battle that would excite, delight, and infuriate. Goodwin, and his equally deft counterpart editing the *Deseret News*, Charles W. Penrose, engaged in an inky war of vitriol, sarcasm, and humor. The competition would sharpen the talents of both men, and because of the "Mormon problem" they would gain national and international status.[2]

Malmquist, in his study of the *Salt Lake Tribune,* wrote that "there are reasons to suspect that they privately respected and admired each other." Penrose would later refer to Goodwin as "[m]y friend, the enemy."[3]

Goodwin expanded the political coverage of the paper and was stanchly a supporter of the Liberal, or anti-Mormon, party. His Liberal Party support appeared to be a valiant but quixotic cause; in the congressional election of 1880, People's Party voters elected the Mormon apostle George Q. Cannon with 18,568 votes to Liberal Allen G. Campbell's 1,370 votes.[4]

However, the Liberals now had a new territorial governor, Eli H. Murray, and he would lead an assault on Mormonism, first by declaring Campbell the winner of the election. He based his decision on the premise that George Q. Cannon was an unnatural alien (born in England), made further ineligible because of his polygamous relationships (he was in violation of the 1862 Morrill Anti-Bigamy Act). Cannon fired back. The clerk of the House of Representatives placed Cannon's name on the roll based on his huge plurality of votes. Cannon continued to draw a salary. It created an uproar locally and nationally. The seat remained vacant.[5]

During the conflict between Cannon and Campbell, President James A. Garfield was assassinated. From July 2, 1881, when he was shot, to September 19, when he died, the event dominated the press. Instead of producing a lull in the conflict, Mormonism got dragged onto the national stage once again when the *Boston Watchman* claimed, "It is an interesting fact that on the day set apart for prayer by the President . . . the *Deseret News,* organ of the Mormons, declared that the 'Praying Circle' of the Mormon Church was engaged in continual supplication for the death of President Garfield." The *News* called it an "atrocious untruth."[6] It is representative of the no-holds-barred conflict of the Mormons and the anti-Mormons.

In 1882 the tempo of the conflict picked up. The *Tribune* slashed away at polygamy and the church's economic system. The Edmunds Act was passed, an anti-polygamy law designed to plug loopholes created by Supreme Court decisions. It would be followed five years later by the Edmunds-Tucker Act, which would finally bring polygamy to heel.

Perhaps tired of the constant battling, Lockley and his associates sold the *Tribune* in 1883. Its buyers were its editor, Goodwin, and Patrick H. Lannan, a Nevadan, with the purchase likely financed by John W. Mackay, founder of the rich Comstock Mine in Virginia City, Nevada. The net worth of the paper was listed as $39,483.44, and the buyers probably paid about that for it. The *Tribune* would be sold for more than $730 million 114 years later.[7]

Goodwin's acerbic tongue was somewhat curbed by Lannan, but the paper clearly was on the side of the non-Mormons. In an editorial on New Year's Day 1884, the paper declared that "it is the only real missionary journal, its mission work being the attempt to convert this region to full allegiance to American laws."[8] The issues that created the paper were still the issues of the day, with added attacks on the "Word of Wisdom," which had become more emphasized by the church after Brigham's death and after John Taylor became president. (The Word of Wisdom advises Mormons to eschew coffee, tea, tobacco, and alcohol.) The *Tribune* frequently snarled its disapproval of the liquor stances of the church and continues to do so to the present day.[9]

The moderated tone of Lannan's *Tribune* was short-lived. By the end of 1884 the "Great Divide" reached new heights. One lacerating editorial began with the following:

The Beast of the *News*

The bastard in charge of the [*Deseret*] *News* again last evening filled his dreary columns with an attempt to convict a man before trial, to advertising a young girl's shame and everlasting disgrace and to seek to make out that the *Tribune* was trying to conceal and apologize for a crime.[10]

The *Tribune* was angry that a local doctor had been named by the *News* for procuring an abortion for a young woman.

About this same time an editor at the *Deseret News*, John Q. Cannon, was charged by the *Tribune* with taking a young, plural wife and arranging for a rival to be sent on a faraway church mission. Cannon sought out the *Tribune* city editor, Joseph Lippman, on the street, demanding an apology. The late Utah historian Harold Schindler wrote,

Cannon said: "I want you to get right down here on your knees and apologize for the lie you published about me last Sunday."

"I never published any lie about you."

"You did! Now, I want you to apologize."

"I will not!" That is as far as Lippman got. Before the words were out of his mouth he found himself "flying through the air as if a cannonball had struck him." He was knocked about ten feet and landed on the back of his neck and shoulders. Before he could scramble to his feet, Cannon was on top of him with a "little rawhide" and was about to give him a taste of it, when the prostrate reporter "began to cry most piteously and beg for his life." Cannon gave him a couple of strokes across the head and hands and was about to apply some more, when police, alerted by Lippman's howls, arrived on the scene. Cannon pleaded guilty in court and was fined $15 for his "infraction of the law." He then hustled back to the *Deseret News* city room—to write the story for the next edition.[11]

The upturn in venom was due to a crusade by the *Tribune* to enforce the anti-polygamy acts.

The Edmunds Act of 1882 and the Edmunds-Tucker Act of 1887 were milestones in a virulent conflict between Mormon and non-Mormon,[12] with the *Tribune* pouring fuel on what it hoped would be the death pyre of polygamy and the end of the Mormon grip on the Utah Territory. The *Tribune* would be the rallying flag for the anti-polygamy crusaders and would press home vitriolic attacks on the church and its leadership for failure to bow to the government.

While the first Edmunds act made polygamy a felony, the Edmunds-Tucker Act of 1887 gave teeth to the anti-polygamy laws, directing the US attorney general to seize real estate and personal property of the church.[13]

Over the next several years the government's campaign to eradicate polygamy became an ordeal for all but the most insensitive and vindictive of Mormon-haters. Fathers were taken to prison, leaving wives and children destitute. Families were hunted down like quail as they attempted to find safety from pursuing federal marshals. Many church officials went into hiding.[14]

Mormons were plunged into despair, and non-Mormons were jubilant with the announcement that Apostle George Q. Cannon, on the run for weeks, had been caught in Humboldt Wells, Nevada, 180 miles west of Salt Lake City.[15] While John Taylor was president of the Mormon Church (and in hiding), many non-Mormons believed Cannon to be the guiding hand of the church.

Cannon consented to return to Salt Lake City, and Marshal E. A. Ireland took a train to Nevada to pick up the fugitive apostle. But while training with marshals back to Salt Lake City, Cannon came up missing.[16]

He next showed up in the custody of a deputy marshal at Promontory, Utah, with a broken nose, a large gash over the left eye, and most of the skin scuffed off the left side of his face. He explained he had accidentally fallen off the train. Journalists at competing papers faced off: "fallen" or "jumped" became arguable terms. Trial was set for Cannon, but he jumped bail and went missing again.[17]

A few weeks later Cannon popped up from hiding and returned to court to face his charges, pleading guilty to two counts under the anti-polygamy laws. Cannon was sentenced to 175 days in jail and fined $450.[18]

Hundreds of Mormons would also be fined and jailed for putting ecclesiastical beliefs ahead of federal law.

After the death of John Taylor on July 25, 1887, Wilford Woodruff became the fourth president of the Mormon Church. It was Woodruff who would bring a conciliatory position to end the "irrepressible conflict."[19] On September 25, 1890, the *Salt Lake Tribune* published a twenty-seven-line dispatch from the Associated Press in Chicago:

> President Woodruff further says that inasmuch as the law forbidding polygamy has been pronounced constitutional by the court of last resort he hereby declares his intention to submit to those laws and use his influence with members of the church to have them do likewise. . . . I now publicly declare that my advice to Latter-day Saints is to refrain from contracting any marriage forbidden by the law of the land.[20]

It astonished Mormon and non-Mormon alike. Thereafter it would be called simply, the "Manifesto." It was sustained by the church membership at the next semiannual LDS Conference.[21]

If statehood came, would Mormons control the political system? This and other worries jammed the political process. Finally, an agreement was reached; the Mormon People's Party and the non-Mormon Liberal Party were no more. Instead, there were Republicans and Democrats. It may be apocryphal, but the enduring story is that ward bishops divided their membership in half: those sitting on one side of the chapel would become Democrats. The other side would become Republicans. Utah was declared a state on Saturday, January 4, 1896.[22]

Chapter 20

ENTER THOMAS KEARNS

> Remember, remember always, that all of us, and you and I
> especially, are descended from immigrants and revolutionists.
> —Franklin D. Roosevelt

The presidential election of 1900 found the *Tribune* supporting the Republicans. In January the Utah Legislature convened to select a man to become a full-term senator, and after much contention between Mormons and non-Mormons, the compromise appointee to emerge was Thomas H. Kearns, a Catholic mining magnate. Reed Smoot, a Mormon apostle, had withdrawn from the race, and church president Lorenzo Snow essentially "allowed" Kearns to go to the Senate.[1]

"Kearns was the greatest surprise that has ever occurred in Utah politics," penned an editorialist for the *Bingham Bulletin*.[2] Utah was at the time 70 percent Mormon.

Tom Kearns was second generation Irish Catholic born in Ontario, Canada. He arrived in Park City in 1883 with a grammar school education and much ambition. He was tough, both physically and mentally.[3]

Kearns had worked in mining camps around the West before making his way to Park City, thirty miles east of Salt Lake City. He and a partner acquired a lease on an undeveloped mining property called the Mayflower. They struck ore, which was 30 percent lead and contained about one hundred ounces of silver per ton. The first ore shipment put $20,000 in Kearns's pocket. The Mayflower led to the discovery of the main vein of the Silver King Mine.[4]

On the day Kearns was due to leave to take his Senate post in Washington, the Silver King announced it was increasing its monthly dividend from $75,000 to $100,000.[5]

Kearns married Jennie Judge, winner of Father Galligan's contest as the most popular girl in Park City.[6] They would move to South Temple Street in Salt Lake City, and the home they built is now Utah's Governor's Mansion.

When Senator Kearns purchased the *Tribune* secretly in 1901 (for an estimated $200,000),[7] he wanted to reach out to Mormon and gentile alike. Kearns, who began in the mines as a mucker (ore shoveler), had an egalitarian streak.

Stories circulated about his lack of education and his hardscrabble beginnings. His gaffes included referring to Alaska as an island; he mispronounced the Philippines as "Filliponies" and referred to indigents as "indignants."[8]

He founded an orphanage, championed miners, and refused to cut their wages when metal prices dropped. Kearns had a down-to-earth appraisal of himself. Meanwhile, in Washington, Senator Kearns was erasing the image given him by his political foes—that he was graceless, a hard-rock miner.[9]

Kearns and his descendants would own the *Tribune* for the next hundred years. Kearns would build it, an adopted son would manage it, and his children and grandchildren would enjoy the prestige and profits of what would become a respected, Pulitzer Prize–winning newspaper. All would be lost to the family through the manipulations of the Mormon Church.

Senator Kearns returned to Salt Lake City in the fall of 1902 to find the political scene chaotic. He was accused of supporting Mormon apostle Reed Smoot for Senate. He was also accused of *not* supporting Smoot. Political alignments were fractured.[10]

Kearns chose no side, but he did have doubts that Smoot would be seated by the Senate if elected. He was right.

Smoot's election sparked a bitter four-year battle in the Senate. Was he eligible to serve? Did his position as a Mormon apostle disqualify him from the Senate?

Meanwhile, Thomas Kearns had to decide whether to seek another term as senator, or to retire. In the 1900 election Kearns had essentially bought his Senate seat.

At the time, the LDS Church was destitute. In an agreement with President Lorenzo Snow, Kearns agreed to buy from the church an option on Saltair (a resort on Great Salt Lake) for $50,000 and also agreed never to exercise the option.[11] In return, President Snow "allowed" Kearns to go to the Senate. Kearns wanted badly to return for a second term, but by then, Snow was dead and Joseph F. Smith was LDS president. Smith hated Kearns for, among other things, railing against polygamy on the floor of the Senate and accusing the Mormons of continuing the practice in secret even after the Manifesto and statehood.

Kearns was well regarded, and his chances appeared favorable for reelection. It was an unwritten maxim of the time that of the two senators from Utah, one would be Mormon and one would be non-Mormon. His seat should be filled by a non-Mormon.[12]

When the Republican Legislature met in early 1905, the Mormons refused to reelect Kearns and instead chose George Sutherland for a full six-year Senate term. (Sutherland had been elected to Congress in 1900; he was raised as a non-Mormon by a father who had left the Mormon Church. In 1922 Sutherland would be appointed to the US Supreme Court and would become one of Franklin Delano Roosevelt's disdained "nine old men.")[13]

Kearns's parting speech upon leaving the Senate dripped with anti-Mormon vitriol. The *Deseret News* called the speech "his dying wail."[14]

By 1903 Kearns's ownership in the *Tribune* had become public knowledge. The anti-Mormon watchdog barked out big headlines during local elections, and frequently Kearns was on the winning side.

Mormons and non-Mormons were mingling more, crossing the religion barrier to vote for candidates on principle and softening their stance on ecclesiastical matters. In the 1912 election, candidates from all three parties—Democratic, Republican, and Bull Moose—were treated by the *Tribune* with an impartiality that puzzled long-time readers. All in all, the *Tribune* had achieved a kind of maturity under Kearns and pursued a course of reconciliation.[15]

John F. Fitzpatrick, who would serve as publisher from 1924 to 1960, joined the *Tribune* in 1913 as secretary to Kearns. Born in 1887 in Pennsylvania, he was an enigma—tough, autocratic, and shy.[16]

He was disciplined and determined to learn, delving into every aspect of the newspaper business—mechanical production, circulation, distribution, advertising, business management, news gathering, and the editorial departments.[17]

The *Tribune*, under Fitzpatrick, was building its circulation and getting advertising from Mormon firms, as well as non-Mormon. Its fight with the *Deseret News* was quiescent. The quelling of the old political war was paying off on the bottom line.

Only occasionally were barbs exchanged with the Mormons, although the *Tribune* was ever ready to harpoon Senator Reed Smoot. Any politician supporting Smoot could be on the receiving end of a *Tribune* editorial punch.[18]

The year 1918 proved eventful. The Spanish flu closed down Salt Lake City. Long lists of dead and missing from the trench war in France appeared in the *Tribune*. For Thomas Kearns, the year ended early. On October 18 he died eight days after he was struck down by an automobile near the base of a monument to Brigham Young on Main and South Temple Streets.[19]

The responsibility for running the paper shifted to Fitzpatrick, and he consigned to the past some of the old animosities that had festered for years. The paper grew in circulation and profits, and the editorials grew blander. In 1924, Fitzpatrick reluctantly agreed to be given the official title of publisher.[20]

In 1930, the morning *Tribune* reacquired another local newspaper, the evening *Salt Lake Telegram* (sold in 1914 by Kearns), which competed for afternoon readership with the *News*. The *Tribune* didn't want it. Nor did the church's *News*. However, neither paper wanted outsiders to take it over.[21] The *Salt Lake Telegram* would be among the cast of characters when the joint operating agreement made its appearance on the stage in 1952, and it would disappear shortly thereafter.

In spite of the Great Depression and the diminution of advertising, the *Tribune* survived with Fitzpatrick guiding the paper through tough times.

The New Deal came to Utah in 1932–33, with voters turning against both the church and the *Tribune* by casting ballots for Franklin D. Roosevelt. Smoot, whose demise as senator had been loudly predicted by the *Tribune* in three prior elections, lost in the Democratic landslide.[22] Smoot's name lives in a kind of infamy as a sponsor of the Smoot-Hawley Tariff Act, considered a factor causing the Great Depression.

The *Tribune* and the *News* would editorialize for Wendell Willkie in 1940, but when war broke out, both papers stood behind President Roosevelt.[23]

+++

Shortly after the election of 1936 a young Notre Dame graduate came to the *Tribune*. John W. "Jack" Gallivan was the only son of a half sister of Jennie Judge Kearns, the senator's widow. Jack's mother died when he was five, and Jennie assumed responsibility for him and his two sisters. He attended private schools in California, and while attending Notre Dame University he was campus correspondent for the *Chicago Tribune*.[24]

He started at the Salt Lake paper on August 1, 1937, as a full-time employee. He was hard working and popular, soon dispelling any mutterings of nepotism. For a brief time he fed the homing pigeons kept by the *Tribune* on its roof. Only the adoption of a two-way radio system by the paper saved him from the dovecote.[25]

Gallivan was clearly marked for higher calling. Soon he moved into Fitzpatrick's office as assistant to the publisher.[26]

Post–World War II brought prosperity but also rising costs. The three newspapers of the Mormon's capital city (the morning *Tribune*, the *Trib*-owned afternoon *Telegram*, and the afternoon *Deseret News*) were vying for advertising and circulation. Editorially there was more tolerance between the two papers, primarily because of the détente established by John F. Fitzpatrick during his years as publisher. It was a time when radio was popular and television was on the horizon.

In 1947 the *Tribune*'s circulation in the primary Retail Trading Area (basically Salt Lake County) was 84,895, more than twice the circulation of the *News*, which stood at 40,147.[27] Any circulation outside that area would be money-losing, since about 95 percent of the profits of a newspaper come from retail and classified advertising. The folks in Pocatello, Idaho, might get a Salt Lake newspaper, but that didn't do the Salt Lake advertisers much good.

The facts didn't deter the *Deseret News*, which made a gambit to increase its circulation, primarily to reach its Mormon audience in Idaho. It was a bruising war, fought with turtles, bicycles, toy race cars, and yo-yos, all given to children as incentives to sign up family and neighbors as subscribers.[28]

For a time the *Deseret News* was able to outspend the *Tribune* in promotion. Both papers expanded their circulation areas. At one time the *Tribune* was reported by *Editor and Publisher*, the industry's trade journal, to cover the largest geographical area of any daily in America—Utah, eastern Nevada, southern Idaho, eastern Oregon and Wyoming.[29]

At the same time, *Tribune* staffers heard rumors of other newspapers being interested in buying the *Tribune*. One rumor that shook the paper in 1950 was that it had been sold to the Mormon Church.[30]

The *Deseret News* leaned on its Mormon business owners, and the pressure resulted in increased advertising lineage. They spent heavily promoting themselves in trade magazines. The *News* gave church-approved books to LDS wards selling the most subscriptions. For thirteen weeks one of the *Tribune*'s major Mormon advertisers, ZCMI department store, withdrew its ads from the morning paper.[31]

Business fell at ZCMI, to the loud cheers of the *Tribune*'s ad salesmen, who quickly restored ZCMI's advertising to the pages of the *Tribune*. The paper gave away live turtles with subscriptions, until crying children called the city desk reporting the death of a turtle.[32]

David O. McKay, president and leader of the Mormon Church (1951–1970), was a tall man, marked by his full mane of silver-white hair even at age seventy-nine. He strode through the halls of Holy Cross Hospital in 1951, a Catholic institution, his figure turning the heads of nurses and nuns.[33]

John F. Fitzpatrick, *Tribune* publisher, now sixty-five and recovering from a heart attack, looked up from his bed and saw the silvery mane of the prophet leaning over him. In that hospital room McKay suggested that they work out a joint operating agreement (JOA) for printing, advertising, and circulation that would cover both the *Tribune* and the *News*. The *Tribune* would become the sanctuary for the survival of the *News*.[34]

A JOA deal went into place on October 1, 1952.[35] It would become known as the "Great Accommodation." Many saw it as a symbol of a healing of the breach between the active LDS community and on the other side, the dissidents and non-Mormons. It was a cultural melding of sorts.

However, the JOA deal was "[h]ated by Mormons for its long fight against various church policies; and scorned, immediately after the accommodation, by the more hard-nosed gentiles who considered it cowardly for giving up the fight," wrote *Tribune* biographer O. N. Malmquist.[36]

The new JOA entity was named the Newspaper Agency Corporation, known locally by its initials, NAC. In the original agreement the JOA would have three representatives from the *Tribune* and two from the *Deseret News*. Since it had the greater circulation, the *Tribune* selected the president of the JOA. Profits were allocated according to each paper's percentage of the total JOA circulation. Fifty-eight percent went to the *Tribune*, 42 percent to the *News*, even though the stock was split fifty-fifty. The *Deseret News* was given a benchmark by which it could split the profits fifty-fifty, if the *News* could increase its circulation to the level of the *Tribune*. Historically the *Tribune* had always enjoyed about twice the circulation of the *News*, and the numbers were based on the figures provided by the newspaper industry's credible third party, the Audit Bureau of Circulation.[37]

The power held by the *Tribune* in NAC essentially was the power to control the business policies of the newspapers. The level of revenue the *Tribune* received from NAC dictated how many reporters it could hire, how many investigative stories it could pursue, and how many editorial writers it could employ.[38] The JOA of 1952 was further affirmed in 1970 by the congressional passage of the Newspaper Preservation Act, in which Gallivan played a major role (Fitzpatrick died in 1960).[39] The Newspaper Preservation Act, in essence, waived monopoly restrictions for cities in which competing newspapers needed the economies of joint operation. It was again affirmed in a JOA in 1980.

In the founding agreement of the JOA was a clause thought relatively innocuous: both parties to the contract must approve any transfer of stock to any other party. Lawyers might have called it "mere boilerplate."

The JOA, and the veto power inherent in the transfer of stock clause, would be the Achilles heel that the *News* would spike in 2013 in its attempt to drive the *Tribune* into its death spiral. Yet "[w]ithout the 1952 agreement," said Jack Gallivan, at the time assistant publisher of the *Tribune*, "[t]he *Deseret News* would have gone down the drain." It had lost an estimated $9 million in the circulation war of the postwar years.[40]

By early 2016, it would be the *Tribune* circling the drain, and while the *Tribune* was still the larger and more profitable of the two newspapers, the maneuverings of the Mormon Church had managed to turn Salt Lake City's newspaper profit structure topsy-turvy.

With the death of John F. Fitzpatrick, Jack Gallivan became publisher of the *Tribune*. Gallivan was a community builder, a man with a puckish sense of humor, who, like Fitzpatrick before him, was a Catholic who counted LDS Church leaders among his friends.[41]

The *Tribune* was no longer in relentless pursuit of Mormonism. Gallivan aimed his editorializing at making tourism Utah's largest industry, rebuilding the aging heart of downtown Salt Lake City, and to bringing the Winter Olympics to Utah. He was also instrumental in reviving a largely abandoned and dying mining town—Park City. His Kearns roots were there, and he envisioned it becoming a winter sports destination resort. He established the first condominium in Park City in 1963, the Treasure Mountain Inn, and it sparked life in a moribund mountain town where just two or three years before a Main Street property could have been purchased for back taxes of $500.[42]

Gallivan also encouraged Utah's bid for the 1976 Winter Olympics and built a consortium of interests to support it. This group would grow until finally, in 2002, Salt Lake City hosted the Winter Olympics.[43]

With an eye to the future, Gallivan began expanding the holdings of Kearns-Tribune Corporation (K-T), owner of the *Tribune*. As assistant to the publisher and on behalf of K-T, he purchased the Elko, Nevada, city cable TV franchise in 1956. He saw cable TV as the wave of the future. He continued to build microwave and cable companies across northern Nevada through the fifties and sixties, eventually merging these systems to another group of western cable companies owned by Bob Magness, naming the combined companies TeleCommunications, Inc. (TCI). Shortly thereafter, John Malone was brought on as TCI president.[44]

While Gallivan grew the Kearns-Tribune's cable business, he also shrank the size of the geographical circulation of the *Tribune*, resulting in greater profitability. Although these years were relatively harmonious and profitable, the *Tribune* and *News* opposed one another in several major clashes. There was a face-off over a law to close all businesses on Sunday, supported by the Mormon Church. The church lost. Most heated was a 1968 plebiscite over serving liquor by the drink (in Utah you could take a full bottle of whisky into a restaurant and pour yourself a dozen drinks from it, but a restaurant was not allowed to serve liquor by the drink).[45] The church prevailed in the liquor vote, but this contentious issue drew battle lines between the active LDS members and the dissidents, inactives, and non-Mormons. It would reverberate in one of the church's salvos to kill the *Tribune* many years later.

Chapter 21

BATTLE ROYAL FOR THE *TRIBUNE*

If you have to keep a secret it's because you shouldn't be doing it in the first place.

—David Nicholls

In 1985 the LDS Church's *Deseret News* served the first of several notices to its JOA partner that it wanted to publish mornings. It was a *News* aspiration that went back at least to the 1970s and possibly earlier, according to one former *Deseret News* staff writer.[1] The paper felt hamstrung by its afternoon publication as required in the JOA.

At the time the *News* was a solid, if conservative newspaper, and its reporting was kept separate from the views of the church that owned it. Its demands were built around the assertion that the evening *News* circulation was being eroded by the changing habits of readers brought on by television news. The paper hoped a morning edition would increase circulation.[2] This was the spark that would smolder in the minds of church officials and would eventually erupt into conflagration.

On June 9, 1989, the church again announced its intention to go mornings, but subsequently backed away. Jack Gallivan (by then semiretired but carrying the title publisher emeritus) and publisher Dominic Welch had to dissuade the church from going mornings time and again. Historically the *News* had never been able to achieve much more than one-third to one-half of the *Tribune*'s circulation, in spite of many attempts to increase its readership. The *Deseret News*'s strength and weakness was its own credibility. A Brigham Young University poll found that 70 percent of Utah voters thought the *News* slanted its coverage in favor of the church.[3] It was again a matter of active LDS members already knowing what the *Deseret News* would print; they wanted to know what others were saying about them.

Thomas Monson (who would later become president of the Church of Jesus Christ of Latter-day Saints) had worked for the *Deseret News* and sat as a board member on the JOA for forty years. He clearly saw the economic benefits of the JOA to the church. The church's newspaper was making a lot more money under the JOA. The advertising rates were designed in a way that made it foolish for any advertiser to place his notices in just one of the papers. If advertisers insisted on buying an ad in just one paper, they would pay a premium. As an example, for a hundred dollars you got your ad in the *Tribune*; for $110 you got the combined circulation of both papers to carry the same ad and get one-third more readers. Monson could explain the finances and dynamics of the JOA to those in the church who wanted a more aggressive attack against *Tribune* control. But as Monson rose in the church hierarchy he resigned from the JOA board. His departure ended the regular reeducating of the LDS Church leadership as to the needs and benefits of the joint publishing business in Salt Lake City.[4]

Again in 1990–91 the *News* sought to shift to morning circulation and even tested the waters by circulating mornings in mostly Mormon Utah County.[5] Jack Gallivan compiled statistics that showed that newspapers shifting from evening publication to morning publication had failed to generate a single new reader after the change, and those papers in fact suffered a loss in circulation of 3 percent, which requires an average of ten years to recover.[6]

Gallivan, in his June 14, 1999, memo to John Malone, wrote of his dealings with Gordon B. Hinckley, by then president of the LDS Church: "A very vicious circle exists. President Hinckley tells me that the *Deseret News* management has assured him of success [by publishing] in the morning. The same management tells me that they are mandated by President Hinckley to make morning distribution a success."[7]

As Jack Gallivan would later write in a plea to have Utah billionaire Jon Huntsman Sr. buy the *Tribune*, "The Salt Lake JOA, as the annual financial and circulation audits of NAC for 49 years disclose, it has been the most successful JOA partnership in the United States in profitability and in maintenance of historical circulation averages and share of market circulation."[8] (Gallivan's plea for Huntsman to buy the *Tribune* would echo until Jon Huntsman's son, Paul, stepped into the *Tribune's* picture in 2016.)

Why, in the face of evidence that afternoons switching to mornings died aborning, did the LDS Church persist in pursuing this illusion?

With the existing JOA the *Deseret News* had done very well, since it was supported by the *Tribune*. During the period from 1988 to 1999, yearly advertising revenue for the JOA went from $62,262,411 to $102,273,562, an increase of 66.9 percent.[9]

As far back as 1977 the publisher of the *Deseret News*, a former advertising executive and active Mormon named Wendell Ashton, sought answers as to why the *News* had half or less the number of subscribers as the *Tribune*. He reasoned the *Tribune* was not twice as good as the *News*. He looked at the historical fact that the *Deseret News* from its outset was the official newspaper of the LDS Church and appealed to its hard-core, tithe-paying members. The *News* had always been a solid, if conservative, voice. Bob Mullins, one of its reporters, had even won a Pulitzer for spot news reporting in 1962.[10]

Ashton decided to implement the "LDS Stake Promotion" in 1977 (a Mormon stake is roughly comparable to a Catholic diocese).[11] He concluded that the JOA was not properly marketing to its Mormon base because there should be more than 50 percent of all LDS homes subscribing to the *News*.

The *Tribune*, through the JOA, agreed to help finance the LDS Stake Promotion through the use of the JOA's circulation crews. In April 1978, almost four thousand soliciting phone calls made by the *Deseret News* resulted in 1,074 homes agreeing to receive the *News* free of charge for two weeks. Ashton—a high-profile church figure—wrote personalized letters to each of the 1,074 at the beginning of the free delivery and again one week later. He urged subscription renewal. The results were revealing: of 686 stake leaders sampled, seventy subscribed. Of 388 Sandy and East Millcreek stakes sampled in the suburbs of Salt Lake City, twelve subscribed. There were no renewals, according to Gallivan's memo.[12]

One can speculate that church members got all they needed in terms of LDS news from their attendance at the multiple weekly meetings the church asks of its members. On the other hand, said Rod Decker, a long-time Salt Lake City television reporter, low *Deseret News* readership might be blamed on the idea that "Mormons don't understand how dull they are."[13]

It was in the 1990s that the LDS Church felt that the *Tribune* could be silenced. If so, the Mormon leadership could tell their story without pesky contradiction from the Catholics and their cohorts, the dissidents, who led in criticizing the church and its social and political clout. They could run the newspaper business as they saw fit. While the LDS Church officially denied any interest in obtaining the *Tribune*, court documents would later show this was untrue.[14] The church watched, waited, and planned its takeover.

Mike Korologos, former assistant editor of the *Tribune*, had been hired away to head the public relations arm of one of Salt Lake City's biggest advertising agencies, David W. Evans and Associates. "It was after I went to the Olympic Committee—which was in 1994—that Glen Snarr took me to lunch at the New Yorker [a local restaurant] and asked me point blank what I thought about the LDS Church buying the *Tribune*," said Korologos. "I told him it would be a PR disaster for the church."[15] An astute observer of the Salt Lake scene, Korologos was ignored.

Snarr was the architect of the church's strategy against the *Tribune*, a secret attack being conducted by the First Presidency of the LDS Church, including Gordon B. Hinckley. Snarr had retired from advertising, and in the tradition of the church sending its people on missions (see "Iron Mission" and "Indian Mission" in earlier chapters), Snarr was assigned the "Tribune Mission."[16]

Meanwhile, since 1993, the owners of the *Tribune* were contemplating the future of the paper. Its profits had grown significantly since supporting the JOA, which had also provided sanctuary for the church's *Deseret News*. By 2000 the Salt Lake City JOA showed a profit of $60 million.[17]

Not only did the newspaper make a profit, but the Kearns-Tribune Corporation, parent of the newspaper, had come to own about 15 percent of TeleCommunications Inc. TCI had grown into the largest cable company in the world.[18]

By now 80 percent of the ownership of Kearns-Tribune was in the hands of two elderly widows, descendants of Senator Thomas Kearns.

When they died there could be tax consequences to their children of up to $150 million.[19]

In 1995 a plan was suggested to swap stock with TeleCommunications Inc. so that K-T shareholders could hold their stock interests individually.[20] The Kearns-McCarthey widows and their children were not sure this was a good idea. The newspaper was a family heirloom and a profitable one at that. They felt it was also an institution needed for balance in the community.[21]

The major shareholders balked but left the door ajar when they heard there might be a way to have their cake and to eat it too.

Jack Gallivan as publisher emeritus was still active in the business affairs of the paper. He was in fact so prominent in the community that many believed he owned the *Tribune*, an assumption that grated on the McCartheys.[22] Gallivan spent many hours conferencing with the *Tribune*'s legal counsel. Together with his friend John Malone, the president and major shareholder in TCI, they came up with a plan to trade and sell shares in both companies in a way that would benefit the Kearns-Tribune's elderly shareholders and their heirs while at the same time avoiding onerous tax consequences. It was a clever but complicated deal.[23]

The transaction would include a management agreement that allowed the Kearns family heirs and their publisher to continue to run the *Tribune*. It also provided an option agreement for the Kearns family to buy back the *Tribune* after a period of five years, which was the time required by the IRS to keep the stock exchange tax-free.[24] And the deal would give Kearns-Tribune liquidity through the TCI stock. The critical element was the agreement for the family to buy back the paper after five years.

The McCarthey family held a very large piece of the Kearns-Tribune Corporation, and they didn't trust any of the deal makers. There were shouting matches as the options were encouraged by Gallivan's side and questioned by the McCarthey side.[25] Adjustments to the deal were dialed in as talks progressed, and as the McCartheys became more interested, the TeleCommunications stock swap heated up.

The McCarthey siblings were children of the senator's oldest grandson, Kearns McCarthey. He had been the only one of Senator Kearns's children or grandchildren to make the newspaper his career, working in the advertising department for forty years. On several occasions, Gallivan is said to have talked Kearns McCarthey out of selling his interest in K-T as had so many of his siblings and cousins. As a consequence, by holding on and exercising buy-sell agreements, Kearns McCarthey's ownership had grown.[26]

The unassuming Kearns McCarthey, as a major shareholder on the board of directors, was actually Gallivan's boss. On one occasion he took Gallivan for a ride in his car and told Gallivan that a decision he had made was not his to make, but that of the board.[27]

By 1997, attorneys for K-T had reworked and refined the plan for the TCI deal, and the corporation decided the time was ripe to execute it. While several newspapers, including the *Chicago Tribune* and *Los Angeles Times*, had expressed interest in the *Tribune*, it made sense, according to publisher Dominic Welch, to make a deal with TCI, since it already held much of its stock. And it looked as though the family could save a bundle in taxes.[28]

McCarthey family members were still wary. They were eventually persuaded to go along with the deal. After all, it was their fortune that was most threatened by the inheritance dilemma that triggered the merger talks in the first place.[29]

During the Kearns-Tribune–TCI negotiations, the *News* believed it had an important legal weapon it could invoke should the *Tribune* be sold. This was the clause in the JOA that said that neither partner could independently transfer or sell its interest in the JOA. It came to be described as the veto power, or the right to consent to any sale of the *Tribune* via its stock in the JOA.

Family reluctance notwithstanding, the deal was made in July 1997, and the papers were signed between K-T and TCI.[30] K-T shareholders got more than $730 million in nonvoting TCI stock, a management agreement to continue to operate the *Tribune*, and an option agreement to buy back the newspaper in five years.

Philip McCarthey, one of the heirs, said, "We were told . . . the management and [buy-back] options were rock solid."[31]

Meanwhile, the McCartheys bought out other heirs and formed the Salt Lake Tribune Management Company (SLTMC).[32] Gallivan had proposed that he and Dominic Welch run the management company and the paper, but the proposal "infuriated the McCarthey family. Board members Sarah, Tom, and Philip McCarthey felt left out of the newspaper's future."[33]

The McCartheys paid $1 million for an option to buy back the newspaper five years down the road.[34] The SLTMC, with the involvement of the McCartheys, continued to run the newsroom and got the long-standing 58 percent *Tribune* to 42 percent *News* profits from the JOA. The *Tribune* people viewed it as a temporary sale of the newspaper.

"We always meant to get the paper back," said Bob Steiner, a shareholder and great-grandson of Senator Kearns. "What we didn't expect was that TCI would be shopping around the *Tribune* within three months."[35]

On the day the sale to TCI was final, the *Tribune*'s law firm, Jones, Waldo, Holbrook & McDonough, dispatched a letter suggesting that there might be a catch. In their July 31, 1997, letter they explained, "We note in this regard that, if this option is exercised by [the *Tribune*] . . . the transfer . . . of [Kearns-Tribune's] shares in NAC will require consent of the Deseret [News] Publishing."[36]

The letter was written to TCI. Philip McCarthey says he never saw it. If he had seen the qualifier about the consent of the *Deseret News*, he "would absolutely have stopped the deal." Apparently, Jack Gallivan never showed him the law firm's letter.[37]

The deal was supposed to reduce the tax burden on the McCarthey family, but according to former editor Jay Shelledy, it was also designed to work Gallivan's sons into the management of the *Tribune*, with Michael Gallivan as publisher and John W. Gallivan Jr. as editor.[38] Michael, or "Mickey" as he is known, was a prominent civic figure and advertising man. John, known as "Champ," had extensive experience in television production and news direction. Certainly both had the credentials.

Speculation aside, Jack Gallivan gave assurances that he could easily obtain consent to exercise the buy-back agreement from the LDS Church.[39]

The deal was signed. It made instant millionaires of twenty-four of the *Tribune* writers and editors, used to living paycheck to paycheck. This was thanks to an employee stock ownership plan that held a lot of TCI stock. Shareholders in the Kearns-Tribune Corporation received a very big, tax-free payday and retained management of the paper.[40]

But the door to the takeover by the Mormon Church was now open, and preparation for it was well underway.

"*News* executives carefully planned to portray the purchase of the *Tribune* as their own acquisition, not an initiative by the LDS Church," according to a story the *Tribune* would later publish.[41]

+++

After the sale of the *Tribune*, Leo Hindery Jr. had become president of TCI, replacing John Malone. Hindery was a businessman, a Democratic political operative, and a sometime race car driver.[42] He was a friend of the Mormon Church, having nearly joined its ranks earlier when he coached an LDS Church basketball team in Farmington, New Mexico. Hindery placed himself on the board of the Kearns-Tribune Corporation.

On March 10, 1998, less than a year after the sale by the *Tribune*, an explosive announcement hit the communications world: AT&T had just purchased TCI for $55 billion.[43] As part of the package AT&T got the *Salt Lake Tribune*. AT&T was not interested in being in the newspaper business.

After the sale to AT&T, Hindery then became CEO at AT&T Broadband and was involved in liquidating the unwanted asset. On May 13, 1999, Hindery sent a letter to the publisher of the *Tribune*, Dominic Welch, demanding that the recently formed Salt Lake Tribune Management Company buy the *Tribune* immediately or it would be sold elsewhere.[44]

In a memo to Hindery, Gallivan put his finger on Hindery's motives: "John Malone has indicated, Leo, that your anxiety to sell the *Tribune* to the *Deseret News* is motivated by your fears of political or other reprisals against AT&T [by the church] if it does not make such a sale."[45]

Unbeknownst to anyone in the *Tribune* camp, Hindery was also secretly negotiating with the LDS Church. He said it should consider buying the *Tribune*. Hindery was suggesting to the LDS Church that the *Tribune* could be purchased for about $175 million. He also put out a secret feeler to Dean Singleton, owner of MediaNews Group, a publishing empire that included the *Denver Post*.[46]

In spite of published denials, the church's Glen Snarr (whose title was president of the LDS Church's Deseret News Publishing Company) jumped at the chance to buy the church's long-time foe and rival from AT&T. His mission was approved by the highest offices of the church, certainly with the involvement of Gordon B. Hinckley, first counselor to the president of the church.

"If the church wants to strengthen its voice, this may be the opportunity we have been looking for," Snarr wrote at the time.[47] *News* executives crafted a number of scenarios to take over the paper. News editor John Hughes even proposed firing *Tribune* columnist Robert Kirby, "whose Johnny-one-note stuff is Mormon bashing." He would also "clean up" other *Tribune* columnists.[48]

Meanwhile, Snarr was working behind the scenes with AT&T's Hindery to purchase the *Tribune*.[49] Flying in the face of Snarr's testimony in later court records, the *Deseret News* ran a lengthy article, "20 Questions: Trying to Make Sense of the Newspaper War":

> Does the Deseret News want to own the Tribune?
>
> Answer: Absolutely not, in the words of L. Glen Snarr, chairman of the Deseret News board of directors. The News, he says, believes Salt Lake City should have two competing newspapers, independent of each other.[50]

AT&T did not want to be in the newspaper business. They made a secret, tentative deal with the Mormon Church, but hearing about it, the *Tribune* threatened a suit and predicted the public relations disaster forecast by Mike Korologos in his conversation with Snarr in the 1990s. Meanwhile, AT&T's Hindery, according to Peter Waldman writing in the *Wall Street Journal* in 2000, had insisted that the *Tribune* had brought on its own demise "by treating their church-owned business partner, the afternoon *Deseret News*, unfairly and by making bigoted comments to visiting AT&T executives."[51]

Gallivan and Welch, the *Tribune*'s chief contacts with AT&T during this period, were perplexed by Hindery's statement. Welch denied that he or his staff made "antiracial or antireligious remarks in public or private."[52] Quoted in the *Journal*, he said the *Tribune* tried hard to resolve its business differences with the *Deseret News* until Hindery came in and threw his weight behind the church.[53] Later, under oath in court, Glen Snarr admitted he had never heard Gallivan or Welch make any bigoted or antireligious statements.[54]

"I regard Glen Snarr, Leo Hindery, and Gary Gomm as the axis of evil," Welch said.[55] (Gomm was a newspaper broker who had inserted himself into the melee.) As court documents would later reveal, while Hindery postured as representing the *Tribune* interests at AT&T, he was actually working behind the scenes on behalf of the LDS Church.[56]

John Malone, the former head of TCI who had drafted the 1997 deal with Gallivan, and was now on the board of AT&T, spoke out against a sale to the church. It was poor policy for AT&T to seek ways around the intent of the agreement, he said. The intent being that the Kearns-Tribune interests could buy the newspaper back in 2002.[57]

By late 1999 AT&T was caught up in a deteriorating situation. Hindery resigned under pressure, leaving behind an eager buyer in the LDS Church and an angry *Tribune*. A date of submission of a firm offer to purchase the paper was set by AT&T for September 30, 2000.[58]

James E "Jay" Shelledy, an aggressive journalist from Idaho, had been brought in by Kearns-Tribune as managing editor of the *Salt Lake Tribune* in 1991. He found what every newcomer to Utah finds: a friendly, industrious, and conforming people.[59]

Shelledy liked to ride buses and question readers of the *Tribune*. He moved around town and got to know the politicos and the business leaders. When he visited the thirty-five-acre grounds of the Salt Lake Temple and the LDS Church Office Building in the heart of the city, he noticed a marked difference between the tourists in T-shirts and flip-flops and the dark-suited men and conservatively dressed Mormon women in their calf-length dark skirts.

A tour of the two-block Temple Square complex is a delight to the senses. A team of gardeners make certain fresh seasonal flowers grow in breathtaking abundance. In spring the tulips and petunias abound; in fall vast fields of mums dazzle the eye.

The focus is the LDS Temple, topped by a golden figure blowing a horn. This building is closed except to Mormons in good standing—those who have paid their tithing and have passed their bishops' questioning about morals, attendance, and tithing in order to receive a "recommend." Designed in a sort of Greek revival style, the temple was completed in 1893 after forty years of construction.

Inside the temple is a large, bowl-like baptismal font, supported on the backs of twelve metal oxen. Rooms in the temple have symbolic representation. Here the various church rituals are conducted, including marriages. On pleasant days a visitor can see a half dozen temple-married couples being photographed with the temple in the background.

Across Temple Square the visitor views the silver dome of the Tabernacle, where the Mormon Tabernacle Choir has broadcast "Music and the Spoken Word" each Sunday since 1929 (some broadcasts today are made from the nearby LDS Conference Center). It is the longest uninterrupted network broadcast in the world. The broadcasts are open to the public, and a tour of the Tabernacle is available every day but Sunday. The Tabernacle's architecture was praised by Frank Lloyd Wright.[60]

Conversely, Oscar Wilde noted that the building had the appearance of a soup kettle; he added that it was the most purely dreadful building he ever saw.[61]

A few paces from the Tabernacle the visitor finds what may be the world's only monument to a bird: the bronze California gulls top a pedestal over a reflecting pond in commemoration of the miracle of 1848 when gulls descended on advancing hordes of crickets, eating them before they could destroy the Mormon crops. The church describes this in biblical terms.

Enter the Visitor Center and see the story of the founding of Mormonism in Teutonic-style paintings by Arnold Freiberg. At the top of a ramp is a startling eleven-foot-tall Christus, the universe spiraling behind him, planets and stars twinkling.

You will be asked to write your name and contact information in a registry, and if you do, count on a call—and maybe several—from the Mormon missionaries, no matter where you live. (An acquaintance of the author takes impish delight in placing the names and addresses of people she dislikes in this registry.)

The Mormons are great recorders of genealogy, and two buildings directly east of Temple Square provide an opportunity for visitors to look up their lineage and family tree. The Joseph Smith Office Building, once the church-owned Hotel Utah, welcomes visitors with a bank of computers and knowledgeable genealogists who provide assistance in searching for ancestors. Once again a visitor is asked to sign a register, and if she does, she can count on contact from the church's missionaries.

The tallest building is the Church Office Building, rising twenty-eight stories. Visitors may enter the building to take in the views from an observation platform.

From here they look down on the unobtrusive beating heart of the Mormon Church: the Church Administration Building, a small Greek revival structure in which the general authorities have offices. Frequently referred to by only its address—47 East South Temple—it is where the president and prophet of the Mormon Church holds sway, surrounded by his counselors. From here the major decisions are made.

The Mormon Church is the largest landowner in the city and the state's largest employer.[62] It owns most of the real estate on the north end of Main Street in downtown Salt Lake City, including the City Creek Center, a shopping mall with a trout stream. It is across the street from Temple Square.

By default, the gentiles, especially those who made money in Utah's mines where Mormons were forbidden to toil by Brigham Young, took over the south end of Salt Lake City. They established their own hotel, the Newhouse, to compete with the Mormon Hotel Utah, and erected buildings to house gentile businesses.

Shelledy's Tribune Building at 143 South Main Street stood almost dead center between the Mormon and the gentile geography of the city. Its location was symbolic of the paper's institutional balance wheel of the community.

Wearing his ubiquitous bow tie, in 1991 Jay Shelledy arrived at a successful business created by the JOA in 1952, and run profitably ever since.

The JOA had been signed thirty-nine years before, and under this agreement both papers flourished. It would seem that it was simply good business to maintain a degree of harmony. *Tribune* reporting on the church had generally been soft until Shelledy's arrival.

Shelledy was about to change the tenuous balance that had profitably served both papers. Mormon history and the editor's aggressive style would begin the unraveling of the era of gentlemanly competition.

The tone of vengeance set by Brigham Young is critical to interpreting the underlying resentments of LDS Church leaders—antipathy that was carried into the twenty-first century. The church frequently claimed to be misunderstood by its critics.

Utah Newspaper Project/Citizens for Two Voices described Jay Shelledy as the "*Tribune's* pugnacious editor from 1990 to 2003. *Deseret* [*News*] executives might have many words to describe Shelledy, but 'discreet' was probably not one of them."[63]

A former *Tribune* staff writer described an automobile ride he took with Shelledy. "Jay Shelledy controlled the heat by turning it as high as it would go when he got cold, and turning it off when he was too warm."[64]

That was how he practiced journalism too. "There was no middle. He was all on or all off," said the reporter.

Patty Henetz, a reporter and editor who was working for the *Deseret News* when Shelledy took the helm of the *Tribune*, said, "Jay Shelledy improved the *Tribune*. When he arrived the *Deseret News* had been a better paper."[65]

He covered the LDS Church as a major beat; he made the paper edgier. "We were just doing our job," he said.[66] He thought complacency was bad for creativity. Shelledy shifted personnel and restructured editorial management. He changed the look of the paper. He brought in new people and aggravated many of the old *Tribune* people, who had to either learn new ways or find new jobs. He did not endear himself to Publisher Emeritus Gallivan, and they sometimes clashed, since even in retirement Gallivan kept an oar in the water as the *Tribune* moved on.

"We had a contentious relationship," said Shelledy. "I thought Gallivan was a great community builder. He was a good guy but not a publisher."[67]

An outsider, Shelledy was quick to put his finger on the "Great Divide" as the differentiation between the *Tribune* and the *News*. The church was startled by his aggressive attitude. The dissident subscribers to the *Tribune* were delighted to see the gloves off.

Said Jim Woolf, a retired staff writer and editor at the *Tribune* for thirty-two years, "Shelledy didn't know or didn't care that many Mormons were our readers. He also believed that the joint operating agreement was bad for the *Tribune* and stifled competition."[68]

Shelledy wanted improved journalism, and he unleashed his reporters and editors.

"In the beginning it was fun and scary," said Woolf. "We were kicking the monster."[69]

Chapter 22

MORMONS VS. THE OUTSIDE WORLD

Anyone not paranoid in this world must be crazy. . . . [I]t's true that I do not know exactly who my enemies are. But that of course is exactly why I'm paranoid.

—Edward Abbey

"**U**s against them" is a feeling that is pervasive among Mormondom's fifteen million members, creating a defensiveness that bonds the faithful and circles the wagons against outsiders and critics.

When Shelledy arrived in 1991, the president of the Church of Jesus Christ of Latter-day Saints was Ezra Taft Benson, a former US secretary of agriculture. Gordon B. Hinckley, a public relations–minded leader, was Benson's first counselor, and as Benson grew frail, Hinckley grew more powerful. Hinckley held a grudge against the *Tribune*, specifically against publisher Jack Gallivan. His grudge went back to 1968 when Gallivan had urged that Utah's tourism could be increased if the state allowed sale of liquor by the drink.[1]

After Utah ratified the repeal of prohibition in 1933, the Utah Legislature set rules for alcohol consumption: a drinker could purchase beer with a 3.2 percent alcohol content at a tavern or grocery store. At any restaurant, individuals could bring their own bottle of liquor for cocktails and wine to accompany their dinner. The restaurant would provide glasses, ice, and a mixer, called a "setup." Restaurateurs hated it. They were not allowed to have bars. They couldn't make money on liquor. Travelers hated it. They didn't want to have to go to a state liquor outlet, buy a whole bottle, and take it to a restaurant for one or two drinks. The

LDS Church thought the existing system was fine; it didn't want liquor by the drink. The church felt it would reflect poorly on the image of the state and it would encourage more drinking.[2]

However, many claimed it did just the opposite. You bought a liquor license at a state liquor store and purchased liquor in "fifths," one-fifth of a gallon. You then brought your bottle to a restaurant in a brown bag, drank as much of it as you wanted in cheap setups, plugged the jug, and wobbled from the restaurant, risking a citation and jail for driving under the influence. It was also illegal to have an open bottle in your automobile, so if the seal had been broken you could be arrested for that. The drinking half of the community said it encouraged overconsumption. Drunks loved it. "Utah is the cheapest place I know to do your drinking," said a tippling *Tribune* staffer during that time.[3]

Jack Gallivan's *Tribune* spearheaded a little-used initiative petition to change the liquor laws, declaring them obsolete and unenforceable. A campaign was begun to get signatures from 10 percent of the voters in fifteen of Utah's twenty-nine counties. It was successful, and the initiative went on the ballot for the fall election.[4]

The Mormon hierarchy felt challenged politically and philosophically. It gathered a formidable assembly of church officials and gentile community leaders to create a committee opposed to liquor by the drink.

It is seldom that two newspapers, operating under a joint agreement, enter into the kind of bitter fight that Salt Lake City saw in 1968. The church, through the *Deseret News*, opposed any changes in the law while the *Tribune* vigorously supported liquor by the drink.[5]

For the first time in many years, both papers would use front-page editorials, the *Tribune* on May 1 supporting the petition initiative, the *Deseret News* on May 11 with an editorial signed by church president David O. McKay in opposition. As it turned out, during the drive for signatures, the *Tribune* devoted a significant percentage (a total of 29 percent) of its coverage of liquor-by-the-drink news items and editorials to Sunday readers. The *News* did not publish Sundays, but the *Tribune*'s circulation on Sunday jumped from about 80,000 circulation to nearly 120,000 circulation. This increase was comprised of Mormon *News* readers who opted to get the Sunday *Tribune* as part of their subscription. In the Sunday *Tribune* during the run-up to the election would be five major pro-liquor advertisements.[6]

Gordon B. Hinckley, then an LDS apostle writing for the church's *Improvement Era* magazine in October 1968, called on members of the church to vote down the initiative, regarding it as a moral issue, therefore transcending the arguments of his opponents. He emphasized its effect on the image of the state (and concomitantly, the church that runs it), its effect on youth, traffic, and crime problems, and increased consumption.[7]

The proposal to ease the liquor laws was defeated resoundingly at the ballot box, and Shelledy maintained Hinckley never forgave Gallivan for running an advertisement the Sunday before Election Day urging a yes vote on liquor by the drink.[8] Hinckley had a long memory, and soon he would be in a position of ultimate power within the church.

Ezra Taft Benson became the thirteenth president of the LDS Church in 1985, the last of the church's presidents to be born in the nineteenth century. He'd been in the cabinet of President Dwight D. Eisenhower. He succeeded Spencer W. Kimball, who as church leader in 1978 had bowed to the inevitable and decreed that African Americans should no longer be denied the priesthood and the temple rites that other Mormon males were granted.[9]

Benson's health declined. The *Tribune* covered Benson carefully, delicately referring to the heart attacks, strokes, and dementia that relegated him to a figurehead. Two other leaders were also in poor health.[10]

Moving into the power void was Apostle Hinckley. A graduate in English from the University of Utah, he was a scholar. He studied Latin and could read ancient Greek. Hinckley was a missionary for two years in Britain, 1933–35. Upon his return he went to work for the church and would spend his life as an employee or a leader of the church. He was executive secretary of the LDS Church's Radio, Publicity and Literature Committee before being called to be an apostle in 1961. He was trained and duty bound to protect and enhance the church's image.[11]

In the early 1980s, Hinckley was about to meet a young Mormon counterfeiter named Mark William Hofmann, who would turn from forgeries to murder.

Mark Hofmann's murders were the biggest Salt Lake City news story of the mid-1980s and a national embarrassment to the Mormon Church and Hinckley. Hofmann was born in Salt Lake City and was an active Mormon. As a youth he was a below average student but had an interest in stamp and coin collecting. By Hofmann's own account he forged a rare mint mark on a dime and then presented it to an organization of coin collectors who declared it authentic.[12]

Like many young Mormons, Hofmann in 1973 was called to a two-year mission to England. He later told investigators that he had lost faith in Mormonism when he was fourteen, but he went to please his parents. Based in Bristol, he wrote to his parents claiming he had baptized several people into the church. He loved the English bookstores, where he explored musty, old historical tomes. He began buying early Mormon material as well as books critiquing Mormonism. It may have been here that he discovered Fawn McKay Brodie's *No Man Knows My History*. Still, he professed to be a faithful member of the church. Returning from his mission, he enrolled as a premed student at Utah State University in Logan. He married, and the couple would eventually have four children.[13]

Hofmann began his criminal forgeries in 1979–80. He stole blank pages from nineteenth-century library books, created his own inks that closely matched those commonly used in the 1800s, and studied the handwriting of the early Mormons and the handwriting of those with whom they interacted. He became a consummate forger. His goal was to blackmail the LDS Church with documents that indicated the church was founded on false pretenses.[14]

In 1980 he created the "Anthon Document," which he said he had found in a gummed envelope inside a seventeenth-century Bible. This document was purported to be the transcript of Joseph Smith's "reformed Egyptian" characters presented by Martin Harris to the Columbia classics professor Charles Anthon in 1828 (see chapter 4 on Joseph Smith and the papyri). The Historical Department of the LDS Church concluded it was a "holograph" done by Joseph Smith and paid Hofmann $20,000 for the forgery.[15]

Mormon academic Hugh Nibley predicted that the discovery promised "as good a test as we'll ever get of the authenticity of the Book of Mormon."[16]

Hofmann dropped out of school and set himself up as a dealer in rare books. He fabricated other documents of historical significance to Mormons. According to Richard and Joan Ostling, in their book *Mormon America: The Power and the Promise*, Hofmann had become a "closet apostate."[17]

By now, Gordon B. Hinckley was running the LDS Church as its de facto leader. During the early 1980s, a significant number of Hofmann's Mormon documents came into the marketplace. Sometimes the church received these as donations, with some of the wealthy faithful directed to purchase them. The Ostlings, in *Mormon America*, said, "The church publicized some of the acquisitions; it orchestrated public relations for some that were known to be sensitive; others it acquired secretly and suppressed."[18] In other words, Hofmann was creating many documents that made the church look bad, and the church or its surrogates were paying to make sure they were never seen.

The documents he created included the "Joseph Smith III Blessing." Ostensibly written by Joseph Smith, the forged document called for the leadership of the church to go to Joseph's descendants. This was what the Reorganized Church of Jesus Christ of Latter-day Saints (now known as the Community of Christ) had been claiming since Brigham's take-over of the leadership in the 1840s. It struck at the heart of the legitimacy of succession, therefore the very foundation on which the Utah church had been built.[19]

There was also the "Salamander Letter," supposedly written by Martin Harris, the secretary to Joseph's translations, which offered a version of the recovery of the golden plates in marked contrast to the official version of the church.[20]

Hofmann realized that through his counterfeits he wielded enormous power to manipulate the church. To make this sudden flood of important Mormon documents seem plausible, Hofmann explained that he relied on a network of tipsters. He said he had methodically tracked down modern descendants of early Mormons and had mined collections of nineteenth-century letters that had been saved by collectors for their postmarks rather than for their contents.[21]

In 1983, Hofmann sold directly to Apostle Gordon B. Hinckley an 1825 Joseph Smith holograph purporting to confirm that Smith had been treasure hunting and practicing black magic five years after his first vision. Hofmann had the signature authenticated by Charles Hamilton, the contemporary "dean of American autograph dealers." The sale price was $15,000. He also gave his word that no one else had a copy.[22]

Then Hofmann leaked its existence to the press, after which the church was virtually forced to release the letter to scholars for study, despite previously denying it had it in its possession. Hofmann also sold forged signatures unrelated to Mormonism: George Washington, John Adams, John Quincy Adams, Mark Twain, Abraham Lincoln, Miles Standish, and Button Gwinnit, the rarest signature on the Declaration of Independence. He forged a "previously unknown poem" by Emily Dickenson.[23] His tour de force was a forgery of "The Oath of a Freeman." The "Oath" was the first document printed in the United States in 1639 and is probably the most famous missing document in US history. Hofmann expected to get $1 million for it.[24]

No one knows exactly how many documents he created in the 1980s or how many were purchased by the church. Some may still be in the hands of unwitting buyers. In spite of all the money rolling in, Hofmann was spending lavishly, including buying genuine first edition books. He was deeply in debt.

Desperate, he attempted to broker a sale of the "McLellin Collection," supposedly a cluster of documents written by William E. McLellin, an early Mormon apostle who left the church. Hofmann hinted that the McLellin collection would provide revelations unfavorable to the LDS Church.[25]

Hofmann had no time to forge a suitably large group of documents. Those to whom Hofmann had promised documents or repayments of debts began to hound him.

Meanwhile, questions arose about the authenticity of his "Oath of a Freeman." In a desperate effort to buy more time, Hofmann began constructing bombs. On October 15, 1985, his first bomb killed document collector Steven Christensen, the son of a locally prominent clothier, Mac Christensen, known for the missionary wear he sold at his chain of stores, Mr. Mac. The nail bomb killed Christensen in his office in downtown Salt Lake City. Later the same day, a second bomb exploded at the home of J. Gary Sheets, killing his wife, Kathy.[26]

As Hofmann had intended, police initially suspected that the bombings were related to the impending collapse of an investment business of which Sheets was the principal and Christensen his protégé.[27]

The following day, Hofmann himself was severely injured when one of his bombs exploded while he sat in his car, which was parked near the Salt Lake Temple. In a letter written to the Utah Board of Pardons and Parole in 1988, Hofmann wrote he was trying to kill himself with the third bomb.[28]

Said Jim Woolf, a *Tribune* reporter at the time, "I ran up the street from the *Tribune* as soon as I heard it on the police radio. Hofmann's car was still smoking, debris were all over the road. They had Hofmann in the ambulance."[29]

As law officers knitted the parts together, the story began to take shape in the pages of the *Tribune.*

For readers of both the *Tribune* and the *Deseret News,* the welter of information on the various documents, as well as the church's public statements, seemed to create a chaotic, disjointed narrative of events.

Woolf said, "I was totally confused by all of the revelations." However, *Tribune* reporters Mike Carter and Dawn House methodically researched and unraveled the mysteries and intrigue for *Tribune* readers, to the embarrassment of the LDS Church leadership.[30]

Several books would be published on Hofmann, his murders, and the LDS Church, before the details came into focus: the Mormon Church had been complicit in a scheme to hide documents detrimental to the faith.

Hofmann was tried and convicted under a plea bargain that sealed specifics of the court records, thus sparing the church more embarrassment. He got five years to life at the Utah State Penitentiary, where, after a suicide attempt, he still remains.[31]

In a speech on August 6, 1987, Dallin Oaks of the Quorum of Apostles blamed the media for the church's loss of face and credibility:

> According to investigators, the church leaders purchased from Mr. Hofmann and then hid in a vault a number of nineteenth-century letters and other documents that cast doubt on the church's official version of its history.
>
> This kind of character assassination attributed to anonymous "investigators" has been all too common throughout the media coverage of this whole event. One wonders why the *New York Times* would not mention in its long article that almost a year earlier the Church had published a detailed list of its Hofmann acquisitions? Is the *Times'* motto still "All the news that's fit to print," or has it become "All the news that fits a particular perspective?"[32]

A historian for the church, Richard E. Turley, would write a book with the title *Victims: The LDS Church and the Mark Hofmann Case.*[33]

According to Richard and Joan Ostling, the Hofmann forgeries could only have been perpetrated "in connection with the curious mixture of paranoia and obsessiveness with which Mormons approach church history."[34] Persecution is proof of the righteousness of the church's position.

After Hofmann's exposure, the LDS Church tried to correct the record, but the "public relations damage as well as the forgery losses meant the church was also a Hofmann victim."[35] Robert Lindsay, author of *A Gathering of Saints: A True Story of Money, Murder and Deceit*, suggested that Hofmann "stimulated a burst of historical inquiry regarding Joseph Smith's youthful enthusiasm for magic [that] did not wither after his conviction." Richard Lyman Bushman's *Joseph Smith: Rough Stone Rolling* includes a continuation of the exploration of magic.[36]

Hofmann had found the most vulnerable part of the LDS Church: the incongruities of its nineteenth-century beginnings and history.

Chapter 23

MOUNTAIN MEADOWS REDUX

The life of the dead is set in the memory of the living.
—Marcus Tullius Cicero

Jerry O'Brien was publisher of the *Tribune* when Jay Shelledy arrived. O'Brien, in the tradition of *Tribune* publishers, was a Catholic and was a veteran newsman. Unlike Jack Gallivan, he was also somewhat shy. He had come to the *Tribune* after serving as an Associated Press bureau chief. O'Brien gave Shelledy a free hand, and the *Tribune* began reporting aggressively on the church.

In 2000, Chris Smith, one of his reporters, discovered a story that led from the Mountain Meadows Massacre of 1857 directly to the door of the modern Mormon Church. It started with an archeological dig at the site of the massacre. It opened old wounds and infuriated officials of the church. Shelledy directed that the story run in three installments (see the appendix to read the full articles). Before publishing, Shelledy invited a representative of the LDS Church to read a sample of the series. The church representative arrived, "saw the thrust and went away."[1] The first installment hit Salt Lake City doorsteps and newsstands early on Sunday, March 12, 2000. The headline read the following:[2]

Bones of Contention:
Unearthing Mountain Meadow Secrets: Backhoe at S. Utah
Killing Field Rips Open 142-year-old Wound

Smith's first installment told of the desire in 1999 of the LDS Church president Gordon Hinckley, and descendants of the victims of the Mountain Meadows slaughter, to build a new monument to the 120

Arkansans who died at Mountain Meadows. The dedication would occur on September 11, 1999.

On August 3, 1999, a backhoe operator from Brigham Young University was excavating for the monument when he unearthed the remains of twenty-nine of the 120 Fancher party emigrants killed in 1857.

The *Tribune* article also reported that, initially, the LDS Church and Ron Loving, president of the Mountain Meadows Association (MMA), hoped to prevent the public from knowing anything about what was found. However, a faction of the descendants of the victims, led by Burr Fancher, suspected Loving was working with the church to "sanitize a foul deed."

There was a third group, the Mountain Meadows Monument Foundation, headed by Scott Fancher, who said, "What we understood in every correspondence, and we thought we had made perfectly clear to the church, was that under no circumstances would the remains be disturbed." Meanwhile, Brigham Young University's staff archeologist, Shane Baker, explained that in spite of ground-reading radar and other tests, the site where the thirty pounds of bones were excavated was somehow overlooked. The man on the backhoe felt he had no choice but to bring the bones to the attention of authorities.

The Utah State archeologist, Kevin Jones, hearing of the find, informed BYU that Utah law required a basic scientific analysis when human remains are discovered on private property. Failure to comply was a felony.

Tribune reporter Chris Smith wrote that BYU's Baker transferred the remains to the University of Utah's forensic anthropology lab in Salt Lake City, "which BYU had subcontracted to do the required 'osteological' analysis."

Loving, vowing to keep things quiet, managed to get Governor Mike Leavitt to order the bones transferred—over the objections of the state archeologist—back to Baker at BYU.

The governor "did not feel that it was appropriate for the bones to be dissected and studied in a manner that would prolong the discomfort," said Leavitt's press secretary later. Asked if he was aware that this was against the law, she replied, "I don't think he was knowledgeable of all the details."

Utah Division of History director, Max Evans, got an email from Governor Leavitt and, over the objections of Jones, personally rewrote BYU's state archaeological permit to require immediate reburial of the bones. Jones raised numerous questions over the political power play, including a concern that it was "ethnocentric and racist" to rebury the bones of white emigrants without basic scientific study when similar Native American remains are routinely subjected to such analysis before repatriation.

It was clear that a complete analysis of the bones could not be finished by the September 10 deadline. After a tense meeting with Loving, Jones agreed to a compromise. Long bones and skulls would be examined, but all would be turned over for reburial.

During this time, other relatives of the dead had heard about the find. The factions within the Fancher descendants were mad as hornets, threatening suits, saying the bones should have been tested for DNA and returned to the families of origin, and castigating the LDS Church and Ron Loving for trying to cover up the find.

Resentment over the discovery and of the remains caused a schism in the descendants' families, with at least one group asking why civil or criminal penalties were not brought against the LDS Church or the MMA for desecrating the grave.

There was confusion over who was in charge of the MMA. Gene Sessions of Weber State University said he'd been elected president of the MMA. He avowed that Loving was voted out of office in November 1999, in the wake of the controversy. Loving said not so fast: "I wasn't voted out of a damn thing. I was moved up. It was my methods and my way of doing business that got that monument done."

The second installment of the Mountain Meadows Massacre series led the front page of the *Tribune* the next morning, Monday, March 13, 2000. It was headlined, "Voices of the Dead."[3]

Smith wrote, "The *Tribune* and archeologists believe the full truth has never been told" as new findings came to light.

While the bones were at the University of Utah, forensic anthropologist Shannon Novak's findings were at variance with official church narratives. Written accounts generally claimed that the women and older children were beaten or bludgeoned to death by Native Americans using crude weapons. Novak looked at twenty different skulls of the newly found Mountain Meadows victims and found that at least five adults had gunshot exit wounds in the posterior of the cranium, clearly showing they'd been shot while facing their killers.

The article would go on to report that women were also shot in the head at close range. And at least one youngster, believed to be ten to twelve years old, was killed by a gunshot to the top of the head. There was other forensic evidence that a three-year-old was killed by blunt-force trauma to the head—in contradiction to the church's claims that children under eight were spared.

Smith wrote that bones "began to morph into individuals" as Novak studied the remains. Soon she could identify individuals, including a child's remains with a distinctive reddish tint. They called him "red boy."

When the Division of History Director, Max Evans, had overruled Jones, Novak had only a few more hours to examine the remains. "We worked through the night to get as much done as we could. This data had to be gathered," said Novak.

The official church history of the massacre, that John D. Lee and Native Americans killed the Fancher party, no longer held up. Gene Sessions, now claiming to be president of the MMA, said it didn't matter. Dead was dead.

But David Bigler, author of *Forgotten Kingdom* and a former member of the Utah Board of State History, said, "People want to have the truth, they want it with a capital T and they don't like to have people upset that truth. True believers don't want to think the truth has changed."

The third installment of the series appeared on Tuesday, March 14, 2000.[4]

Church president Gordon B. Hinckley delivered the dedicatory address at the new monument on September 11, 1999, adding a legal disclaimer on the advice of attorneys: "That which we have done here must never be construed as an acknowledgment of the part of the church of any complicity in the occurrences of this fateful day."

The *Tribune* article asked, if the church held no responsibility, then whom should history hold accountable?

"[L]ocal people," Hinckley responded. "I've never thought for one minute—and I've read the history of that tragic episode—that Brigham Young had anything to do with it."

For descendants of John D. Lee, the church's position added to many of their uncertainties from that autumn 150 years before. Now there was an unwanted reminder of the horror. The *Tribune* reported that those who believed an apology was forthcoming from the church had "come up short." Scott Fancher of the Mountain Meadows Monument Foundation in Arkansas, a group of direct descendants of the victims, said that instead of an admission of guilt, they got "an acknowledgement of neglect and of intentional obscuring of the truth."

Apologies will never be forthcoming, said Gene Sessions, president of the Mountain Meadows Association, "one of which is that as soon as you say you're sorry, here come the wrongful death lawsuits."

Utah writer Levi Peterson explained another difficulty, especially about Brigham Young's ordering the murders: "If good Mormons committed the massacre, if prayerful leaders ordered it, if apostles and a prophet knew about and later sacrificed John D. Lee, then the sainthood of even the modern church seems tainted. Where is the moral superiority of Mormonism, where is the assurance that God has made Mormons his new chosen people?"

Said Will Bagley, whose *Blood of the Prophets: Brigham Young and the Massacre at Mountain Meadows* was still unpublished at the time the series was written, said the church "was on the horns of a dilemma. It can't acknowledge its historic involvement in a mass murder, and if it can't accept its accountability, it can't repent."

The *Tribune* story also brought up blood atonement again and said its shadow still reaches across Utah, the only state today that offers execution by firing squad. Blood atonement, say some historians, is central to understanding why faithful Mormons would conspire to commit mass murder. The article went on to recapitulate some of the reasons that Brigham Young ordered the massacre.

But LDS Church president Hinckley said, "Let the book of the past be closed."

Dominic Welch, who became publisher of the *Tribune* at the death of Jerry O'Brien in 1994, was a Korean War veteran and a Catholic from Carbon County, Utah, notable for its mix of non-Mormons, descendants of Europeans who immigrated to Utah to work the coal mines. He also sat on the board of the Newspaper Agency Corporation, the company formed by the joint operating agreement. Dominic was considered a tough negotiator and had consistently turned down the church's request that the JOA pick up the costs of the *News* publishing mornings. Dominic dug in his heels. The *Tribune* was not going to pay out of its JOA profits to help the *News* get new presses required for its morning venture.[5]

On March 15, 2000, just after Bones of Contention was published, Dominic got a call: LDS Church president Gordon B. Hinckley wanted Dominic in his office. Welch said,

> When I arrived there were three men: President Hinckley, James Faust [a lawyer before becoming second counselor to the First Presidency of the church], and Thomas H. Monson [first counselor to the First Presidency and at this writing president of the church].
>
> Tom Monson had been president of the Deseret News Publishing Company and had sat on the Newspaper Agency Corporation board with us for many years. Monson was a fine man and a good partner.
>
> So I go in and Hinckley demands an explanation for the stories on Mountain Meadows.
>
> I said the wrong thing about Mountain Meadows. I told Hinckley, "You should have left the bones with the state instead of giving them to BYU."[6]

It made Hinckley angry, Welch said. The president of the church also expressed anger about a 1998 *Tribune* article on polygamy and a 1991 article on baptizing certain dead people.[7]

Welch continued: "Jack Gallivan used to be able to go in to the church leaders and apologize. He was the spear catcher, although all he had to do to enrage the church authorities was to mention the *Nauvoo Expositor*. I should have just gone in and apologized. So maybe I screwed up."[8]

He added, "If you meet with the LDS Church leadership, there will always be three of them in the room. Any correspondence will not contain individual names in any narrative, but will say 'it was related.'"[9] Whatever else happened that day in March 2002, it didn't take long for Hinckley's anger to mount.

"This is enough," Hinckley was later reported to have said in fury after Welch had left.[10] There were those who knew exactly what the words meant: the church's desire to see the *Tribune* expire was amplified by the Mountain Meadows stories, and maneuvering behind the scenes would make sure it happened.

Said Welch, "The church needed to get even. They were entitled."[11]

William B. Smart, the *Deseret News*'s editor and general manager from 1975 to 1988, cited the series on the Mountain Meadows Massacre as a "particularly telling example of the *Tribune* becoming overblown and needlessly abrasive."[12]

Fifteen years later, Jay Shelledy mused on the three-part story that set off the firestorm: "Looking back I think we overplayed Bones of Contention. It should have been a single, long piece."[13]

Chapter 24

MediaNews GROUP
BUYS THE *TRIBUNE*

Be leery of silence. It doesn't mean you won the argument.
Often, people are just busy reloading their guns.
—Shannon L. Alder

After the three-part series of articles, Bones of Contention, was published fierce squabbling reached a crescendo between the *Deseret News* and the *Salt Lake Tribune* over the *News*'s desire to buy the *Tribune*.

In 1996, Glen Snarr, a retired Salt Lake City advertising executive and chairman of the board of the Deseret News Publishing Company, had been appointed to sit on the board of the JOA, the Newspaper Agency Corporation (NAC). He filled the seat that had been occupied by Thomas H. Monson, whose other church duties consumed his time.[1]

According to the *Tribune*'s publisher, Dominic Welch (Snarr died in 2012), Snarr was assigned to silence the *Tribune* as part of a mission for the church starting in the 1990s. "Serving the church was Snarr's only interest," said Welch.[2]

Snarr had a media background. As a young man he had worked as a reporter and editor at the *Deseret News*. He had worked in advertising and public relations. He chaired the Deseret News Publishing Company for nine years.

Then came a Texas entrepreneur and an active Mormon named Robert Gary Gomm (1938–2011), born in Ogden, Utah.[3] "He was a newspaper broker from San Antonio who had assisted negotiating certain amendments to the JOA when it was renewed in 1982," said Welch. His sole desire was to serve the church, added Welch, and "he would do anything to achieve his goal."[4]

Gomm made it clear to all who would listen, including AT&T and TCI, that he was speaking for Gordon B. Hinckley, president of the church.[5]

Behind the scenes the church was shuttling confidential memos from Snarr to the First Presidency and, after AT&T acquired the *Tribune*, to Gomm and Hindery, strategizing on how best to torpedo the repurchase clause held by the family who had owned the *Tribune* for more than a hundred years. In June 1999, the church had even prepared a press release announcing that the *Deseret News* had purchased the *Tribune* as a result of a transaction with AT&T and that the result would be "two locally-owned, independently-edited newspapers." It was marked as confidential and would come to light during later court proceedings.[6]

Publisher Emeritus Gallivan by now realized Hindery was under the sway of the Mormon Church. He wrote Hindery a letter on July 7, 1999:

> John Malone has indicated, Leo, that your anxiety to sell the *Tribune* to the *Deseret News* is motivated by your fears of political or other reprisals against AT&T if it does not make such a sale.
>
> I have no idea who or what generated these fears but I guarantee you these fears have no foundation in fact. I can only speculate that you have been deceived by the members of the LDS Church who believe the end justifies the means and will stop at nothing to achieve an end they believe will please the First Presidency.[7]

The church's secret plan involved buying the *Tribune* outright or, barring that, taking control of the JOA, although the church initially denied it. Only later would court documents reveal its secret plans.[8]

The First Presidency of the church, responding to a letter from Gallivan questioning their good faith in the long-standing JOA agreement, responded that while they regretted the difficulties faced by the newspapers, the *Tribune* was at fault due to its owners selling to TCI without permission from the church. James Wall, then the *Deseret News* publisher, says the church never planned to take over the *Tribune*'s news department, only the joint papers' business operations. Yet in a November 1997 letter to Snarr, *Deseret News* editor John Hughes offered detailed proposals for content and personnel changes at a church-owned *Tribune*. One proposal read, "Exploit the presence of a non-Mormon editor (assuming you keep him) to reassure faint-hearted non-Mormon subscribers." Mr. Wall dismissed that letter as just "an editor's musings."[9]

In February 2000, *Tribune* reporter Chris Smith said he learned that Senator Orrin Hatch (R-Utah), a devout Mormon, had met with AT&T officials on behalf of the *Deseret News* regarding possible acquisition of the *Tribune*.[10] Hatch, chairman of the Senate Judiciary Committee, which has broad oversight on mergers, told the phone company he did not see any antitrust problems if the *Deseret News* acquired another Salt Lake paper. AT&T had been the fifth-largest contributor to Hatch's last campaign for the Senate in 2000.[11] He had interceded at the request of Gary Gomm.[12]

Senator Hatch also made contact with the office of Governor Mike Leavitt, where he talked to his chief of staff, Ted Stewart.[13] Stewart, who would later sit as a judge involved in the case, had to be aware of the church's desires in the matter.

Hatch would later concede, after the *Tribune*'s revelations about his conversation with AT&T, that the meeting was an "error, as it created what he said was the false appearance that he was trying to influence AT&T."[14]

By now, the church's bitterness (and its eagerness to control or cripple the *Tribune*) was intensified by the Mountain Meadows Massacre series.

In CFO Michael Huseby's letter of June 22, 2000, AT&T had told the parties they were accepting open bids for the *Tribune* on September 30.[15] They extended the deadline by six weeks. The *Tribune* managers bid $175 million and were advised by AT&T to increase it to $180 million. They did. They thought the deal was done. They didn't know the church was bidding too.[16]

The church leadership denied that it was trying to buy the *Tribune* but later admitted it when court documents made it public.[17]

"They were lying for the Lord," commented Patty Henetz, the former Associated Press, *News*, and *Tribune* reporter who covered the church and has been on the board of directors of the Utah Newspaper Project/Citizens for Two Voices.[18] In fact, the church already had plans for the *Tribune* once its takeover was complete. In one memo, as was discussed in chapter 21, John Hughes, then news editor of the *News*, suggested that they fire the *Tribune*'s humor columnist, Robert Kirby, an active Mormon. Hughes called him a "Johnny-one-note" for his acerbic views on community, church, and culture.[19]

Kirby has been called on the carpet by Mormon leaders, once for writing that Mormon Church president Gordon B. Hinckley didn't scare him because Kirby could probably win in a fist fight. Another time was when his column ruminated about attending the LDS Church in the nude. One church leader told him to tone down the "racy language" in his columns (hells and damns are infrequently used). He said, "[N]o, because that is my yard."[20]

The *News* also planned to "clean up other columnists."[21] Paul Rolly and Joanne Jacobsen Wells were then writing the Rolly and Wells column. Some were certain Pat Bagley, the *Tribune* cartoonist who taught members of the church to laugh at themselves, would be the first to go.

For AT&T the deal was becoming more complicated, and they didn't like it. The Mormon Church was prodding AT&T, reminding them what a very large client the church was for the company's wireless and landline business. As the *Wall Street Journal* reported in 2000, "Ultimately, AT&T decided not to sell the *Tribune* to the church. But Mr. Snarr and church officials still had plenty of leverage. They threatened AT&T with a $200 million lawsuit related to their business grievances against the *Tribune* and warned that they would use the veto power granted by the joint-operating agreement to kill any *Tribune* sale they didn't like." The *Tribune* also threatened suit.[22]

AT&T was caught up in a nasty squabble in which both sides were intractable. Steven Garfinkel, AT&T general attorney and deal negotiator, wrote that "we were caught in the middle of an impossible and deteriorating situation."[23]

Perhaps AT&T saw a way to sidestep the rancor when they began talks with Dean Singleton, head of MediaNews Group, an empire of forty-nine dailies and ninety-four non-daily newspapers. Singleton, in late October 2000, sent a written proposal to AT&T offering $200 million cash for the *Tribune*. He also delivered a written promise from the *Deseret News* that it would drop any plans to sue AT&T, solving any indemnification problems.[24] Because of apparent assurances from Singleton, the church agreed not to oppose a sale to MediaNews of the *Tribune*. How this happened is unclear, and nobody is talking about it.

AT&T's board accepted Singleton's offer, and it went into effect on November 30, 2000. On December 16, 2000, the *New York Times* announced Singleton had purchased the *Salt Lake Tribune*.[25]

There has always been speculation about the church paying for, or arranging for, part of the purchase by Singleton. Philip McCarthey, one of the selling shareholders of Kearns-Tribune in 1997, believes this is true.[26]

"There had been other interested newspaper groups—Gannett, Pulitzer, McClatchy, Knight-Ridder. Why did AT&T and the church decide to go with a bottom-feeder like MediaNews Group?" asked McCarthey.[27]

On the other hand, Dominic Welch does not think the church underwrote or paid Singleton.[28] It merely opened the door and said, "Enter, but never forget who opened this door for you." Welch admits that he and Randy Frisch, former CEO of the *Tribune* and former treasurer of the JOA operating committee, were newcomers to the rough-and-tumble world of corporate mergers and negotiations.[29]

"We're not financial people; we're newspaper people. The main point is that we were honest and felt we were dealing with honorable people. . . . [W]e were rubes, no question," said Welch.[30] Via a surrogate, the church felt it had the *Tribune* in a position where the next steps could be taken. The church might not be able to buy the *Tribune*, but it could certainly neutralize the paper.

On January 2, 2001, Singleton told *Tribune* publisher Welch, "MediaNews Group owns the *Salt Lake Tribune* now." Even so, the managers would not let Singleton in the Tribune Building.[31]

Eventually he did get to address the *Tribune* staff, and when he did he called the church "our partner," raising the hackles of many reporters.[32] "They [the church] eventually screwed Singleton over as much as anybody," said Pat Bagley, the *Tribune's* political cartoonist and a former member of its editorial board.[33]

Where to put the blame for the messy and costly fight?

Michael D. Gallivan, son of former *Tribune* publisher Jack Gallivan, claimed Shelledy made a bad move in publishing, among other articles, the Mountain Meadows series: "He failed to follow my father's *Guide for Publishers, Editors, Writers, Reporters, Columnists, Cartoonists and all Editorial Contributors*." The guide was written by Jack Gallivan in 1983. In it he said, "The *Tribune* remains vigilant of the LDS Church political activities to guard against possible infringement upon the general welfare. The

Tribune, however, should treat the LDS Church as a friend and essential partner in advancing the social, cultural and economic progress of the state. The *Tribune* must ever cover the LDS Church in the news in meticulous objectivity, striving never to needlessly embarrass the church or its leaders. When it or they embarrass themselves in this manner that affects the general public then, of course, the *Tribune* must report the facts."[34]

Some observers said the *Tribune*'s lawyers at the firm of Jones, Waldo, Holbrook & McDonough should have examined the veto clause more rigorously during the sale in 1997. "I told the *Tribune* owners they should be using a take-no-prisoners law firm from out of state," said Jay Shelledy. "They [the local firm] will only go so far because of local clients who are members of the church or are influenced by the church. They've got to live here."[35]

Suits and countersuits were initiated in December 2000, filed in federal and state courts. The family owning the *Tribune*, as well as its managers, asked rescindment of the *Tribune* sale to Singleton. The *Deseret News* sought veto power in a state court jury trial to block any future sale of the *Tribune* by the family and to transfer all litigation to state courts.[36]

The Utah State Supreme Court moved jurisdiction back to Salt Lake County District Court, and eventually the case went to federal court.

In October 2001, Jack Gallivan wrote a memo to billionaire industrialist Jon Huntsman, an active Mormon and father of Jon M. Huntsman Jr. (who would become governor of Utah, US ambassador to China, a 2012 presidential candidate, and in 2017 ambassador to Russia).[37] In his memo, Gallivan pleaded with the elder Huntsman to buy the *Tribune*. Gallivan explained how the JOA between the *Tribune* and the *News* had been the most successful JOA partnership in the United States in profitability and in its maintenance of historical circulation averages and share of market circulation:

> The determination of the LDS Church, owner of the *Deseret News*, to block Tribune Publishing Company ownership of the *Tribune* and continued management of NAC cannot, therefore, be a business reason. Repeated requests by Dominic Welch and me for meetings with the First Presidency to discover the real reason have been denied "on advice of counsel."
>
> It can only be concluded that the true reason for the LDS Church to block the sale is its desire to silence the newspaper voice that has

been the balance wheel of Utah for 100 years and the salvation of the
Deseret News for 50 years.

The solution: you, Jon, purchase the *Tribune* and, 1) save the LDS
Church world-wide embarrassment. 2) restore and preserve peace in
this community. 3) Make yourself an excellent investment and maximize your leadership power to promote the social, cultural and economic welfare of the State of Utah for the well-being of all its people.[38]

The Huntsman name would come up with recurring frequency
during the years 2012–2016 as a suitor for the purchase of the *Tribune*
after Singleton went bankrupt. The Huntsman family wanted it. The
church didn't want them to have it. It seems Jon Huntsman Sr. had
enemies among the church's First Presidency. For Jack Gallivan, the sale
and the events around it was a disaster: "My mission in life is maintaining
control and ownership in that newspaper" for Senator Kearns's descendants. "If I fail, then my life's effort is a failure."[39]

On December 1, 2000, Singleton walked into the lobby of the
Tribune Building to announce that AT&T had accepted his offer to buy
the newspaper.[40]

"The next day *Tribune* editorial page editor Randy Frisch's desk was
cluttered with gifts left by consoling colleagues: a lit religious candle,
and a voodoo doll with a picture of Singleton. 'Pins are inside,' read a
note."[41]

Chapter 25

THE *TRIBUNE'S* BUY-BACK OPTION

Bitterness is like cancer. It eats upon the host.
But anger is like fire. It burns it all clean.

—Maya Angelou

The McCarthey family, heirs to Senator Thomas Kearns and owners of the *Salt Lake Tribune* for nearly a hundred years, insisted they had a buy-back option that was valid. As far as they were concerned Singleton was an interloper and the church had turned its back on a partnership that had endured since 1952.

On July 30, 2001, Philip McCarthey climbed up on a reporter's desk and addressed the *Tribune* staff: "I object like hell to some outsider coming in here who doesn't know this community."[1]

"The five McCarthey siblings had been dubious about the TCI merger from the beginning. Tom McCarthey, older brother to Philip, writing in early 1997, said 'Once ownership of the paper is out of our hands, it seems highly unlikely that we would ever see it again. Are these honorable people we are dealing with?'"[2]

There have always been whispers about the mutual disdain between the LDS Church and the Roman Catholic McCartheys. The McCartheys felt wronged, and they were not about to give up. They continued to seek legal regress, their attorneys focusing on the validity of the repurchase agreement.

While the sprawling suit worked its way through the courts, the McCartheys, with Dominic Welch, Randy Frisch, and others, continued to run the paper under the management banner of Salt Lake Tribune Publishing Company (SLTPC), with Singleton on the outside looking in. By now the spikey dispute had spilled onto the pages of both newspapers. "The *Tribune*'s editorial pages became more strident as the paper's ownership grappled with the prospects of a Singleton takeover," the *Columbia Journalism Review* reported.[3]

An article in the *Tribune* quoted Dean Singleton as telling *Tribune* management, "You will not win against me and the *Deseret News* with a Mormon judge." Dominic Welch confirmed the quote, while Singleton denied it.[4]

The Tenth Circuit Court reviewed the case and upheld the veto power of the *Deseret News*. "But deep in the decision the court went out of its way to make a rather startling point," the *Columbia Journalism Review* noted. The court thought the McCartheys could very well win at trial.[5]

The McCarthey family fought on, appealing the earlier court's jurisdiction. The contentious case over the buy-back option went to trial before federal judge Tena Campbell in the US District Court for Utah. There was an especially telling point in a filing by the family's company that cited a legal precedent: "Delaware law [the place of incorporation for the family management company] recognizes that every contract contains an implied covenant of good faith and fair dealing that requires parties to a contract to preserve the spirit and the bargain rather than the letter, and adhere to the substance of the contract rather than its form. . . . A party violates the implied covenant when 'without violating an express term of the agreement, one side uses oppressive or underhanded tactics to deny the other side the fruits of the parties' bargain.'"[6]

The LDS Church didn't like the way the case was now heading. It made a crafty move. Judge Campbell's lawyer husband, Gordon, was working for a Salt Lake law firm. The church hired the firm, thus requiring that Judge Campbell remove herself from the case.[7]

The new federal judge hearing the case was Ted Stewart, former chief of staff to Governor Leavitt and an active Mormon. He'd been involved in the Mountain Meadows dispute in 1999 that was covered by the three *Tribune* articles in 2000. He had been in communication with Senator Orrin Hatch at that time. He was appointed to the bench at the behest of the senator. In spite of protests, Stewart refused to recuse himself in the *Tribune* case.[8]

Joan O'Brien of Citizens for Two Voices is blunt: "If Tena Campbell had stayed on the case it would have changed the outcome."[9]

During the trial, Tom and Philip McCarthey watched Judge Stewart taking frequent recesses. "You just knew he was going into his chambers to call the LDS Church authorities," said Philip.[10]

An observing lawyer (not involved in the case) explained that Judge Stewart had been appointed to the bench with very little lawyering experience: "He came directly from government. Ted had been political and was used to seeking advice. In the judicial world individual judgment is essential."[11]

Said another well-placed lawyer who observed the case, "There was a concerted, orchestrated effort by the church to make this case go its way."[12]

Philip McCarthey remembers one of the court sessions in which John Malone bumped into Dean Singleton as they were leaving the chambers.

"I'm Dean Singleton," said the MediaNews Group mogul, extending his hand.[13]

Malone, refusing to take his hand and looking Singleton in the eye, said, "When are you going to sell the paper back to the family?"

"I don't think I can," responded Singleton.

Malone brushed by him to a waiting car. He was never allowed to testify.[14]

It was a bitter eighteen-month court battle, but in the end Judge Stewart ruled that the *Deseret News*'s consent was required for any sale of the *Tribune*. In dueling conclusions, Stewart also ruled that the McCarthey family held a valid option to buy the newspaper back. The LDS Church had decided its best gambit was to let church-friendly publisher Singleton buy the *Tribune* and work to veto the McCartheys' option.[15]

Judge Stewart insisted on removing portions of the public court record that might have embarrassed the Mormon Church, and ordered that certain documents be sealed. It is unknown if these redacted sections have gone missing forever. Whatever legal documents remain are in a Tenth District Court repository in Denver. The judge's blackout can be removed only by filing suit with the court. Meanwhile, lawyers who worked on the case back in 2000–2002 are forbidden to comment on the locked documents.[16] "All the missing court records sound like tinfoil hat stuff, but it's true—there's page after page about the church and the *Deseret News* that have been scrubbed," said Joan O'Brien.[17]

In its entirety, the McCarthey–LDS Church litigation came to an estimated $40 million, the largest amount ever spent on legal fees and costs in Utah.[18]

In the spring of 2001, Brigham Young University had invited *Tribune* publisher emeritus Jack Gallivan to be a commencement speaker, even as church president Gordon B. Hinckley refused to meet or speak with Gallivan as the church pursued control of the *Tribune*.[19]

Thomas Monson, who had been a close friend of Gallivan's through his years of working for the JOA, was now second counselor to Hinckley. At a reception prior to the event Monson sought out Gallivan and with tears in his eyes said, "Jack, I am so very sorry. I cannot help in the *Tribune* matter. My hands have been tied." Mickey Gallivan was a witness to the exchange.[20]

"Monson was friendly to the Gallivans, the Kearns, and the McCarthey families during the forty years he had been a board member of the JOA," said Philip McCarthey. "He understood the business and how important the JOA was. He realized that people with differences came to work together under the JOA. He understood that it was good for the community, and that it allowed for different points of view. We became aware of differences between President Monson and other high authorities in the church. The other apostles were at odds with Monson because of this."[21]

Monson became president of the Church of Jesus Christ of Latter-day Saints on February 3, 2008, six days after Gordon Hinckley's death at age ninety-seven.

And Singleton firmly controlled the *Salt Lake Tribune.*

Chapter 26

SINGLETON BANKRUPT, ALDEN GLOBAL CAPITAL SWOOPS IN

A man who fights you as he does
is no better than an opportunist and no worse than a thug.

—Kristin Cashore

Dean Singleton assured *Tribune* staffers that nothing would change and that he would put more money into the paper.

"Singleton was a wannabe and a contemptible person," said Tom McCarthey. "Singleton wrecked this community in concert with the church."[1]

In 2003, Jay Shelledy resigned in the fallout after it was revealed that two of his reporters had sold false information to the *National Enquirer* during the sensational kidnapping of fourteen-year-old Elizabeth Smart from her home in Salt Lake City.[2]

Singleton replaced him with the first woman editor to lead the paper's newsroom, Nancy Conway. A former Peace Corps volunteer who worked on newspapers in Massachusetts, Pennsylvania, and at Singleton's *Denver Post*, she brought a calm competence to the paper.

Ad lineage dropped significantly at the *Tribune* during Conway's tenure due to digital inroads. Beginning in 2007, the paper reduced its page numbers. What once was a fifteen-pound Sunday paper was down to two pounds and shrinking. Staff was laid off in round after round of cuts. The classified ads were particularly hard-hit.

The digital *Tribune* was late entering the market, already being preempted by church-owned ksl.com (named for its flagship radio station

KSL founded in 1922, originally an arm of the *Deseret News*), and by craigslist. The website of the paper was messy and difficult to access. It continued to create major problems for web searchers and failed to keep pace with the rapid changes in the digital world.[3] In 2016, former editor Shelledy judged the *Tribune*'s website to be "awful."[4]

Dean Singleton was focused on the big picture of building his MediaNews empire. This was at a time when digital fragmentation was on the rise and print media revenues were in a downward spiral. Singleton, who had a debilitating illness, had over-leveraged his empire.[5] By 2009 it was a house of cards. The financial squeeze on MediaNews hit the *Tribune*'s newsroom and the rest of Singleton's papers.[6]

"Dinky Swindleton," as he was called by some of the *Tribune* staff, was seldom seen in Salt Lake City,[7] and left his *Tribune* property in the hands of Conway with the support of some long-time *Tribune* staffers, including Terry Orme, who would be a well-liked publisher during the paper's most difficult times, 2013–2016. Tim Fitzpatrick (grandson of former publisher John F. Fitzpatrick and today the executive vice president of the *Tribune*) shaped the editorial voice along with writer George Pyle.

Peggy Fletcher Stack, an active Mormon and the paper's award-winning religion editor, reported on the church's stand against gay marriage and its emphasis on the traditional family, while also covering its conflicts with the LGBT community.[8] She evenhandedly reported on the expansion of Mormonism under its new president, Thomas Monson, and on its greater emphasis on being a Christian church. She covered the church's conflicts with breakaway women Mormons like Kate Kelly and her group, Ordain Women. She covered the church's support of compassionate laws to allow illegal immigrants to gain citizenship.

Shelledy claimed that while most church officials appreciated Stack's reporting, Russell M. Nelson, president of the Quorum of Twelve Apostles (and possibly the next president of the church), did not like her reporting on church matters, since she sometimes wrote about subjects controversial within the church.[9] A couple of non-Mormon observers think she favors the church. Most *Tribune* people feel Stack does a good job in her tight high-wire act of reporting about the church and also of being one of its active members.[10]

+++

In 2010 MediaNews had announced the bankruptcy of its holding company, Affiliated Media, Inc., with some 89 percent of its assets going to its major creditor, Bank of America. The bankruptcy deal was structured so that when the bankruptcy ended after two months, Singleton received 20 percent of its stock plus $994,000 a year in salary with bonuses of up to $500,000 if the company met its profit targets. But his empire-building days were over.[11]

"In the beginning Singleton's mantra was 'the church is our friend, the church is our friend.' It didn't take too long to change [to] 'the church is the enemy, the church is the enemy,'" said one *Tribune* insider who asked for anonymity.[12]

Control of MediaNews and Affiliated Media had passed into the hands of Alden Global Capital, the hedge fund. They had acquired, for an unknown sum or trade of stock, a significant share of Singleton's holdings. The new entity was called Digital First Media.[13]

It was at this time that the balance of the JOA changed, with the church's *Deseret News* representatives achieving a majority of its management. Hedge funds do not run newspapers. In this case Alden specialized in taking stressed properties and turning their assets into cash before bankrupting them.

They "hedge their risky investments by selling the assets of some companies . . . to make up the deficiencies of other companies," is how Utah blogger Arvid Keeson described Alden.[14]

"Alden managed a declining resource by making sure the newspaper's costs were always lower than revenue. When it finally reaches the point of no return, they close it. Pioneer Press in St. Paul is an Alden/ Digital First property. That's what they are doing to them," said a *Tribune* editor in 2017 who requested anonymity.[15]

Chapter 27

THE NOTE AND ITS CONSEQUENCES

Disruption is, at its core, a really powerful idea.

—Clayton M. Christensen

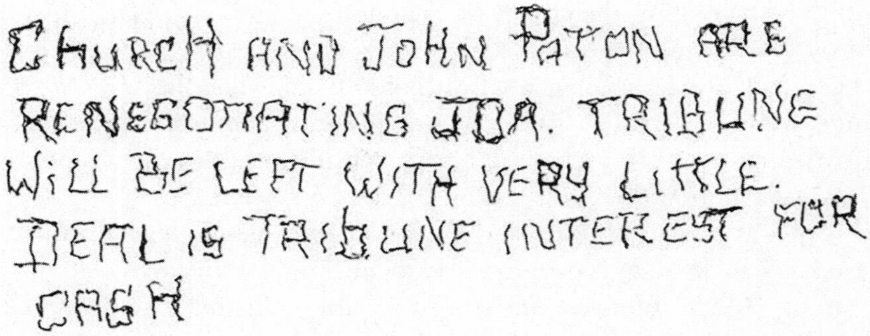
CHURCH AND JOHN PATON ARE
RENEGOTIATING JOA. TRIBUNE
WILL BE LEFT WITH VERY LITTLE.
DEAL IS TRIBUNE INTEREST FOR
CASH

Fig. 27.1. The "Note," arrived in the *Salt Lake Tribune* newsroom anonymously.

On Monday, October 21, 2013, Tom Harvey, *Tribune* business reporter, arrived at work and saw an envelope on his desk. In the envelope was the "Note." But what did it mean, exactly?

Said Harvey, "So I read the note on Monday when I got back from vacation. I showed it to Lisa Carricaburu, who was managing editor at that time. She took it to publisher Terry Orme. He called Paton and said we were getting these anonymous notes in the office and asked him what was up. Paton told him they would issue a press release later in the day. So I wrote that first story based on the press release and two short interviews with Paton."[1] Paul Rolly, the *Tribune*'s political columnist, as well as reporter Robert Gehrke, received the same cryptic note.

The negotiations the year before between the LDS Church and the New York owners of the *Tribune* had been conducted in secrecy. *Tribune* reporters started digging and obtained the secretly negotiated and executed contract from the Department of Justice. Later that day Harvey revealed for readers an article explaining the possible implications for the public: Paton was John Paton, who ran Digital First Media for its owners, Alden Global Capital. They had struck a deal with the LDS Church, owners of the *Deseret News*.[2]

The church, under pressure, made a statement.

Clark Gilbert, president of the *Deseret News*, was quoted as saying that selling the *Tribune*'s interest in the printing plant was "a good investment for the *Deseret News*, and a signal of our commitment to the state of Utah. It helps ensure two strong and independent voices, while allowing our partner to follow an investment pattern that fits what they have done in other markets." In an act of noblesse oblige, Gilbert said the "*Tribune* will gain sole control of sltrib.com and other aspects of its digital operations and their profits."[3]

Alden/Digital First had sold the *Tribune*'s presses in the jointly owned printing plant and other assets, "which involved an undisclosed but sizable cash payment by the *News*."[4] In fact, it was sold for $23 million.[5] The sale negotiations also resulted in reducing the *Tribune*'s share of the joint operating agreement from 58 percent to 30 percent. The *News* would get 70 percent of the profits.[6]

"It was a death warrant for the *Tribune*, which for sixty five years had shared business operations with the *News*," said Joan O'Brien of the Utah Newspaper Project/Citizens for Two Voices.[7]

With the selling of the printing plant, the only assets the *Tribune* had left were its masthead and its poorly performing digital operation.

Gilbert, the devout Mormon president of the *Deseret News*, had engineered the deal for the church. Gilbert wanted the money from the profit points acquired from the *Tribune* through the JOA in order to achieve his dreams of expansion. It would kill the *Tribune*, but that was part of the plan.[8]

Gilbert was a former professor at Harvard. While there he studied under Clayton Christensen, a Mormon and creator of a popular management theory called "innovative disruption." Christensen's theories have been disparaged by a number of critics, including a devastating article in the *New Yorker* by Jill Lepore, and by the *M.I.T. Sloan Management Review.* Lepore calls many of Christensen's cases "murky." She says "Christensen's sources are often dubious and his logic questionable."[9]

What Christensen really did was turn the word *disruption* into a brand he could call his own. Until Christensen came along, business had called it "competitive challenges," or simply, "change." Christensen put lipstick on it.

When Gilbert took over the *Deseret News* for the church in 2010, he came with accolades. Wrote Netnewscheck.com, "No one has yet tagged Clark Gilbert as the 'oracle of Salt Lake,' but to some local media, the nickname might be coming."[10]

Gilbert had a strategy of what he called "dual transformation."[11] It consisted of "disrupting" his flagship product, the print version of the *Deseret News,* while at the same time using the name to expand the brand and the church's internet presence. He started "hundreds of websites," said one insider, "until he realized the money was in classifieds at ksl.com."[12] (The source was referencing the popular local website that was a magnet—along with craigslist—that drew virtually all classified advertising from the printed Salt Lake newspapers.)

Gilbert's innovative disruption in 2010 included laying off almost half of the *Deseret News*'s staff and combining staffs of the newspaper and KSL Television.[13] The television station's news audience went into decline. It dropped from a powerhouse first place in the ratings when Gilbert took over to second or third place in a four-station news market in 2016.[14] Said one highly placed former church executive, "Gilbert was the real mastermind behind the layoffs, utilizing Christensen's 'disruptive innovation' theories. It was brutal, and morale hit rock bottom."[15]

Gilbert's mission statement was "Trusted voices of light and knowledge reaching hundreds of millions of people worldwide." The vision of the *Deseret News* was to be the nation's largest news publication focused on faith- and family-oriented audiences. His announced vision included making the *Deseret News* a top twenty-five newspaper publication and a top ten newspaper website by 2015.[16]

"We want to own faith like the *Washington Post* owns politics," he said.[17]

The LDS Church, ever conscious of its public image, was already media heavy; its subsidiary, Bonneville International Corp., owned at least eleven radio stations in different markets. They owned a television station in Salt Lake City, a publishing and distribution arm (through the JOA), and the successful digital media company—ksl.com.[18]

Back in 2008 the church had launched the Sunday *Mormon Times*, alleging it would appeal to all denominations with its emphasis on the family, financial responsibility, excellence in education, care for the needy, values in the media, and faith in the community. It gave an artificial bump to Sunday circulation, but Gilbert was later quoted as saying that "Mormons read Mormon content, Catholics read Catholic content, Baptists read Baptist content."[19]

Gilbert rebranded the Sunday *Mormon Times* newspaper as the *Deseret News National Edition* and reset it to target Mormons living outside of Utah. The *News* claimed the Sunday print circulation jumped in 2011 from about 69,000 to 129,000. The *National Edition* included the insert, "Church News."[20]

While the *National Edition* may have increased the Sunday print circulation of the *News*, it came at a steep price. Observers say it cannot possibly be profitable. Out-of-area circulation for either of the Salt Lake newspapers was tagged at $175 per subscription by John W. Gallivan, publisher emeritus of the *Tribune*, who wrote an analysis of the circulation of the two papers in 2000.[21] In 2016 a subscriber to the church's Sunday *National Edition* could get it mailed out of state once a week for thirty-three dollars a year. A subscriber to the *Salt Lake Tribune* would have to pay $308 a year for each Sunday's paper to be mailed out of state.[22] In a recent copy of the *National Edition*, there was very little advertising, and what there is consists largely of house ads for the *Deseret News*.[23]

The *Deseret News* had been comparable to the *Christian Science Monitor* for many years. Reporting could reliably be considered unbiased. Gilbert's actions, however, took the paper into the realm of "church newspaper," with an agenda appearing to advance the LDS Church.[24]

+++

John Paton was head of Digital First Media (formerly Singleton's Media One) under Alden Global. Paton and Gilbert were acquaintances, and both had gone to Harvard. According to talk, they didn't much like each other, but they were useful to one another.[25]

Recalled the highly placed former church executive, "Digital First Media [Paton] had come to Clark Gilbert and implied they could sustain the *Tribune* on 30 percent of the profits if Gilbert paid them enough."[26] Apparently, $23 million was enough.

What was happening at the highest levels of the LDS Church at this time?

> Gilbert sold Keith McMullin on the idea [McMullin was CEO of the church's business arm, Deseret Management Corporation]. McMullin had been a long-time member of the Presiding Bishopric, which is the executive management committee for Deseret Management Corporation. The others sitting on the Deseret Management Corporation board included the three members of the First Presidency, the Presiding Bishopric, three rotating members from the Quorum of Twelve [Apostles], and someone from the law firm of Kirton and McConkie.
>
> This group meets twice a week. They were told by McMullin the plan was in place to sell off *Tribune* assets and cut the percentage of the JOA. McMullin persuaded them to proceed. The First Presidency could have said no to it. They did not.
>
> Once it became public, it was definitely a concern for the church. I do think Clark Gilbert put more trust in Paton than was warranted.
>
> Do I think it was a great idea? From the *Deseret News*'s perspective, absolutely, the sale of the *Tribune*'s plant and equipment sustained the *News* for several more years. However, it was painful for the community. The *Tribune* had "doubled down" as a watchdog of the church, and they alienated a portion of the market where they could grow. They'd been poking the church in the eye for a while.[27]

The "Note" was possibly scrawled by former *Tribune* owner Dean Singleton, who was in a position to know what was happening. He was also angry with the Mormon Church, which had rebuffed combined offers by Singleton and Jon Huntsman Sr. to buy the *Tribune* in 2011–2012.[28] It is more likely to have come from an anonymous source inside the church-run JOA.[29]

The secret act by the church described in the "Note" touched a raw nerve in the community—among active, inactive, and non-Mormons (60.7 percent of Utahns are counted as members of the Church of Jesus

Christ of Latter-day Saints, although only 41.6 percent of them are active members. Mormons now make up an estimated 34 percent to 41 percent of Salt Lake City, while rural areas of Utah tend to be overwhelmingly Mormon. Utah has a total population of about three million).[30]

One of those most alarmed by the crippling of the *Tribune* was Joan O'Brien. Her father, Jerry, had been its publisher from 1983 to 1994. She'd worked in the newsroom as a reporter and editor. When she left the *Salt Lake Tribune* it was to take a law degree, marry *Tribune* reporter Tom Harvey, and have a daughter.

O'Brien has a law degree but does not practice law. She quickly realized that Gilbert's new JOA had sent the *Tribune* on its death march.

"Gilbert and Paton had created a flaming mess," said O'Brien. "I was really angry."[31] Harvey encouraged her to act, and for several days they mulled the options. The upshot was that O'Brien, who considers herself shy, stepped into the public arena and formed a citizen's group called the Utah Newspaper Project/Citizens for Two Voices. A group of about seventy supporters joined O'Brien (thirty of them former *Tribune* reporters, and a board was formed, consisting of O'Brien; Harry Fuller, former editorial editor of the *Tribune*, Janet Goldstein, a lawyer; Edward "Ted" McDonough, a grandson of John W. Gallivan; and Patty Henetz, the reporter who had worked for the Associated Press, the *Deseret News*, and the *Salt Lake Tribune*.[32]

O'Brien wrote a petition letter on October 28, 2013, to the US Department of Justice. It contained thirty signatures of former staff members and *Tribune* readers, as well as citizens. It called for antitrust action against the Alden, Digital First/MediaNews Group, and the LDS Church's *Deseret News*. Its first paragraph laid out the case:

> As former employees and current readers of the *Salt Lake Tribune*, we respectfully request an investigation into the 2013 amendments to the Joint Operating Agreement between MediaNews Group, Inc. and Deseret News Publishing Co. The changes threaten to undermine an important journalistic voice in Utah's unique marketplace of ideas, represent an intolerable consolidation of news media ownership here, and violate the spirit and letter of the Newspaper Preservation Act.[33]

One church insider at the time said, "If Citizens for Two Voices think the US Department of Justice is going to step in and oppose the LDS Church, they are kidding themselves."[34]

O'Brien began combing the files from the suit that resulted from the old sale of the *Tribune* by the McCartheys. She was helped by Henetz, who had done a lot of reporting on the church. "It was clear the *Deseret News* and the church had been messing with the *Trib* for years." Henetz was indignant that a "very insecure" LDS Church was using its power and position to kill the *Tribune*.[35]

"I don't think the *Tribune* staff was initially cognizant of the fact that they had a situation on their hands that threatened the paper's existence," O'Brien explained. "We had an existential question as well as a freedom of the press question."[36]

Jay Shelledy, by now professional in residence, and Fred Jones Greer Jr., endowed chair at Louisiana State University's Manship School of Mass Communication, was in Salt Lake City frequently during the years since he had left the *Tribune*. He had helped Jon Huntsman Sr. write his biography, *Barefoot to Billionaire*, as well as a second book, *Winners Never Cheat*. During this time he was also consulting with a frustrated Huntsman, who made repeated attempts to buy the paper beginning in about 2011 but was angry because the church refused to negotiate.[37]

Shelledy watched the unfolding drama of the renewed battle between *Tribune* allies and the church. Said Shelledy, "Joanie's group petrified the church. They had real leverage, and they put the fear of God into the church that the Department of Justice would get involved."[38]

The church's fears were well founded. O'Brien in fact hoped to depose the First Presidency of the Mormon Church, the pinnacle of its leadership.[39]

On November 13, 2013, the Justice Department responded that they would consider the complaint as they reviewed changes to the JOA of the *Tribune* and the *News*. In February 2014, determined to add more pressure after reading the non-redacted files of the old case, O'Brien prepared another petition for the US Department of Justice. This time it ran fourteen pages.[40]

O'Brien scraped together enough money to hire legal counsel. After vetting several firms, she selected high-profile Utah lawyer Karra Porter, a former working journalist from Kansas. Porter had been president or general manager of the law firm of Christensen and Jensen for nineteen years. She and a colleague, David Richards, who would work the case. Porter had also represented the LDS Church in past litigation.[41] Said Porter,

I talked to Dave Richards and my other partners and asked, "Should we take this on?" It was a high-risk case, especially for a midsize firm like Christensen and Jensen. We had a discussion at the firm. Finally, an active Mormon partner said, "It's your responsibility to the community. Salt Lake needs two voices."

It was daunting, taking on the limitless resources of the LDS Church. Meanwhile, a number of prominent members of the community, including highly placed active Mormons, encouraged us to become involved.

We had active Mormons remind us that Salt Lake was unlike any other two-newspaper cities in the US. We are unique here. If the *Tribune* went under, things would boil over in the valley.[42]

Porter took on the case with her associate, Richards, and quickly suggested that O'Brien's group use the "Citizens for Two Voices" tagline as part of their Utah Newspaper Project name. "It really described more of what we were about," said Porter.[43]

O'Brien was reluctant to tap friends and acquaintances for financial aid, and she invested heavily in the legal case using personal money. Said one friend of Utah Newspaper Project/Citizens for Two Voices, "You almost had to force donations on her."[44]

One Democratic Utah legislator, Senator Jim Dabakis, jumped into the fray and generated a petition that garnered seventeen thousand signatures.[45] It went to the Department of Justice. Pressure on the church was mounting.

By spring of 2014, many Salt Lakers had heard of the "Note." But even after nearly eight months the LDS Church seemed to pretend nothing was going on. Finally, the church could ignore the ruckus no longer. Under pressure, *Deseret News* president Clark Gilbert issued a statement on April 21, 2014:[46]

- Gilbert claimed the new agreement would protect the independence of both papers.
- He announced that now the *Tribune* would pay no rent for use of the printing plant that was purchased by the *Deseret News*.
- He claimed the revisions to the JOA were initiated by the owners of the *Tribune*.
- He insisted that news organizations' future profits were in digital formats.

It sounded as though the *Deseret News* was dealing with local *Tribune* representatives. In this release the Church of Jesus Christ of Latter-day Saints was never mentioned. "*Tribune* Ownership" and "*Salt Lake Tribune*" would actually be Alden Global Capital/Digital First in faraway New York City. The concept of selling the *Tribune*'s presses and calling it a significant financial advantage seems ironic, especially when they cut the share of income to the bigger and more profitable paper by half.

"Gilbert's statement showed mastery of Mormon flimflam," said Mickey Gallivan.[47]

Later, Porter would ask the court to have Gilbert and the church share the financials, "if they thought this was such a good deal for the *Trib*." They were never produced.[48]

Arvid Keeson, commenting on the statement in Utah Stories, said, "Gilbert has made a statement that the *Tribune* should essentially feel glad that it is printing the paper rent-free." Meanwhile, the *News* got 70 percent of the profits.[49]

Joan O'Brien, responding for the Utah Newspaper Project/Citizens for Two Voices, said on local public radio that the new profit split—combined with the *News*'s veto powers of any potential sale—weakened the prospects of a buyer making an offer for the *Tribune*. "Completely one-sided, shockingly unfair," said O'Brien. "I can't imagine why they have so deliberately undercut the *Tribune* in this way."[50]

The church, the JOA management, and the *Deseret News* clamped a blackout on any interviews that might have provided an additional dimension to the story.[51]

Calls and email questions were sent to Clark Gilbert, then president of Brigham Young University Idaho in Rexburg. In March 2016, Gilbert responded graciously but did not answer any of the author's questions, which were as follows:

- Have you read Jill Lepore's article regarding the validity of Clayton Christensen's destructive innovation theories? In her *New Yorker* article of June 23, 2014, titled "The Disruption Machine," she writes, "Our era has disruption, which, despite its futurism, is atavistic. It's a theory of history founded on a profound anxiety about financial collapse, an apocalyptic fear of global devastation and shaky evidence." Would you comment on this?

- Were Christensen's theories behind your dealings with Alden Global and Digital First Media when you restructured the JOA to favor the *Deseret News*? Please explain how this theory applies to a reinvigorated and profitable *Tribune*?
- When you cut the profit split, you left the *Tribune* little in the way of resources to make the change for a digital future. If you were publisher of the *Tribune*, what would you do to create the change necessary for them to become profitable digitally? The *Tribune* has continually reduced its reportage and features since you restructured the profit split. The staff continues to be reduced.
- Did you answer directly to the First Presidency while heading Deseret News Publishing?
- If you had the restructuring of the 2013 JOA to do over again, would you do it, in light of the public relations impact?[52]

President Gordon B. Hinckley died in 2008. Thomas Monson, the long-time JOA representative of the church, succeeded Hinckley as leader of the LDS Church.[53]

The hierarchy of the church seemed above the fray, yet they certainly had to be discussing the uproar. There was some hope that Monson might bring wisdom to what was seemingly becoming a church blunder of considerable proportion. Monson, however, was by 2014 eighty-seven years old and in declining vigor.

The dissident and non-Mormon half of the "Great Divide" seethed with anger and held demonstrations, while the devout leadership seemed to pretend that there were no Goths or Vandals battering at the gate. Adding fuel to the fire were others who spoke against the deal, including several state senators and retired *Tribune* editor Nancy Conway.[54]

On June 16, 2014, attorney Porter filed a complaint on behalf of the Utah Newspaper Project/Citizens for Two Voices in the US District Court of Judge Clark Waddoups. The complaint said that the action by the *Deseret News* and Alden/Digital First Media were illegal in light of the Sherman and Clayton antitrust acts.[55]

The complaint asked the court to rule that the 2013 JOA be declared an illegal restraint of interstate trade. It claimed that the Deseret News Publishing Company had unlawfully engaged in action to monopolize the Salt Lake City daily newspaper market. Further, it said the revised JOA was illegal, and its effects would lessen competition, or to tend to create a monopoly. The complaint specifically pointed out the "veto clause," if exercised by the *News* against a *Tribune* buyer, would be in violation.[56]

"It was a flaming antitrust violation," said Porter.[57]

"The veto power of the church to exclude any buyer they wished was the single, most egregious part of the case. I had one billionaire who was very interested in buying the *Tribune*. He was sipping red wine and told me he was sure the church would veto any offer from him," said Porter.[58] Her law firm received offers to purchase the paper from several qualified buyers.

The attorneys for the church quickly filed a complaint asking for dismissal. The next step in the legal process, if the judge decided the case could proceed, was discovery—the revealing of pertinent facts and background. The church did not want this to go any further.[59]

"The response to our complaint by the church's attorneys was interesting. Virtually all of it was marked 'attorneys eyes only.' We couldn't even show the documents to our client," said Porter.[60]

Judge Waddoups said he would announce his ruling on whether to dismiss or go ahead to discovery on September 8, 2014. That afternoon the courtroom was packed with Citizens for Two Voices followers, journalists, and church officials.[61]

The LDS Church, Alden Capital and Digital First, and the *Salt Lake Tribune* were represented by nine attorneys opposing Citizens for Two Voices.[62] Five of them flew in from Washington, DC, and Chicago. For some bystanders, the case seemed odd: supporters of the *Tribune* suing the *Tribune?*

Only Porter and her partner, Dave Richards, represented Citizens for Two Voices. They were sitting in the front row. Directly behind them was Justin Dempsey, a trial attorney for the Department of Justice's Anti-Trust Division. Dempsey was the DOJ's specialist in newspaper antitrust. He focused on the case and was following every move.[63]

"Nobody in the US knows more about newspaper and trust laws than Dempsey," said Porter.[64]

Waddoups, peering down at his papers, dismissed the counterclaim of the church and gave the go-ahead for Utah Newspaper Group/Citizens for Two Voices to proceed with discovery. The room hummed. Cell phones lit up.[65]

To the dismay of the lawyers for the church, O'Brien and her group were punching above their weight.

Waddoups's ruling was what Citizens for Two Voices hoped for. They believed the discovery process would eventually allow them to examine documents ordered sealed by Judge Ted Stewart in the old McCarthey case, documents they believed might show collusion by the church, and would be able to show disregard for Sherman and Clayton antitrust acts. "It was a wonderful moment, but also daunting," said Joan O'Brien. "Now we'd have to come up with some real money to enter into discovery."[66]

One thing seemed certain: the LDS Church was fighting hard to keep those documents sealed. It didn't like holding a light up to the past.

Porter and O'Brien had every intention of issuing subpoenas to depose the First Presidency of the LDS Church because "it wasn't clear who was making most of the decisions."[67]

On September 28, 2014, attorneys for the church filed another suit to stop the proceedings. Meanwhile, Porter was in regular contact with Justin Dempsey at the Department of Justice, sometimes arguing law and frequently getting suggestions.[68]

Some prospective buyers of the *Tribune* in 2016, including the McCartheys, expressed concern that even if the LDS Church lifted its veto power, there would be a lot of cash required to revive the newspaper.[69]

Even so, would the LDS Church let the McCartheys repurchase the paper that had been its nemesis for so many years?

The McCartheys made a lot of money when they made the TCI deal, but feel like they were lied to and manipulated by the LDS Church, and that much of the manipulation went on behind the scenes through the Mormon underground. They have especially harsh words for Judge Ted Stewart. They also resented Jack Gallivan for his handling of the initial sale.[70]

"I can't cry for the McCartheys," says one person active in Citizens for Two Voices who requested anonymity. "They made a shitload of money, almost three quarters of a billion dollars, when they sold the paper in 1997."[71]

Another project member disagreed: "The McCartheys were betrayed by a partner of sixty years. The LDS Church has never had any ethics or honesty."[72] This party also requested anonymity.

Phil and Tom McCarthey live relatively modestly. While not exactly reclusive, neither are they extravagant. Philip has a penchant for designer clothes. Tom worked his way up the *Tribune* ladder from police reporter to music critic, then to travel editor, and finally he retired as associate editor under Jay Shelledy. He likes to travel. The McCartheys have restored several historic buildings in Salt Lake City. They are significant donors to Gonzaga University (where the McCartheys went to college), the University of Utah, the YWCA, the Ronald McDonald House, the Volunteers of America, numerous recovery programs treating drug and alcohol, many Catholic charities, and arts groups. They annually sponsor the McCarthey Series for Independent Journalism at Rowland Hall School, which in 2016 brought Tom Brokaw as guest speaker. Most recently the McCarthey Plaza at the new downtown Eccles Theater was a gift of the McCartheys.[73]

While they freely acknowledge they made a lot of money on the sale, they are bitter about the maneuverings of the LDS Church and of Dean Singleton that prevented them from buying the paper back.[74]

They viewed the paper as an institution as much as a business.

Chapter 28

ENTER AND REENTER THE HUNTSMAN FAMILY

Damn. It looks to me like I just missed the best reunion since
Sherman got together with Atlanta.

—Susan Elizabeth Phillips

In the autumn of 2015 Alden Capital/Digital First asked Utah Newspaper Project/Citizens for Two Voices to stay their discovery process
for three months. A prospective buyer, whose name was secret, was negotiating to buy the *Tribune*.[1]

Citizens for Two Voices agreed to the stand-down in its lawsuit, hoping
the *Tribune* could be removed from the grip of the venture capitalists.
They particularly hoped the rumors were true that a local group or person
would buy the paper. The buzz on the street was that industrialist billionaire Jon Huntsman Sr. was again negotiating to buy the *Tribune*.[2]

Weeks later, the rumored proceedings between Huntsman, Alden, and
the church, gauzy with obfuscation, were revealed to have broken down.

Terry Orme, the publisher and editor of the *Tribune* since 2013,
began secret meetings with Jon Huntsman Sr. in 2014. He was encouraged by Huntsman's desire to own the *Tribune*. Said Huntsman to Orme,
"We're going to get this done."[3]

Since Orme was in constant conflict with the budget cuts ordered
by Alden/ Digital First Media (DFM), he was anxious to see the paper
change ownership. At one time he was told he was about to be fired by
DFM in New York, only to be saved by a DFM human resources woman
in Denver who fought for his retention. Meanwhile, Orme had grown to
like Huntsman and was reassured by Huntsman's "hang in there, help is
one the way" messages.[4]

There was one rough spot in the relationship between Orme and the Huntsman family: the publication by the *Tribune* of the book *Mormon Rivals: The Romneys, the Huntsmans and the Pursuit of Power*.[5] The book, by two *Tribune* writers, told of the "friends-to-foes" relationship of the two families and how it culminated in the 2012 presidential campaign when Mitt Romney and Jon Huntsman Jr. squared off as GOP contenders.

"They [the Huntsmans] didn't like the book. Jon Sr.'s wife, Karen [Karen Haight Huntsman], wrote a letter to the editor calling it 'tabloid trash.' We published it on a Sunday, but after that, things smoothed out again," said Orme.[6] He resumed his clandestine meetings with Huntsman Sr.

In the autumn of 2015, after the stand-down, Orme met with a much more pessimistic Jon Huntsman.

"The LDS Church had failed to negotiate in good faith," according to Patty Henetz, a member of the board of the Utah Newspaper Project/Citizens for Two Voices. "The church used the stand-down to their benefit."[7]

Henetz, in her years of reporting on the church, had a jaundiced view of the maneuverings of the LDS Church.

"You remember the parable of the frog and the scorpion?" said Henetz. "When the scorpion convinces the frog to carry it across the river, then stings the frog? The LDS Church is the scorpion. Of course the frog gets stung halfway over. When you ask, 'Why did you sting me?' they answer, 'Because that's what scorpions do.'"[8]

Orme said that in the autumn of 2015 he felt like the deal might be dead.[9] Huntsman had made several offers before (including in partnership with Dean Singleton, who had, through his original contract, an exemption from the veto clause held by the church). Alden was willing, but each offer was blocked. Only someone at the very top of the church hierarchy could do this—someone in the First Presidency. The questions were, who and why?

Dominic Welch said that when he was *Tribune* publisher he heard Huntsman speak with irony of his relationship with the church's higher-ups. He loaned the church his private Gulfstream jet, and church authorities flew all around the world on it. Yet Huntsman was blocked from positions on the church's business boards. Someone in the church hierarchy had it in for him.[10]

Jon Meade Huntsman Sr. is reportedly Utah's richest citizen. Born in

1937, he was a White House aide under Richard Nixon. Leaving government, he made billions by providing Styrofoam clamshells to McDonald's and panty hose containers to L'eggs. He is a philanthropist who has shed much of his wealth in the search of a cure and of treatments for cancer. Huntsman is widely recognized for his humanitarian giving. The *Chronicle of Philanthropy* placed Jon and Karen Huntsman second on their 2007 list of largest American donors to charity.[11] His contributions to the homeless, the ill, and the underprivileged exceed $1.2 billion.

An active Mormon, Huntsman served as an LDS Area Seventy (one of the church's elite general authorities) from 1996 to 2011. He also served as president of the church's Washington, DC, Mission from 1980 to 1983.[12] His son, Jon Huntsman Jr., was elected Utah governor in 2004 and served till 2009. Jon Jr. was well regarded by both major political parties. He served as ambassador to Singapore in 1992–93 under George W. Bush, ambassador to China in 2009–2011 under Barack Obama, and ambassador to Russia under Donald Trump.[13]

Huntsman Sr. had eight other children, about whom the public knew little until 1987 when his son James, sixteen, was kidnapped by a classmate and held for $1 million ransom.[14] James was successfully recovered by FBI agents, although one agent was stabbed during the rescue.

Many Americans had heard of Jon Huntsman Jr. due to his run for president in 2012. His daughter, Abby, was a television personality on MSNBC and later a general assignment reporter for Fox News.[15]

Few Utahns had heard of Jon Sr. and Karen's son, Paul Huntsman, an active Mormon who is CEO of the $1.1 billion Huntsman Family Investments. The sixth of Huntsman's nine children, he had appeared as a surrogate for his father at a number of charitable events.[16]

Jon Huntsman Sr., in a partnership with former owner Dean Singleton as previously mentioned, reportedly tried on several occasions to buy the paper as early as 2011, only to be thwarted at every turn.[17]

The obstructionist was reportedly Henry B. Eyring, first counselor to the president of the Church of Jesus Christ of Latter-day Saints. Eyring and Jon Huntsman Sr. had a long-standing enmity, origin unknown.[18]

Apparently aware of the enmity of Eyring, and holding an exemption to the veto power of the church, Singleton felt it best to make the first approach without Huntsman in about 2012, and offered $18 million. The church countered with $20 million. Singleton would not budge on the $2 million difference, and apparently fur flew.[19] Singleton report-edly called Eyring "a prick to beat all pricks. He hates the *Tribune.*"[20]

Jim Dabakis, the gadfly Democratic Utah legislator, announced in April 2016 that he was prepared to buy the paper.[21] He claimed to have the backing of several wealthy Utahns. Dabakis had been a vocal critic of the Mormon Republican establishment.[22] It stretched the imagination to visualize Dabakis going to the First Presidency of the LDS Church and asking them to approve his purchase of the *Tribune.*[23] However, he was part of the pressure on the church and may have proved an ally to the efforts of Citizens for Two Voices.

During the winter in early 2016, a blanket of pessimism settled over the *Tribune* deal. It looked like an obituary for the city's paper of record would soon be written.

"The church is just waiting until the current JOA runs out in 2020. The *Trib* will have nothing left but its masthead. No delivery system, no sales reps, no printing facility," said Patty Henetz of Citizens for Two Voices.[24]

At this point several members of Citizens for Two Voices saw the paper failing, probably before 2020.

Jill Lepore, writing about the "disruptive innovation" theories that seemingly influenced the church's moves against the *Tribune* in 2013, described it as a "theory about why businesses fail. It's not more than that. It doesn't explain change. It's not a law of nature. It's an artifact of history, an idea, forged in time; it's the manufacture of a moment of upsetting edgy uncertainty. Transfixed by change, it's blind to conti-nuity. It makes a very poor prophet. . . . Forget rules, obligations, your conscience, loyalty, a sense of the commonweal. If you start a business and it succeeds . . . sell it and take the cash. Don't look back. Never pause. Disrupt or be disrupted."[25] The attempted takeover of the *Tribune* had disrupted not only a newspaper but a community.

The church's botched attempt to still the voice of the *Tribune* had created a public relations disaster. No matter how the church's PR staff spun it, Mormonism was once again trying to silence the voice of a critic. Will Bagley, the Western historian, said it immediately brought to mind the 1844 burning of the *Nauvoo Expositor.*[26]

The man who engineered the *Tribune*'s 2013 sale, Clark Gilbert, was sent to Rexburg, Idaho, where he would run BYU Idaho and be out of the storm. Then came a surprise.

On April 20, 2016, *Tribune* readers awakened to a news story: "After almost three years of uncertainty about the *Salt Lake Tribune*'s ownership and financial status, officials announced Wednesday that the Huntsman family is buying Utah's largest daily newspaper."[27] The article quoted Digital First Media's CEO Steve Rossi as having "great respect" for the new owners. (Rossi had replaced Paton.)[28]

Ten paragraphs down was this assertion from officials of the Mormon Church:

"In a brief statement, the Utah-based faith said that 'while The Church of Jesus Christ of Latter-day Saints has not participated in negotiations relating to a sale of the *Salt Lake Tribune* by Digital First Media, we wish both the *Deseret News* and the *Tribune* the best as they move forward.'"[29]

Paul Huntsman was the buyer. He made it clear that it was not his father or family buying the paper. He would assume the role of publisher.[30]

The deal was forged behind the scenes, with pressure from the Department of Justice when it announced to all parties—the church, Alden/DFM, Citizens for Two Voices, and the buyer—that they wanted the deal done. They believed in the validity of the antitrust questions raised by O'Brien and her group. Each party had to sign off. Utah Newspaper Project/Citizens for Two Voices had to agree to drop their suit to allow the deal to be consummated.[31]

On April 27 the board of directors of the Citizens for Two Voices met in the offices of attorney Karra Porter and came face-to-face with the proposed buyer. Porter said that during the three-hour session the group grilled Huntsman, wanting to determine how he intended to run the paper. "Paul was honest. We got some answers we didn't want to hear, but it showed me his integrity," said Porter.[32]

"Paul Huntsman was very gracious," said O'Brien. "I offered an olive branch and told him we were on the same side. We needed to be reasonable. But since the Department of Justice had already announced they wanted the deal done, we were hamstrung in terms of leverage to get the best deal."[33]

The *Tribune*'s preferred solution would have been for the church to restore the *Tribune*'s 58 percent profit in the JOA. Instead, the negotiators had to settle for 40 percent.[34] The settlement did not bring joy to the hearts of many who could run the numbers and from them and draw a picture of the future.

In February 2016, when the *Tribune* was getting 30 percent of the profits from the JOA, it showed a $1.9 million loss for that part of the fiscal year beginning June 2015, until the end of February 2016. By extrapolation that would mean the newspaper would lose at least $2 million for the fiscal year 2015–2016. To continue extrapolating, if the *Tribune* deal was increased to 42 percent (the old *Deseret News* share), it would lose about a million a year under current conditions. At 50 percent it would show an annual profit of $240,000, and at the *Tribune*'s old rate of 58 percent of the JOA, it would show a profit of about $1.1 million.[35]

The 40 percent would buy the paper time, but little more.[36] The terms included a payment of an estimated $5 million by Huntsman.[37]

Said O'Brien, "We signed off on the deal and dropped our suit because newspapers were dying everywhere, and we didn't want the *Trib*'s obituary written. People's jobs were on the line. They were our friends."[38]

O'Brien said she personally had paid a high price for taking the case to court. There was stress. "My daughter had a grumpy mom. Tom [husband Tom Harvey] and I were on edge. I was so angry it made us crazy. But I couldn't start a fight and not see it through."[39]

All parties signed off on the deal, including the unhappy LDS Church and an unhappy Alden Global Capital, who had expected to continue to milk the *Tribune* until the cow was dead.

Said Karra Porter, "The case was one of the most gratifying experiences of my career."[40]

On June 3, 2016, Paul Huntsman printed a letter to readers in his new acquisition, saying, "Returning the ownership back to Utah could provide the *Tribune* the ability to think creatively, move quickly and celebrate its unique role in this state."[41]

He praised the professionalism of the staff but warned that there was no clear path to financial success in the rapidly changing world of digital media. He finished by writing,

> So let's now address the elephant in the room. I am an active member of the Church of Jesus Christ of Latter-day Saints and have been a bishop. I make no apologies for this. I embrace the belief that Hindus, Catholics, Protestants, Mormons, Jews, Muslims, Unitarians, atheists and every person of goodwill has a right to a shot at this planet's brass ring without undue pressure to change. I also believe in the independence of church and state and press.

So here is my promise to Utah: As long as I am the owner/publisher, the *Salt Lake Tribune* will never be held hostage by ideology, political persuasions, business pressure or particular dogma.

We will hold every person of influence and entities accountable for their actions as we will hold ourselves responsible for fairness, accuracy and independence.[42]

Paul Huntsman later said, "This is a generational investment for me. . . . The *Salt Lake Tribune*—and what we represent here in the community—is going to go on for generations."[43]

Former editor Shelledy had been consulting with the Huntsman family during the negotiations. On May 25, 2016, a blog, *Utah Policy*, intimated Shelledy might be brought back as editor.[44]

Mickey Gallivan, son of the late publisher Jack Gallivan, was alarmed. He believed that Shelledy's prickly coverage of the LDS Church had amped up the maneuvering by the church to kill the *Tribune*. Also close to Huntsman Sr., Mickey Gallivan wrote to him that if they were thinking of returning Shelledy to the editorship, he hoped that Huntsman would reconsider. Huntsman Sr. wrote back, quoting a famous Mormon hymn: "All is well. All is well."[45]

"Mickey's never liked me," said Shelledy, "and I have no intention of returning as editor of the *Tribune*."[46]

After Huntsman's purchase, Citizens for Two Voices wrote, "The events of the last three years should put to rest concerns that Paul Huntsman is a *Deseret News* stooge. In fact, Citizens for Two Voices alleged in its public-interest antitrust lawsuit that the Huntsmans were prevented from buying the *Tribune* in 2013, and the community got that rotten 'Joint Operating Agreement' instead."[47]

In spite of the church's refusal to deal with Huntsman Sr., he may have taken a role in the negotiations, if only as a consultant to his son. He was quoted in a May 13, 2016, *Tribune* article:

"He [Paul] actually spent more than a year and a half of his life being inundated with very tough negotiation points," said the elder Huntsman. "And he did a terrific job of it and everybody trusted him and felt that his word was his bond.". . .

Paul Huntsman said the extended family also agreed it made more sense for him to be the sole owner, because he lives in Utah and has no intention of ever moving. It also avoids the "too many chefs in the kitchen" problem if the newspaper decided to endorse a candidate or take a strong stand on its editorial page. . . .

Paul Huntsman said a family as large and diverse as his would have a hard time reaching agreement on an editorial stand.[48]

The Huntsmans' journey to purchase the *Tribune* was an arduous one. First, the Eyring factor came into play, and the church refused to deal with Jon Huntsman Sr. Several times during the negotiations lower-level church officials agreed to a deal; once the deal was taken "upstairs" for approval, it was rejected.[49] "We were never sure who at the church we were dealing with," said Karra Porter.[50]

And just who was Paul Huntsman?[51]

A University of Utah graduate, Paul moved to Australia to work for the family's chemical company. He moved to Houston for three years where eventually he became Huntsman's vice president responsible for base chemicals. He earned an MBA from Wharton, then worked for Deutsche Bank in New York City. Returning to Utah he worked for other family entities until becoming CEO of Huntsman Family Investments, of which his father is chairman.[52]

Paul Huntsman is a cosmopolitan man but with deeply planted Utah roots. He is married to Cheryl Wirthlin Huntsman, and together they had eight children. Cheryl's parents, LeRoy and Mary Wirthlin, had seventeen children.[53]

Paul runs in marathons, hikes, and likes to be outdoors. He is said to be quiet, even tempered, and without ego. He is a Republican, at least around the edges. His first political donation was to Elizabeth Dole in 1999, a friend of his father who was running for president. Ron Wyden, the Democratic senator from Oregon, was one of the recent recipients of his political donations.[54]

"And I would say that socially the Huntsmans tend to be liberal, but fiscally they are conservative," said one observer who knows the family well and wished to remain anonymous.[55]

On Paul's Facebook page he "sided 81 per cent with Green candidate Jill Stein" (posted in 2012) and "likes the *Colbert Report*" (posted 2011).[56]

Pat Bagley, the *Tribune*'s political cartoonist, sat down for a private chat with Huntsman, emerging to say later, "I think he's a closet liberal."[57]

Terry Orme, relieved to be back in his editor's role after Paul Huntsman became publisher, and George Pyle, the paper's liberal-leaning editorial writer, were talking at a garden party celebrating Huntsman's purchase of the paper three months earlier. The previous weekend had seen the mass shooting of gays at a nightclub in Orlando. During a Monday phone conference with Paul Huntsman, they presented the thrust of the next day's lead editorial: Pyle wanted to write a condemnation of the sale of automatic military weapons. There was a pause on the other end of the line. Said Huntsman, "Do you know you are talking to a man whose father-in-law gave him an AK-47 as a wedding gift?"[58]

Orme and Pyle braced. Would he shut down the editorial? On the contrary, he gave his blessing to a blistering piece urging a ban on the sale of military-grade automatic weapons.[59]

On Facebook's "Save the *Tribune*" pages Paul Huntsman wrote, "We hope to ensure the *Tribune*'s independent voice for future generations and are thrilled to own a business of this quality and stature."[60]

Questions flew fast and furious. Was Paul Huntsman really interested in running the *Tribune?* Was Paul tapped to carry out his father's desire to own a newspaper? Jon Huntsman Sr. had always wanted a newspaper. He tried to buy the *Deseret News* years before.[61]

Would Paul Huntsman be a civic-minded, highly visual community leader like Jack Gallivan? Or would he become a hands-off publisher? Or somewhere in between?

Some *Tribune* staffers speculated that Paul Huntsman wanted to see reform within the LDS Church. His ownership of the *Tribune* could be influential. "He really believes that the *Trib* should be a counterbalance—and that's a tricky needle to thread," said another staff writer who wished to remain anonymous.[62]

Paul Huntsman underlined this in a statement: "We can assure you that the *Tribune* will never abandon its purpose as a watchdog over Utah's institutions of power; its positioning as a platform for vivid storytelling and its reputation as a voice for all Utahns."[63]

A note of dissonance was struck on July 29, 2016. Terry Orme resigned. He had been at the *Tribune* for thirty-nine years and had helmed the paper during its darkest times under Alden's ownership. He was "a reporter's editor," said *Tribune* columnist Paul Rolly.[64] Terry had a good reputation and was well liked by those who worked with him.

In July 2016, Orme had been called to Paul Huntsman's office. Winding down a discussion on possible political endorsements, Huntsman said he wanted to bring back Jennifer Napier-Pearce, a multimedia specialist who had recently left the *Tribune* to join the University of Utah's Hinckley Institute of Politics. Orme told Huntsman he wasn't sure Napier-Pearce would come back.[65]

Then Huntsman told him he wanted to bring Napier-Pearce back to replace Terry as editor. He added that Terry could have "any position at the paper he wanted."[66]

Orme was stunned. He'd expected, as promised when Huntsman bought the paper, to stay on as editor. "I was out. That's what happens in business," said Orme. "On reflection, I'd been there for thirty-nine years. It's healthy for the institution and for me. It's sort of necessary, really. And it's karmic. I laid off a lot of people as Alden and Digital kept insisting on cutbacks. For me to shed tears would be selfish. The irony is that under Alden I thrived and had a lot of fun. Then along comes the local billionaire who everyone wanted to own the paper, and I'm out the door."[67] It was a decision that many lamented.

"Terry's departure ruined our happy ending," said Joan O'Brien of Citizens for Two Voices.[68]

Some *Tribune* staff threatened to quit in sympathy with Orme, but Orme cooled the idea. "It wasn't handled well," said a former *Tribune* staffer who has an inside track at the newspaper.[69]

Orme's replacement, Jennifer Napier-Pearce, was a multimedia maven with a master's degree from Stanford who had worked at the *Tribune* as well as for the local NPR station, KUER. According to Jay Shelledy, Napier-Pearce had not "intrigued for the job and was surprised when Paul Huntsman offered it."[70] Napier-Pearce's public statement on taking the editorship was, "This is such a tremendous honor to rejoin an institution that I love with all my heart. . . . I owe a debt to Terry [Orme] and think he is the consummate professional and mentor."[71]

Napier-Pearce was qualified to lead the *Tribune* into the digital frenzy. She was well liked and respected by local journalists. She took her place as editor on August 22, 2016, at a staff meeting at which both Paul Huntsman and his father spoke. The concern of some was that she had little experience as an editor, but on November 23, 2016, Matt Canham, a veteran staff writer, was named senior managing editor and would oversee day-to-day newsroom operations.[72]

Canham was charged with overseeing newsroom operations and content standards that will allow other editors to focus on cross-team investigative coverage and special projects.[73] She would also have the benefit of Tim Fitzpatrick's many years at the *Tribune*. He is the grandson of John F. Fitzpatrick and is executive vice president.

One of the immediate tasks of Huntsman and Napier-Pearce was to oversee improvements to the *Tribune*'s dreadful website, which was begun in 1996. In 2008, when Dean Singleton still controlled both the *Tribune* and the JOA, he established a *Tribune*-owned company called Utah Digital Services (UDS) to handle the website. Content was provided by the *Tribune* staff. However, Singleton turned the UDS operation over to the JOA's advertising people so as to maximize profits from combination web and print buys. After Clark Gilbert assumed JOA control in 2013, UDS answered to Ad Taxi, the digital ad sales company of MediaNews Group/Digital First Media, who were wringing every penny out of the paper and giving lip service to the website. The *Tribune* staff had to provide content while being helpless as to the look, feel, and operation of its own website.[74]

In the 2016 deal, Huntsman acquired control of UDS. "We are rebuilding the website from the ground up," said Napier-Pearce. "We are using Arc Publishing tools from [Jeff] Bezos's *Washington Post*, and we've signed a local firm to do the design work. Additionally, we are going to have a new app that brings more personalization to the reader, and, eventually, perhaps a suite of apps."[75]

One initially voiced concern was that Napier-Pearce was an active Mormon, and the nuances of Mormon dealings can be reported in so many different ways.

To that Napier-Pearce responded, "I trust our reporters to do their jobs—to hold those in power responsible, be it the LDS Church, Rocky Mountain Power [Utah's electricity provider], or government. The *Tribune*'s mission has not changed. I'm not pushing any personal agenda, and I want my reporters to do their jobs."[76]

On October, 3, 2016, the *Tribune*'s front-page headline read, "Leaked LDS Videos Cause Stir." The lengthy story helped allay concerns that the new owner and editor would give the church deferential treatment, although the story was not exclusively the *Tribune*'s. The story told how fifteen secret videos shot from 2007 to 2012 showed high-level LDS Church leaders privately talking about hot-button issues. In the videos the leaders discuss espionage-convicted soldier Chelsea Manning's sexuality and increased proselytizing opportunities among Muslims since the US invasion of the Middle East.[77] "They discussed issues ranging from politics to pot, the 'homosexual agenda' to the housing crisis, marriage to morality, Muslims to Kurds," the *Tribune* reported.[78]

Napier-Pearce had gone big on the story, signaling an independent future for the *Tribune*.

In the autumn of 2016 the newspaper editorialized in favor of Hillary Clinton for president; for US senator Mike Lee, a conservative Republican; for US congresswoman Mia Love, a conservative Republican, for US congressman Chris Stewart (brother to Judge Ted Stewart), a conservative Republican. Confounding this was the endorsement of a Democrat, Steven Tryon, who faced off against congressional gadfly, Republican Jason Chaffetz. (All incumbents were reelected, including Chaffetz.)[79]

The endorsements were loaded with as many criticisms as plaudits; each had the feel of editorial writers holding their noses. This was Paul Huntsman's bailiwick, so the endorsements must be his responsibility.

Four months into her editorship, Napier-Pearce said, "There is a true sense of optimism on the staff. Paul [Huntsman] is a great guy, a great boss, and interested in what we are doing, but he is not a micromanager. He lets us do our job. There's not a reporter on staff who's had anything but encouragement from Paul." As for Jon Huntsman Sr., who has visited the newsroom twice since Napier-Pearce came on board, "He's our greatest cheerleader. Paul has inherited his interest in newspapering."[80] The Huntsmans, said Napier-Pearce, believe in the *Tribune* as an important institution for Salt Lake City and Utah.[81]

In April 2017, Jon and Paul Huntsman showed themselves unafraid to use the *Tribune*'s news and editorial muscle to battle changes proposed by the University of Utah to the Huntsman Cancer Institute, which has received hundreds of millions of dollars from the Huntsman family. Vivian Lee, vice president of the university's hospitals and medical school, had dismissed the head of the Huntsman Cancer Institute, Mary Beckerle, with a "cowardly" email sent by university president David Pershing. Huntsman Sr. called it a "brutal power grab by Lee."[82] Huntsman Sr. minced no words during a KSL radio interview, proceeding to call the University of Utah president "pathetic" and a person who "should have been let go a long time ago."[83]

An April 24 editorial in the *Tribune* called for "new leadership at the University of Utah and its health sciences colleges."[84]

As a result of Huntsman media and financial pressure, Beckerle was reinstated; the president of the university resigned and so did the vice president of the school's hospitals and medical school.[85] Clearly the Huntsmans, through the *Tribune*, had extended the family's leverage in the community.

If the balance wheel of Salt Lake City is being restored, much credit goes to Joan O'Brien and her small group of determined newspaper people and their supporters who became the David that humbled the LDS Church's Goliath.

"We were always careful to refer to our foe as the *Deseret News*, not its owner, the LDS Church," O'Brien said in a speech to the First Unitarian Church in Salt Lake City in June 2016.[86]

In fact, the church and the *News* are impossible to separate.

It was a classic American story of a win by an underdog.

Chapter 29

WHITHER THE LDS CHURCH?

States that are built on a religious foundation limit their own
people in a circle of faith and fear.

—Raif Badawi

Mormons make wonderful friends and neighbors. Millions gain spiritual succor from Mormonism. The church does many good works. It desires to have mainstream acceptance, thus the conservative clothing, missionaries in suits, and a highly effective public relations department. This is a result of its unusual origins and its stormy history. Yet many active Mormons may chafe under the conformity required of its culture.[1]

The Church of Jesus Christ of Latter-day Saints has from its beginning been a political institution, a theocracy. Because Mormonism went against the grain of virtually all sacred American mores—sexual, political, dietary, theological—it has been on the defensive since its founding.

As a result, the church has adapted a cloak of persecuted innocence. Historian Will Bagley calls it "an odd defensiveness [that] still characterizes the 'faithful' version of Mormon history, which occasionally borders on paranoia."[2] Or, as authors Richard and Joan Ostling put it, "the curious mixture of paranoia and obsessiveness with which Mormons approach church history."[3]

Some church leaders certainly held a sincere belief that by silencing the *Tribune*—its most vocal critic—that it could carry out its policies and practices without oversight and comment.[4] They also believed the end justified the means. That the end justifies the means is a constant in the history of the church; it's a given when the continuity of the church is built on divine revelation that must be upheld at all costs. If God revealed it, you can't repeal it.

The effort to mute the *Tribune* started when printed newspapers were still opinion leaders. By 2016 the objective reporting by the *Tribune* about Mormonism—especially by Peggy Fletcher Stack—stood out in the explosion of semi-news and outright lies about the church to be found in the digital world.

Changes within Mormonism are glacial and frequently are forced by outsiders or dissidents. For instance, the *Washington Post* has described recent disclosures about LDS history as opening a new era of transparency in the church.[5] With temple rites and LDS beliefs undergoing scrutiny on millions of sites, blogs, and posts, the church would seem to have no choice but to open up.

In fairness, there is more transparency in the church in recent years. Richard Turley's 2007 article on the Mountain Meadows Massacre in the church's *Ensign* is an even-handed telling of the story—except that Brigham Young is not held responsible for the disaster.[6] In 2016, Peggy Fletcher Stack heralded a new openness in that the church was publishing articles using the bylines of historians with footnotes and references. This had not been done since 1966.[7] The church struggles to find a balance, and its public relations department—said to be 250 strong—strives for ways to be open.

CONFLICTS CONTINUE

Mormonism comes in many flavors: "active" Mormons make up 40 percent of the total 6.5 million members in the United States. That drops to 25 percent outside the country, and only 30 percent for the church as a whole.[8] There are degrees of disagreement within the Mormon community, and as much as mainstream Mormonism would like to be rid of them, they are here to stay.

There are the anti-church thunderers on one end of the spectrum, with the "Mopologists" (Mormon apologists) on the other. There are professional anti-Mormons like the late Sandra and Jerald Tanner and their Lighthouse Ministry.[9] There are a number of those from fundamentalist churches who regularly show up to picket the church's semiannual conference and who post lengthy denunciations of Mormonism in thousands of blogs and postings. The dissident Mormons are represented on such sites as Recovery from Mormonism, ex-Mormons.org, and the Mormon Curtain.[10]

Defending mainstream Mormon scholarship is the Foundation for Ancient Research and Mormon Studies (FARMS) at Brigham Young University. It does what is called "faithful scholarship," and its research and publishing supports official positions of the LDS Church.[11]

The Sunstone Education Foundation publishes a scholarly and critical approach to Mormonism and frequently causes heartburn among the LDS Church leadership.[12] A recent Sunstone article explained, "As a church, we desperately need a transparent two-way process for giving and receiving feedback without judgment or recrimination. At this point, I would be grateful even for a culture that could tolerate feedback without bunkering down or battering the already-bruised messengers. The alternative is grim: continued attrition, greater insularity, irrelevance."[13]

"Many Mormonisms" are part of Salt Lake City's Great Divide. "I believe the people most angered by the secret 2013 deal were the active, inactive, and dissident Mormons," said Joan O'Brien of Citizens for Two Voices.[14] Dissident Mormons are frequently vocal, recoiling against what they believe to be the inconsistencies and tales they consider deceits.

Further splitting the community are the kinds of teachings offered during a conference on faith and intellect at Brigham Young University in 2016, as described in an op-ed piece in the *Tribune* on December 4, 2016. "There were repeated references to doubters and those who leave the LDS Church, with charges that such people 'succumb to spiritual and intellectual laziness' and lack moral character," wrote Christy Money, a Mormon and a PhD counselor.[15]

She views this as part of an "alarming increase in fear-based narratives that distance LDS Church members from unorthodox friends and family."[16]

Said one formerly active church member, "I didn't swan dive into Babylon. I was dragged out kicking and screaming by my own conscience."[17]

MORMON GOVERNMENT AT WORK, THE THEOCRACY

In Utah, the theocracy is alive and well. The Church of Jesus Christ of Latter-day Saints has enormous moral authority.

"Almost entirely the LDS Church believes their motives are benign. They want to be upright, charitable people," said Rod Decker, a former *Deseret News* writer and now a retired political reporter at a Salt Lake television station.[18]

While it claims political neutrality, the LDS Church must take responsibility for the underlying philosophy guiding politics in Utah. All the members of Utah's congressional delegation are Mormon. An estimated 88 percent of the Utah Legislature is Mormon.[19] The governor and lieutenant governor are Mormon. Church and state are melded in Utah as in no other place in America. This creates a kind of exceptionalism.

As part of the theocracy, the politicians, with the implicit consent of the church, offer plenty of targets to the *Tribune;* its political cartoons and editorials frequently reflect this criticism.

"The church has one issue: they focus on the family," said Decker.[20]

And yet the state is last in the nation when it comes to spending per pupil in its public schools. Some of this is due to the large number of children in Mormon families, but some is due to the long-standing mentality of the tight-fisted legislature. The attitude seems to be that teachers are dedicated to their profession and since most of them are Mormon, anyway, they owe it to their church. Largely as a result of this, two in five of all new Utah teachers leave the profession after five years.[21] They are among the lowest-paid college graduates in the state. Many must work two jobs. "You just watch your children grow up without you," said one teacher.[22]

From half to two-thirds of Utah students are not testing as adequate, proficient, or college ready on various state and national measures.[23] These are kids who are part of Mormon families.

Non-Mormons, who tend to have smaller families, pay a disproportionate share of taxes in order to school the children of large LDS families. This inequity festers and occasionally blossoms into rage in letters to the editor published by the *Tribune.*[24]

Another hot-button issue is Wasatch Front air quality, which is frequently cited as the worst in the nation. The American Lung Association lists the Salt Lake–Orem–Provo metro area as the seventh worst in the nation for twenty-four-hour particle pollution out of 220 metropolitan US areas.[25] At times the pollution in Salt Lake–Orem–Provo has become so noxious that national television has featured it on the news. The state legislature and the congressional delegation support the oil and coal industries and block attempts to legislate for better air quality. Could the church exert more influence to better the environment for its families?

+++

Utah officials largely view the federal government as the enemy, and this attitude is on display in the Utah Legislature and by even those elected to federal office. The state clings tenaciously to Hill Air Force Base, yet refuses federal help for the poor, ill, and elderly, many of them Mormon families. The legislature has turned down almost a billion dollars in federal Medicaid money that would serve the less fortunate, especially those without access to the church welfare program. A majority of Utahns polled favored expansion of the Medicaid program but were ignored.[26]

The Utah Legislature and the congressional delegation are adamantly against the establishment of any new national parks or monuments in Utah, yet Utah's "Mighty Five" national parks are major contributors to the $8 billion spent in Utah by tourists. Tourism is the state's largest export industry.[27]

The church comes under intense criticism on gay issues.

The *Tribune* regularly runs articles on gay members of the church and how they face discrimination. Still on the law books are statutes preventing the "advocacy of homosexuality" by teachers who may be confronted by vulnerable LGBT youth undergoing internal pain as they reach a crossroad of life. Utah's LGBT teens are three times more likely than their heterosexual peers to commit suicide.[28]

The church has lobbyists at the Utah Legislature and in Congress, yet it is mum, claiming it takes no role in politics. "The church is very selective regarding the legislation they engage in. This is due to the fact that because most of Utah's legislators are LDS members, the majority of legislation already aligns with the LDS Church position without their influence," wrote Carl Wimmer, a formerly faithful Mormon who served three terms in the Utah House of Representatives.[29]

ELDERLY LEADERSHIP FACES MODERN CHALLENGES

Fundamentalist churches will continue to attack Mormonism as being non-Christian. Polygamy will continue to make headlines, and the mainstream LDS Church will fight the perception that it still practices polygamy. Mormon politics will always be under fire. Questions of separation of church and state will continue to be contentious.

The church also must find ways to rationalize emerging DNA findings that indicate that indigenous Americans came from eastern Asia, not from Israel and the Middle East. This is in conflict with the gospel in the Book of Mormon.

Proselytizing by its young missionaries is anathema to many cultures, and while boys in suits on bicycles remind the world that Mormonism is everywhere, missionaries are also seemingly intrusive, expensive, and becoming less effective. The ratio of converts to missionary is slipping.[30] The Mormon Church's claim to being the fast-growing faith is being challenged by the explosive growth of Seventh-day Adventists, Assemblies of God, and Pentecostal groups.

The church will continue to have trouble with the retention of its newly baptized members, especially in countries where strong family ties may call the Mormon back to his or her original religion.

The creation stories of Joseph Smith's finding and translating of the golden plates will dog the church. It is a story that can make the prospective member—or the existing member—wary or disillusioned.

Many Mormons would like to know how their tithing is spent, but the church books are closed to the membership. From the website MormonLeaks, pay stubs indicating the salaries of Mormonism's general authorities were posted by the *Tribune* in January 2016. In 2014 the "base living allowance" for all Mormon general authorities was being raised from $116,400 to $120,000, certainly not excessive. However, other perquisites were not included in the leaks.[31]

Perhaps the greatest pressure on the church will come from women members, many of whom want to hold the priesthood, or at least have greater say in decisions made by the church. Ordain Women's Kate Kelly was excommunicated for speaking out on behalf of women in the church in 2014. Dissident women within the church are gathering in numbers and in strength of voice.[32] Many will be censured, and more will be excommunicated as they speak out. The treatment of dissidents has not changed in almost two hundred years.

One Mormon female student at Brigham Young University, Madi Barney, was named the *Tribune*'s Utahn of the Year 2016 for speaking out against the school's onerous policy of punishing victims of rape. Women victims of rape were examined under the school's Honor Code to determine if they had "asked for it." She was questioned about the kind of clothing she was wearing, if a male was the only other person at the scene, if alcohol or drugs were involved, and about curfew adherence and chastity. After she reported being raped in September 2015, Barney was placed under investigation and refused enrollment while an inquiry took place. At a rape awareness forum at the school in April 2016, she took the microphone and confronted BYU's Title IX coordinator. The dam of silence broke. She was surprised at the supportive applause of fellow students and at the effectiveness of a petition that more than 117,000 people signed. It seemed that many assailants had explicitly used the threat of the Honor Code system to discourage victims from reporting. A few months later BYU announced sweeping changes on how it will respond to students who report sexual assault.[33]

On April 10, 2017, the *Tribune* staff was awarded a Pulitzer Prize for local reporting for its coverage of BYU's treatment of rape victims.[34]

And who will be shaping the theological decisions and public statements on the difficult questions facing Mormonism?

At the time of this writing, the average age of the top fifteen leaders of the LDS Church is eighty years. "The LDS Church has never had an older First Presidency and Quorum of the Twelve Apostles," wrote Peggy Fletcher Stack.[35]

Thomas H. Monson, the president of the church, turned ninety in 2017. The office usually falls to the longest-serving member of the faith's Quorum of the Twelve Apostles, which means Russell M. Nelson is next in line to replace President Monson.[36] Nelson turned ninety-three in 2017. There is no such thing as retirement, even in the case of ill health.[37]

The church seems to take pride in this ossification. Many of its flock do not. It was not until 1978—115 years after the signing of the Emancipation Proclamation—that African Americans were allowed to become fully churched and hold the priesthood.[38]

With older men in charge, they resist the changes that might make the church more welcoming and loving, as is now being witnessed in its revelation banning baptism of any children of same-sex couple unions unless the child renounces the parents' lifestyle. The child must be at least eighteen and must get approval to be baptized by a high authority.[39]

Some ask of this policy, "Is it discrimination? Or is it abuse?" These are families too.

Insularity besets the leadership, which also lacks diversity. The vast majority are white men, even those general authorities who come from outside the United States.

In an interesting study compiled by a researcher for the blog *Nearing Kolob*, data clearly show a lack of diversity among the leadership of the LDS Church: "[W]e find, of the 103 General Authorities, there are 18 with MBAs (masters of business administration), 20 with JDs (juris doctors, i.e. lawyers), 25 with Masters (not MBAs), 9 with medical degrees (either doctors or dentists) and 9 with Doctorates."[40]

Listed are the degrees held by the First Presidency, the Quorum of Twelve Apostles, the Presidency of the Seventy, the First Quorum of the Seventy, and the Second Quorum of the Seventy. Not a single theological or Bible studies degree is held among the general authorities. As for sciences, there are four engineering degrees, one in physics, one in zoology, two in biology, and one in mathematics; "the majority of this small group went on to business or medical school."[41]

If accurate, the study paints a monochromatic picture of an institution operated in a bubble of successful business and professional men. As psychologist Jonathan Haidt wrote, "In moral and political matters we are often groupish, rather than selfish. We deploy our reasoning skills to support our team, and to demonstrate commitment to our team."[42] Joan of Arc's judges fed off one another's self-righteousness until, of course, Joan had to be burned.

Because of the precedents within the prophetic flow of its history, the church is trussed to itself. The presidents of the church receive word from God; therefore they cannot be wrong. Mormon doctrine moves forward on wheels constructed in the nineteenth century.

The church's utterances will continue to be the source of its self-inflicted wounds into the foreseeable future. As would happen so often in the nineteenth and twentieth centuries, the church leaders ignore the implications that follow their acts of suppression. And when the criticism flows, the leaders say, "Persecution is proof of our righteousness."

Change will come to Mormonism slowly. The church will tweak its Book of Mormon and its other guiding sources to neutralize criticisms, and will in turn be criticized for doing so. "The word of God outranks the word of law" is a statement that will continue to be useful whenever the church disagrees.

And the end will justify the means.

As Will Bagley has written, frontier Mormonism feared dissent as much as it valued unity.[43]

To the membership, faith will be the key to happiness.

Chapter 30

THE *TRIBUNE*'S FUTURE

> It was summer and moonlight and we had lemonade to
> drink, and we held the cold glasses in our hands, and Dad
> read the stereo-newspapers inserted into the special hat you
> put on your head and which turned the microscopic page
> in front of the magnifying lens if you blinked three times in
> succession.
>
> —Ray Bradbury

Newspapers everywhere are struggling to survive. Readers are fewer and older. The daily papers are managing decline. They downsize, try paywalls, and have bloggers and affinity programming with radio and television stations. They involve themselves in social media. Their reporters carry video cameras. They are trying many routes to readership and to increasing profitability. At this writing, no newspaper seems to have found the silver bullet.

The *Salt Lake Tribune* could find a special niche and thrive, suggested Pat Bagley, the *Tribune*'s cartoonist and former editorial board member. "The *Washington Post* owns politics; the *New York Times* owns culture; the *Wall Street Journal* owns business. The *Salt Lake Tribune* is perfectly positioned to own outdoor recreation and travel," said Bagley.[1]

It is conceivable that the *Tribune* could capitalize on its geography and become the go-to website/newspaper for western travel, possibly even international travel, thanks to the cosmopolitan aspects of the Mormon Church and its far-flung members and missionaries.

However, editor Jennifer Napier-Pearce's thinking is more in line with that of Warren Buffett.[2]

Warren Buffett's Berkshire Hathaway in 2013 acquired twenty-eight daily newspapers for $344 million.[3] In Buffett's 2013 annual shareholder letter he explained why newspapers were important and why he believed they will survive and thrive. It is an interesting view:

> Over the years, almost all cities became one newspaper towns (or harbored two competing papers that joined forces to operate as a single economic unit). Contraction was inevitable because most people wished to read and pay for only one paper. . . .
>
> Now the world has changed. Stock market quotes and the details of national sports events are old news long before the presses begin to roll. The Internet offers extensive information about both available jobs and homes. Television bombards viewers with political, national and international news. In one area of interest after another, newspapers have therefore lost their "primacy." And, as their audiences have fallen, so has advertising. (Revenues from "help wanted" classified ads—long a huge source of income for newspapers—have plunged more than 90% in the past 12 years.)
>
> Newspapers continue to reign supreme, however, in the delivery of local news. If you want to know what's going on in your town—whether the news is about the mayor or taxes or high school football—there is no substitute for a local newspaper that is doing its job.[4]

Buffett went on to say that newspapers delivering comprehensive and reliable information to a tightly bound community and having a sensible internet strategy will remain viable for a long time.

There will always be a hard-core readership for newspapers; it may even grow. In the 2016 elections, disinformation, "alternative news," and fabricated reality flooded the internet and television channels. It is possible that a portion of the public will want reliable news sources, and newspapers that separate opinion from news can offer it. Newspapers still produce the vast majority of original news gathering.[5]

There is also a case to be made for printed newspapers. "[B]y its very nature, print is an artisanal product," said Kathleen Kingsbury of the *Boston Globe*.[6] The *Tribune* conceivably could dedicate part of its newsroom to putting out a separate premium product with the kind of quality that attracts upscale readers and advertisers.

+++

The *Salt Lake Tribune* is forced to turn print dollars into digital dimes. And it's starting from deep in the hole, since its resources were starved by the church for nearly four years.

The Huntsmans may have to subsidize it for quite a while; the LDS Church was probably doing this with the *Deseret News* for a hundred years prior to the 1952 JOA. In slashing budgets to meet Alden's continuous demands for economy, Orme had cut one section out of the Monday and Tuesday editions.

To repair some of the damage, Napier-Pearce, in a column written on November 20, 2016, announced that one of those sections would return to the paper on Tuesdays. She also wrote that more staff would be added and that a 5 percent increase in salary would be given to all employees.[7] In January 2017, the paper added a columnist who is a lesbian mother, married to another woman, recognizing a lifestyle that is anathema to the LDS Church.[8]

Meanwhile, assuming that Huntsman, Napier-Pearce, and the *Tribune* staff will create a website that is user-friendly and personalized, the internet could be used for drilling down to get more substance from the shorter stories that run in print, a suggestion mused upon by Jay Shelledy.[9]

Napier-Pearce is also redefining the paper's mission and determining ways to involve readers in real time. She has beefed up business coverage and plans to amplify the paper's coverage of outdoor recreation. "No newspaper has yet found the magic solution. We may have to deal with issues of frequency and delivery of our product," said Napier-Pearce.[10]

Long-time readers will not see the return of the *New York Times*'s syndication services, including columnists Paul Krugman, Thomas Friedman, Gail Collins, and Maureen Dowd. Paul Huntsman, when offered a bargain-basement price to resume syndication services of the *New York Times*, turned it down.[11]

The Mountain Meadows Massacre story continues, and the *Salt Lake Tribune* will be covering it in the near future.

In 2015 California-based archeologist Everett Bassett announced he had found the two rock graves constructed by the US Army about twenty months after the 1857 massacre. He had used old army records to locate the mass graves, which were described as mounds of rocks. They were in a ravine on the Old Spanish Trail approximately a thousand feet from the monuments that the LDS Church erected. They were on land the church does not own.[12]

"The [LDS] church is trying to buy the land, but we think the management of this new site should consist of a consortium of interested parties, and not the church alone," said Bassett. "As one elderly descendent of the massacre explained to me, it would be 'like a Holocaust survivor going to the Auschwitz Museum and discovering it was run by Nazis.' I appreciate that the distrust of the LDS Church runs deep among many massacre descendants," said Bassett.[13]

Bassett intends to publish his findings in a peer-reviewed journal.

In 2020 the joint operating agreement will be up for renegotiation. Will the *Tribune* desire to do business with an unfaithful partner? Because of economics and past meddling it may be forced to stay in a deceitful marriage.

AUTHOR'S NOTE

The church and its various organizations and individuals relevant to this work, including the *Deseret News*, largely rejected the author's inquiries or requests for interviews. Those inside the church who willingly discussed with the author the conflict between the *Tribune* and the LDS Church asked for anonymity.

It's the nature of the LDS Church, when under questioning, to erect barriers of silence. It protects a relatively young organization that is still forming itself, struggling with contradictions of nineteenth-century beliefs in a twenty-first-century world.

Mormonism is my tribe. Like Jews, once a Mormon, always a Mormon. I love the Mormon people, and I count my best friends among the faithful. Many of my devout relatives expressed their love for me regardless of my criticisms. They epitomize the basic goodness of Mormon members.

I am also grateful for the many non-Mormons who I count among my closest friends.

For those who chafe under Utah's exceptionalism, I beg you to view our cultural caprices as theater, with good-hearted players and spectacular props that include everything from alpine mountains to biblical red-rock badlands.

—J. W. U., Salt Lake City, 2017

ACKNOWLEDGMENTS

Joan O'Brien provided her valuable time in helping me understand the tricky spaghetti bowl of legal maneuverings both during the 2013–2016 events and the actions and aftermath of the sale of the *Tribune* in 1997. Were it not for your Utah Newspaper Project/Citizens for Two Voices this book would never have been possible. Joanie, your wisdom and persistence were marvelous. Any errors in interpretation of the legal ramifications are mine, not Joan's.

Karra Porter, thank you for your time and insights as to the legal maneuverings as well as some insights into the role of the Department of Justice. Your lawyering gave this work a happy ending.

Will Bagley provided me with excellent sources and suggestions regarding the Mountain Meadows Massacre, and his book, *Blood of the Prophets: Brigham Young and the Massacre at Mountain Meadows*, stands with Juanita Brooks's book, *The Mountain Meadows Massacre*, as the definitive works about that terrible event.

The late John W. "Jack" Gallivan was generous with his time when I interviewed him in 2012, and provided me with vital information that would later become useful.

Michael D. "Mickey" Gallivan went above and beyond the call in providing me with documents from his father and from other sources that revealed the machinations of the "other side" of this story. He has my deepest gratitude.

Thomas Kearns McCarthey Jr. and Philip George McCarthey spoke freely with me, providing details of the procedure of the court cases in which they lost the *Salt Lake Tribune*. Philip has not picked up a copy of the *Tribune* since the family lost the paper in 2002.

Mike Korologos and I go back to days shared at the *Tribune*. His historical interface with Glen Snarr was helpful in reconstructing what happened in the 1990s as the LDS Church was maneuvering to outflank the *Tribune*.

Patty Henetz, you were a mighty force in keeping me on track and providing me with the benefit of your experience as a reporter covering the church for the Associated Press.

Terry Orme, you are one of the heroes of this book. Few understand how much difficulty you faced as editor and publisher during the 2013–2016 period when the *Tribune*'s future hung on a thread. Thank you also for your help and insights as to where the *Tribune* might go in the future.

I also want to thank Eva Finkemeier for your research help and support for this project.

James E. "Jay" Shelledy, thank you for your remembrances and insights on the relationships of many of the characters in this book. Your directness and willingness to provide certain details were refreshing.

Ed Berkovitch, thank you for your thoughts on the philosophy that guides the leadership of the LDS Church. You are a scholar and a gentleman.

Peggy Fletcher Stack, much of your incisive reporting influenced this book, as the endnotes show. You are a community treasure. It's a balancing act, and you perform very well.

Pat Bagley, you've given me endless hours of pleasure with your cartoons. My wish for next year: a Pulitzer. You deserve it.

To the late Dominic Welch, I owe this man so much for his generous thoughts and memories. His passion was still at work in his well-documented review of the events of the period 1997–2002, which was most helpful.

Jim Woolf, thanks for your recollections. You gave the *Tribune* and its readers so much during your years at the newspaper and continue to provide me not only with information but also with your friendship and your editor's eye.

Tom Harvey, Mike Carter, Paul Rolly, Carol Sisco, Dick Rosetta, Dave Jonsson, Lynn Johnson, Verdo Thomas, Craig Hansell, Shirley Jones, Connie White, Francine Giani, Ann Poore, and John Keahy: all of you made contributions to this work, and I appreciate your time and energy.

Thanks to John Netto, who gave me sage advice and supported this work from the beginning.

To the Utah Historical Society, many thanks for your work on my behalf.

I owe much to my publisher, Prometheus Books. I especially want to thank Steven L. Mitchell, Hanna Etu, Jeffrey Curry, and Liz Mills.

Special thanks for all their hard work go to Janet Rosen and Sheree Bykofsky of Sheree Bykofsky and Associates, Inc.

To my family, my long-time friends, and cheering section, I extend my gratitude and thanks for your support.

Many of my sources wished to remain anonymous, for obvious reasons. They provided invaluable perspective and information. You know who you are, and I have deep appreciation for your willingness to dig at the truth.

To those I've missed in these acknowledgments, I apologize. There were so many helpful people. You cared about an institution that hopefully will continue to be "the balance wheel of Utah."

THREE *TRIBUNE* ARTICLES IN FULL ABOUT THE EXCAVATION AT THE MOUNTAIN MEADOWS MASSACRE SITE

To better examine what the *Salt Lake Tribune* had written about the excavation of the Mountain Meadows Massacre site, and the details, the three full articles from March 2000 are provided below.

BONES OF CONTENTION

Unearthing Mountain Meadows Secrets: Backhoe at a
S. Utah killing field rips open 142-year-old wound[1]

By Christopher Smith

Editor's Note: Mountain Meadows, southwest of Cedar City, is the site of the worst slaughter of white civilians in the history of the frontier West. Last summer, LDS Church officials descendants of the victims sought to finally close the 142-year-old wound. Together they were to build and dedicate a new monument to the 120 Arkansas emigrants who perished in unimaginable violence at the hands of Mormon settlers and Indian accomplices.

The new memorial stands, but the wound still festers. In constructing the monument, workers uncovered remains of 29 victims, a vivid and horrific reminder of that September day in 1857. The story of those bones, and what happened to them last summer, adds another excruciating chapter to the history of a crime that many of Utah's pioneer descendants can neither confront nor explain.

MOUNTAIN MEADOWS—After burying dozens of men, women and children murdered in a bizarre frontier conspiracy, an Army major ordered his soldiers to erect a rockpile and a carved wooden cross swearing vengeance on the perpetrators. Brevet Maj. James H. Carleton then wrote to Congress: "Perhaps the future may be judged by the past."

They were fated words. When a backhoe operator last summer accidentally dug up the bones buried here in 1859 by Carleton's troops, it set into motion a series of cover-ups, accusations and recriminations that continue today. It also caused a good-faith effort by The Church of Jesus Christ of Latter-day Saints—to reconcile one of the ugliest chapters of U.S. history—to backfire.

The Aug. 3, 1999, excavation of the remains of at least 29 of the 120 emigrants slaughtered in the Mountain Meadows massacre eventually prompted Gov. Mike Leavitt to intercede. He encouraged state officials to quickly rebury the remains, even though the basic scientific analysis required by state law was unfinished. "It would be unfortunate if this sad moment in our state's history, and the rather good-spirited attempt to put it behind us, was highlighted by controversy," Leavitt wrote in an e-mail message to state antiquities officials shortly before LDS Church President Gordon B. Hinckley presided over a ceremony at Mountain Meadows.

The widely publicized occasion was to dedicate a newly rebuilt rock cairn monument, crafted with the same stones Carleton's troops had piled defiantly in 1859. They also were the same rocks that were torn down from the grave site by one of Leavitt's own ancestors. Dudley Leavitt, himself a participant in the Sept. 11, 1857, murders, visited the cairn with LDS prophet Brigham Young a year after Carleton's troops left.

After ridiculing the pledge of vengeance, Young lifted his right arm toward the rock pile and "in five minutes there wasn't one stone left upon another," Dudley Leavitt would recall. "He didn't have to tell us what he wanted done. We understood."

The governor's intercession was one of many dramas played out last summer, all serving to underscore Mountain Meadows' place as the Bermuda Triangle of Utah's historical and theological landscape. The end result may be another sad chapter in the massacre's legacy of bitterness, denial and suspicion.

In retracing the latest episode, The Salt Lake Tribune conducted numerous interviews and researched documents obtained under Utah's Government Records Access and Management Act to find:

—Co-sponsors of the monument project—the LDS Church and the Mountain Meadows Association—initially hoped to cover up the excavation, with the MMA demanding any documentation be "kept out of public view permanently." The president of the association, Ron Loving, wrote in an Aug. 9 e-mail to the director of the Utah Division of History: "The families [descended from victims] and the LDS church will work out what we want to become public knowledge on this accidental finding."

—The vain effort to hide the truth gave rise to wild conspiracy theories among some descendants. They suspected Loving was working with the LDS Church to rewrite history by having church-owned Brigham Young University determine the exhumed victims died of disease, not murder. "I call it 'sanitizing' a foul deed," Burr Fancher wrote to other descendants Aug. 24.

—Utah Division of History Director Max Evans, over the objections of state Archaeologist Kevin Jones, personally rewrote BYU's state archaeological permit to require immediate reburial of the bones after receiving the governor's e-mail. Jones raised numerous questions over the political power play, including a concern it was "ethnocentric and racist" to rebury the bones of white emigrants without basic scientific study when similar American Indian remains are routinely subjected to such analysis before repatriation.

—News of the excavation triggered written requests to BYU from people around the nation, seeking to determine if their ancestors were among the recovered victims. Some offered to submit to DNA testing and desired to reinter the remains in family burial plots outside of Utah. Although the Utah Attorney General's Office had advised state officials that "any and all lineal descendants of the Mountain Meadows massacre would appear to have a voice in determining the disposition of the bodies," there is little documented evidence any of the people seeking information about family members were consulted.

—Resentment over the discovery and of the remains has caused a schism in the descendant families, with at least one organized group asking why civil or criminal penalties were not brought against the LDS Church or the MMA for desecrating the grave. There also is confusion over who is now in charge of the MMA. While new president Gene Sessions of Weber State University says Loving was voted out of office in November in the wake of the controversy, Loving says he's still the boss: "I wasn't voted out of a damn thing. I was moved up. It was my methods and my way of doing business that got that monument done."

Other descendants have enlisted the support of Arkansas Gov. Mike Huckabee in calling for federal stewardship of the emigrant mass graves scattered in Mountain Meadows, instead of having the Mormon Church own the land.

"We're doubtful with the church in control this will ever be completely put to rest," says Scott Fancher, president of the Mountain Meadows Monument Foundation in Arkansas. "There's a sense among some of our members it's like having Lee Harvey Oswald in charge of JFK's tomb."

Glen M. Leonard, director of the Museum of Church History and Art and Hinckley's personal representative in the process, said the church endeavored with the MMA to gather comment from all descendants through the association's Web page and newsletter.

"While this was not a perfect method for reaching all members of all branches of all families, it was a practical means for the church and the association to inform most of them with interest in the grave site restoration project," Leonard says. "We are sorry if some descendants of the emigrant families feel left out."

Marian Jacklin, an archaeologist with the Dixie National Forest in Cedar City who has spent years trying to navigate the emotional minefield of Mountain Meadows, says the events of last summer did not yield the desired consequences.

"This whole episode didn't answer anything," she says. "It just asked more questions."

And the question that burns in the minds of many angry descendants is: Why was a backhoe digging at a known, well-marked grave site?

"What we understood in every correspondence, and we thought we had made perfectly clear to the church, was that under no circumstances would the remains be disturbed," says Scott Fancher, whose organization is considering legal action over the excavation. "Never in my wildest imagination did we expect them to set a backhoe on this grave and start digging."

Hinckley had personally launched the effort to stabilize the decaying rock cairn—rebuilt at least 11 times since Carleton's troops placed the stones—after a visit to the site in October 1998. The 2.5 acres was deeded to the church in the 1970s after the landowner reportedly tried in vain to find descendants in Arkansas to accept the donation of land.

Partnering with the MMA—a group of emigrant descendants, historians and interested southwestern Utah residents—LDS Church architects designed a monument with a thigh-high stone wall around the old cairn, perched on a steep stream bank.

There are conflicting accounts of whether descendants understood the wall would require digging a trench around the grave for a concrete footing. Some MMA members, including the contractor, interpreted the "do not disturb" edict to cover the pre-construction archaeological investigation. Once the archaeologists said all clear, crews could dig the footing, they believed.

But Scott Fancher says his branch of the family understood the wall would be "surface-mounted," in keeping with the church's pledge not to disturb the burial ground in any way.

Before beginning, the LDS Church had hired BYU's Office of Public Archaeology to conduct a non-invasive archaeological survey. Using ground-penetrating radar, aerial photos, metal detectors and hundreds of soil-sample tests to search for signs of bones or artifacts, a team of professionals scoured the area.

"The archaeological evidence was 100 percent negative," says Shane Baker, the BYU staff archaeologist who directed the study. "I went to our client, the church, and said either this is not the spot or every last shred of evidence has been erased."

There was speculation that bones buried beneath the cairn had been exposed to the elements and deteriorated. Or, they had been washed down the ravine, the cairn was in the wrong place or the cairn was directly on top of the bones.

But today, Baker admits the archaeological examination at the location where the bones were eventually disturbed was not as complete as it was in other areas. The narrow spot between the cairn and streambank was not probed with radar because the trailer-like unit could not be towed near the precarious edge. Instead, Baker took soil core samples, using a bucket auger, which strained against the impacted earth.

He again found nothing. Witnesses would later draw an analogy to a magician thrusting swords into a box containing an assistant and somehow missing the mark.

"Shane came within inches of the remains and it is amazing that no evidence was determined," says Kent Bylund of St. George, an association board member and adjacent Mountain Meadows landowner who served as project contractor. "I sincerely believe everything was done to ensure the area to be excavated was core sampled and thoroughly examined before excavation was permitted."

BYU's Baker blames the accidental discovery of bones on the restrictions placed on the investigation by the LDS Church.

"We were not allowed to do the kind of testing we would do normally, and I was concerned the whole time we were going to hit bone," he says. "The very fact they wouldn't let me dig with a shovel and a trowel is why a backhoe found those bones."

It was on the second or third scoop that more than 30 pounds of human skeletal remains clattered out of the backhoe bucket as it dug the footing trench on Aug. 3. Bylund looked on in disbelief, his heart in his throat.

His first inclination was to put the remains back in the ground and swear the backhoe operator to secrecy. But it was impossible to unring the bell.

"Once they were uncovered, for this new monument to go in, you really had no choice but to remove them because they were dead center in the middle of the new wall," Baker says.

As Baker delicately removed hundreds of pieces of bone from the exposed trench, Loving and Leonard debated what to do and who to tell.

"My plan was to have them reburied within 48 hours of their discovery," says Loving. The Arizona man, whose ancestor was a brother of a massacre victim, took charge, he says, "because the LDS Church considered me as the spokesman for the families in my capacity as president of the Mountain Meadows Association."

But other descendants more directly related to the victims are outraged the church gave Loving such authority.

"It's offensive to a lot of people to hear Mr. Loving say this is what the family thinks because we put the church on notice repeatedly that Mr. Loving does not speak for the family and never has," says Scott Fancher. "We are very disappointed we did not have a voice in how the remains were treated after they were disturbed."

Church officials and BYU put Loving in charge and agreed with his plan to rebury within 48 hours. But that plan was foiled on Aug. 5 when Jones, the state archaeologist, informed them Utah law required a basic scientific analysis when human remains are discovered on private property. Failure to comply was a felony.

BYU needed a state permit to legally remove the remains. And, by law, such permits require "the reporting of archaeological information at current standards of scientific rigor."

Although LDS officials knew the descendants would be uncomfortable with the required analysis, they agreed it was necessary, says Leonard.

Jones issued BYU's permit Aug. 6, requiring scientists to determine as best possible, age, sex, race, stature, health condition, cause of death and, because the remains were commingled, to segregate the largest bones and skulls of each individual for proper reburial.

Baker immediately began sorting bones with an assistant in his St. George hotel room, then transferred the remains to BYU's Provo lab and to the University of Utah's forensic anthropology lab in Salt Lake City, which BYU had subcontracted to do the required "osteological" analysis.

Throughout, Loving demanded not a word be said to anyone about the discovery. On Aug. 9, he threatened to sue the state Division of History if Evans did not guarantee in writing the state would adhere to several conditions of secrecy, including "none of the contents of the report, in part or in whole, is released to anyone."

Baker of BYU maintains the secrecy was to allow time to notify family members who did not know of the accidental discovery. "To the credit of the church, they always told me they wanted everything to be open and aboveboard," he says.

Yet many descendants involved in the monument project didn't learn of the discovery until the St. George Spectrum newspaper broke the story Aug. 13, 10 days after the backhoe unearthed the remains. Failing to get answers from state officials whom Loving had told not to talk, many descendants bitterly wondered what was really going on.

Burr Fancher, who had supported the monument reconstruction, was incensed. In an e-mail message circulated to several other descendants, he said Loving was a "lackey in the employ of the Mormon Church and caters to Hinckley's every whim."

The news also triggered a flood of requests to BYU and the state from people wanting to know if their family roots could be traced to Mountain Meadows. On Aug. 22, the Utah Attorney General's Office informed state antiquities officials: "Generally, next of kin is privileged in advancing the burial rights of the deceased absent a compelling state interest."

Loving was telling BYU and state officials the families wanted the remains buried Sept. 10 in a private ceremony at Mountain Meadows. But new claims of affiliation complicated matters.

"I went into this blindly and naively assuming the Mountain Meadows Association spoke as a unified voice on behalf of all the descendants and that turned out to be wrong," Baker says today. "On one hand I had descendants demanding I test for DNA, and on the other I had descendants saying they were going to sue my pants off if I did."

By now it was clear scientists would not be able to complete even the baseline scientific analysis in time for the scheduled Sept. 10 reburial ceremony. After a tense meeting with Loving, Jones agreed to a compromise. The examination and segregation of the "long bones" would probably be finished by Sept. 10, and those bones would be placed in the ground at the ceremony. The skulls would require more time, but once that analysis was complete, the cranial material would then be reburied.

Loving says he was "forced to accept" the compromise, but immediately launched an end run. He contacted Dixie Leavitt, the governor's father and a former state senator who played a leading role in the 1990 dedication of another monument overlooking the killing field. Loving warned Dixie Leavitt that unless all the bones were reburied on Sept. 10, there would be an uproar during Hinckley's dedication ceremony.

"I don't recall exactly what I said, but 'disturbance' sounds like a pretty good word," Loving says today.

"I received a call today from my Father (sic) who has been rather involved with the people from Arkansas who are planning to hold a burial and memorial service," Gov. Leavitt wrote in a Sept. 6 e-mail to Wilson Martin, the division's director of cultural preservation and Jones' boss. "Apparently, the State Archaeologist is insisting that some portion of the remains be held from the burial for study. It is apparently causing a lot of angst amongst the family members."

Gov. Leavitt responded to The Tribune's questions about his intercession through his press secretary, Vicki Varela. She said the governor "did not feel that it was appropriate for the bones to be dissected and studied in a manner that would prolong the discomfort."

Leavitt did not speak to any descendants or family members "other than being notified by his father that there was some risk a respectful event may turn into something of a discomfort for the participants," said Varela.

Asked if Leavitt understood there was a state law requiring such study, Varela answered: "I don't think he was knowledgeable of all the details." She said as the CEO of the state, the governor believed "we should find a way to create minimal interference."

Church History Museum director Leonard says it was the decision of the MMA, not the church, to seek an executive exception to the scientific study requirements.

"We were aware of the political implications and the emotional implications of this issue," says Leonard. "In hindsight, it is fair to say that the governor's directive to bury those remains not completely analyzed was a humane response to conflicting needs."

Evans drew up a new state antiquities permit for BYU, removing the previous requirement of analysis "in toto" and replacing it with a new requirement that BYU "shall reinter, by Sept. 10, 1999, all human remains into the prepared burial vaults, near the place of discovery."

Jones, in a memo to the division files Sept. 9, noted his professional objections.

"To rebury the remains at this point would constitute, in the opinion of the Antiquities Section, a violation of professional, scientific and ethical responsibilities," Jones wrote. "It also might indeed be seen as demonstrating disrespect for the victims, to bury them once again with bones of many individuals mixed and jumbled, as they were originally disrespectfully interred, in a mass grave of murder victims."

But Evans also included a notation on the new permit that could lead to another re-opening of the massacre grave.

"Since the remains have been interred in a concrete vault, it is possible that further evaluation can take place if all the parties agree, or if a court so orders at some future date," Evans says today. "This is a matter for the family members and the landowner to address, not one the Division of State History expects to be involved in."

Early on the morning of Sept. 10, Baker picked up the remains from the U. and drove them to a St. George mortuary. There, the unsegregated bones and skulls of at least 29 people were placed inside four wooden ossuaries and later reburied at the rebuilt monument.

On Sept. 29, Baker sent letters of thanks to Division of History officials explaining how many family members at the memorial service appreciated that all the remains were reinterred. "This certainly represents the positive side of Governor Leavitt's action to intercede on the reburial issue," he wrote. At the same time, Baker said he was professionally conflicted by the precedent set with the political decisions.

"The state and its people benefited from this absolutely unique opportunity to, in some small way, try and make amends for the tragic events that transpired there so long ago," Baker wrote in a letter to Jones. "That certainly counts for something. I just hope that some of the other consequences we were all concerned about in connection with the action to rebury do not come back to cause us grief in the future." Again, those would prove fateful words.

Voices of the Dead—Monday, March 13, 2000.[2]
By Christopher Smith
© 2000, the *Salt Lake Tribune*, with permission

University of Utah forensic anthropologist Shannon Novak is piecing together the bones from the Mountain Meadows excavation.

"The truth ends up in sharper focus" in the tug-of-war between the LDS Church, the anthropologists, surviving families of the dead Fancher party and the public as represented by The Tribune.

There is little widespread public knowledge of a crime of civil terrorism that pales in modern U.S. history only to the 1995 Oklahoma City bombing. The slaughter of an estimated 120 white civilians by a cabal of Mormon zealots and Indians is never mentioned in school history textbooks and is not even listed as a "point of interest" on Utah's official highway map. Until recent additions, the interpretive signs at Mountain Meadows were so vague as to how the Arkansas emigrants died that they became a source of national ridicule.

The Tribune and archeologists believe the full truth has never been told. New findings come to light:

For instance, written accounts generally claim the women and older children were beaten or bludgeoned to death by Indians using crude weapons, while Mormon militiamen killed adult males by shooting them in the back of the head. However, Novak's partial reconstruction of approximately 20 different skulls of Mountain Meadows victims show:

—At least five adults had gunshot exit wounds in the posterior area of the cranium—a clear indication some were shot while facing their killers. One victim's skull displays a close-range bullet entrance wound to the forehead;

—Women also were shot in the head at close range. A palate of a

female victim exhibits possible evidence of gunshot trauma to the face, based on a preliminary examination of broken teeth;
—At least one youngster, believed to be about 10 to 12 years old, was killed by a gunshot to the top of the head.

Other findings by Novak from the commingled partial remains of at least 29 individuals—a count based on the number of right femurs in the hundreds of pieces of bone recovered from the gravesite—back up the historical record;
—Five skulls with gunshot entrance wounds in the back of the cranium have no "beveling," or flaking of bone, on the exterior of the skull. This indicates the victims were executed with the gun barrel pointing directly into the head, not at an angle, and at very close range;
—Two young adults and three children—one believed to be about 3 years old judging by tooth development—were killed by blunt-force trauma to the head. Although written records recount that children under the age of 8 were spared, historians believe some babes-in-arms were murdered along with their mothers;
—Virtually all of the "post-cranial" (from the head down) bones displayed extensive carnivore damage, confirming written accounts that bodies were left on the killing field to be gnawed by wolves and coyotes.

Assisted by graduate student Derinna Kopp and other U. Department of Anthropology volunteers, Novak's team took photographs, made measurements, wrote notes and drew diagrams of the bones, all part of the standard data collection required by law.

"I treated this as if it were a recent homicide, conducting the analysis scientifically but with great respect," says Novak. "I'm always extremely conservative in my conclusions. I will only present what I can verify in a court of law."

Beyond the cause of death, Novak was able to discern something about the constitution of the emigrants.

"These were big, strong, robust men, very heavy boned," she says. "We found tobacco staining on teeth, which is helpful in indicating males, and lots of cavities, indicating they had a diet heavy on carbohydrates."

There came a point in the reconstruction where the disparate pieces of bones slowly began to morph into individuals, each with distinct characteristics. One victim had broken an arm and clavicle that had healed improperly. One male had likely been in a brawl that left a healed blunt wound on the back of his head. One youngster's remains all had a distinctive reddish tint; as scientists inventoried the bones they would note another part of "red boy."

"We were at the stage when we were distinguishing them as people, where you were getting to know each one," says Novak. "We could have started to match people up. You would never have gotten complete individuals, but given a little more time, we could have done a lot more."

But time was up. Novak had concentrated her initial work on the "long bones," as part of an agreement reached between the Division of History, Mountain Meadows Association and Brigham Young University. Those post-cranial remains would be re-interred during a Sept. 10 memorial. Because the reconstruction of the skulls would not be finished by then, the agreement allowed Novak until spring—about six months—to do the studies required by state law.

It was late on Sept. 8 that she learned that Division of History Director Max Evans had overruled Jones and re-wrote BYU's antiquities permit, changing the standard requirement for analysis "in toto" to require reburial of all remains on Sept. 10. When BYU asked to pick up the cranial bones on Sept. 9, Novak deferred, saying she had until the next day according to the amended permit.

"It was the only stand I could make because they had changed the rules in the middle of the process with no notice whatsoever," she says. "We worked through the night to get as much done as we could. This data had to be gathered."

BYU archaeologist Shane Baker picked up the remains from Novak early on the morning of Sept. 10, drove them to a St. George mortuary where they were placed in four small wooden ossuaries and then reburied later that day at the newly finished monument.

The dead would say no more. Their remains should never have been queried in the first place, says Weber State historian Sessions.

"This idea of Shannon Novak needing six months to mess around with the cranial stuff, well, I know something about that science and that's a fraud," says the Mountain Meadows Association president, who adds he consulted his WSU colleagues about the time needed for such studies. "I really disagree with anyone who says we should have kept the bones out of the ground longer to determine what happened at Mountain Meadows. The documentary evidence is overwhelming. Whether or not little kids were shot in the head or mashed with rocks makes no difference. They were killed."

But other historians, searching for more information about an event cloaked in secrecy for generations, see value in the empirical evidence that forensic anthropology can offer. On Feb. 15, BYU's Baker made an informal presentation of his own photographs and research on the Mountain Meadows remains to the Westerners, an exclusive group of professional and amateur historians who meet monthly. As Baker flashed color slides of the bones on the screen, the men were visibly moved.

"I've dealt with this awful tale on a daily basis for five years, but I found seeing the photos of the remains of the victims profoundly disturbing," says Will Bagley, whose forthcoming book on the massacre, Blood of the Prophets [*Brigham Young and the Massacre at Mountain Meadows*], won the Utah Arts Council publication prize. "It drove home the horror."

But would it convince those who still believe the killing was done solely by Indians, or was part of an anti-Mormon conspiracy or the work of a single, renegade apostate?

"My own father believed John D. Lee was the one behind it all and if you think you were going to convince him any differently with empirical proof, forget it," says David Bigler, author of Forgotten Kingdom and former member of the Utah Board of State History. "People want to have the truth, they want it with a capital T and they don't like to have people upset that truth. True believers don't want to think the truth has changed."

And according to the leader of the modern Mormon church, the truth has already been told about Mountain Meadows.

The Dilemma of Blame—Tuesday, March 13, 2000[3]

BY Christopher Smith
Tribune reporter Peggy Fletcher Stack contributed to this story.
© 2000, the *Salt Lake Tribune*, with permission

MOUNTAIN MEADOWS—As LDS Church President Gordon B. Hinckley delivered words of reconciliation at the Sept. 11, 1999, dedication of a rebuilt monument to emigrants slaughtered by Mormon militiamen and their Indian allies 142 years earlier, he added a legal disclaimer.

"That which we have done here must never be construed as an acknowledgment of the part of the church of any complicity in the occurrences of that fateful day," Hinckley said. The line was inserted into his speech on the advice of attorneys for the Corporation of the President of The Church of Jesus Christ of Latter-day Saints.

The statement, seemingly out of sync with Hinckley's desire to bring healing to nearly one hundred fifty years of bitterness, caused some in attendance to wonder if any progress had really been made at all. If the Mormon Church leadership of 1857 was not at least partially to blame for the one hundred twenty people slain at Mountain Meadows, then whom should history hold responsible?

"Well, I would place blame on the local people," Hinckley told The Salt Lake Tribune in a subsequent interview Feb. 23. "I've never thought for one minute—and I've read the history of that tragic episode—that Brigham Young had anything to do with it. It was a local decision and it was tragic. We can't understand it in this time."

For families of the slain emigrants and descendants of LDS pioneer John D. Lee—the one participant convicted and executed for the crime—Hinckley's delineation of the church's position on Mountain Meadows compounded many of the misgivings they had about the entire chain of events during the summer.

First, a church contractor's backhoe accidentally exhumed the bones of at least 29 victims Aug. 3 while digging at the grave, even though the church had pledged not to disturb the ground. That was followed by a failed attempt at secrecy, leading to wild speculation and a schism among descendants.

There was a heated debate over whether a state law requiring forensic analysis of the bones should be obeyed, with Gov. Mike Leavitt finally intervening to prematurely terminate the study and ensure that all bones be reburied before the dedication. New forensic anthropology studies done on the bones before reinterment provided the first graphic evidence of the brutality, and a new, unwanted reminder of the horror.

Now, those who had hoped to hear some sort of apology on behalf of the modern Mormon Church from the man who had done more than any of his predecessors to salve the wounds, were left feeling they had come up short.

"What we've felt would put this resentment to rest would be an official apology from the church," says Scott Fancher of the Mountain Meadows Monument Foundation in Arkansas, a group of direct descendants of the victims. "Not an admission of guilt, but an acknowl-edgement of neglect and of intentional obscuring of the truth."

Others closely involved in Hinckley's participation in the new mon-ument project believe the LDS Church went as far as it's ever going to go in addressing the uncomfortable details of the massacre.

"You're not going to get an apology for several reasons, one of which is that as soon as you say you're sorry, here come the wrongful-death lawsuits," says Gene Sessions, president of the Mountain Meadows Asso-ciation, the organization that partnered with Hinckley on the project.

"If President Hinckley ever contemplated he was going to open this can of worms he never would have bothered to do this, because it asks embarrassing questions. It raises the old question of whether Brigham Young ordered the massacre and whether Mormons do ter-rible things because they think their leaders want them to do terrible things."

Noted Mormon writer Levi Peterson has tried to explain the dif-ficulty that Mormons and their church face in confronting the atrocity of Mountain Meadows.

"If good Mormons committed the massacre, if prayerful leaders ordered it, if apostles and a prophet knew about it and later sacrificed John D. Lee, then the sainthood of even the modern church seems tainted," he has written. "Where is the moral superiority of Mor-monism, where is the assurance that God has made Mormons his new chosen people?"

Mormons are certainly not alone in trying to square the shedding of innocent blood in the name of God. In the 13th century, the Roman Catholic Church established courts of the Spanish Inquisition, gaining confessions of heresy through torture and punishment by death. In 1692, Puritans in Massachusetts executed 20 people for allegedly prac-ticing witchcraft.

But acknowledging any complicity in Mountain Meadows' macabre past is fundamentally problematic for the modern church.

"The massacre has left the Mormon Church on the horns of a dilemma," says Utah historian Will Bagley, author of a forthcoming book on Mountain Meadows. "It can't acknowledge its historic involve-ment in a mass murder, and if it can't accept its accountability, it can't repent."

The massacre also shows a darker side to Mormonism's proud pioneer heritage, an element used today to shape the faith's worldwide image.

"The problem is that Mormons then were not simply old-fashioned versions of Mormons today," says historian David Bigler, author of Forgotten Kingdom. "Then, they were very zealous believers; it was a faith that put great emphasis on the Old Testament and the Blood of Israel."

Brigham Young's theocratic rule of the Utah Territory—he wore the hats of governor, federal Indian agent and LDS prophet—was at its zenith in 1857 when the mass murders at Mountain Meadows occurred. Reformation of the LDS Church was in full swing, with members' loyalty challenged by church leaders. Young taught that in a complete theocracy, God required the spilling of a sinner's blood on the ground to properly atone for grievous sins. It was the Mormon doctrine of "blood atonement."

The modern church contends blood atonement was mainly a "rhetorical device" used by Young and other leaders to teach Saints the wages of sin. Yet some scholars see its influence even today, pointing to such signs as Utah being the only state left in the nation that allows execution by firing squad. There is widespread disagreement, but some historians have concluded that blood atonement is central to understanding why faithful Mormons would conspire to commit mass murder.

Alternate explanations have included speculation that Indians threatened to prey on local inhabitants if Mormon settlers did not help them raid emigrant wagon trains. There also are the oft-repeated "evil emigrant" stories, accounts that the Arkansas wagon train antagonized Mormon settlers with epithets, poisoned watering holes that resulted in the deaths of Mormon children and Indians, and boastful claims of one contingent called the "Missouri Wildcats" that they were with the Illinois mob that killed LDS founder Joseph Smith.

Retold as fact in many accounts and in the National Register of Historic Places nomination for Mountain Meadows, the veracity of those stories has been called into question since the earliest investigations of the massacre.

Historian Juanita Brooks, in her seminal book, The Mountain Meadows Massacre, believed the emigrants met their doom in part through their own provocative behavior and because they came from the Arkansas county adjacent to the county where beloved LDS Apostle Parley P. Pratt had recently been murdered.

In his forthcoming Blood of the Prophets, Bagley points to new evidence that seems to blunt this one point of Brooks' landmark research.

"[Noted historian] Dale Morgan alerted Brooks in 1941 to the likelihood that the emigrant atrocity stories had been 'set afloat by Mormons to further their alibi of the massacre's having been perpetrated by Indians,'" Bagley writes, quoting from Morgan's letter to Brooks. "Even then it was well-established that the Fancher party came from Arkansas, and Morgan had never been satisfied with tales that the company included a large contingent of maniacal Missourians."

That a wagon train mainly of women and children would be slaughtered for belligerence and taunting seems too farfetched to many historians today.

"When you have 50 to perhaps more than 70 men participate in an event like this, you can't just say they got upset," says Bigler, a Utah native. "We have to believe they did not want to do what they did any more than you or I would. We have to recognize they thought what they were doing is what authority required of them. The only question to be resolved is did that authority reach all the way to Salt Lake City?"

Fifty years ago, when Brooks broached the question of Young's role and blood atonement in her book, she was labeled an apostate by some and "one of the Lord's lie detectors" by others, such as the late philanthropist O.C. Tanner. Brooks noted her own LDS temple endowment blessing was to "avenge the blood of the prophet," a reference to Smith's 1844 murder. References to vengeance on behalf of slain church leaders eventually were removed from endowment ceremonies.

The journals kept by Mormon pioneers, who considered maintaining diaries a religious duty, continue to shed more light on the questions Brooks raised. Among key developments in the historical record:

—The Sept. 1, 1857, journal of Young's Indian interpreter, Dimick Huntington, recounts Young's negotiations with the Paiute Indians, who were offered a gift of the emigrant wagon train's cattle. When Paiute leaders noted Young had told them not to steal, Huntington translated Young's reply: "So I have, but now they have come to fight us and you, for when they kill us they will kill you."

—Young, as superintendent of Indian Affairs in the Utah Territory, ordered the distribution of more than $3,500 in goods to the natives "near Mountain Meadows" less than three weeks after the massacre.

—The patriarchal blessing given to the commander of the Mormon militia in Beaver, Iron and Washington counties called on Col.

William Dame to "act at the head of a portion of thy brethren and of the Lamanites [Indians] in the redemption of Zion and the avenging of the blood of the prophets upon them that dwell on the earth."

There is also additional support for Brooks' original premise: That Young wanted to stage a violent incident to demonstrate to the U.S. government—which was taking up arms against his theocracy—that he could persuade the Indians to interrupt travel over the important overland trails, thwarting all emigration. She was the first to note a frequently censored phrase from Young's Aug. 4, 1857, letter to Mormon "Indian missionary" Jacob Hamblin to obtain the tribe's trust, "for they must learn that they have either got to help us or the United States will kill us both."

Hinckley has declared, "Let the book of the past be closed" at Mountain Meadows and believes it is pointless to continually speculate on why it happened.

"None of us can place ourselves in the moccasins of those who lived there at the time," he said in an interview. "The feelings that were aroused, somehow, that I cannot understand. But it occurred. Now, we're trying to do something that we can to honorably and reverently and respectfully remember those who lost their lives there."

Sessions, the Weber State University historian who serves as president of the Mountain Meadows Association, says Hinckley's efforts at reconciliation this past summer "may be the most significant event to happen in Mountain Meadows since John D. Lee was executed."

Attitudes are changing, he says, pointing to the church's acceptance of interpretive signs at the Meadows that better explain who did the killing. As to who ultimately is to blame, perhaps that's not for anyone to judge.

"Somebody made a terrible decision that this has got to be done," says Sessions. "I don't justify it in any way. But I do believe it would have taken more guts to stay home in Cedar City on those days in 1857 than it would to go out there to the Meadows and take part.

"You couldn't stay away. You would have been out there killing people."

NOTES

CHAPTER 1: BOMBSHELL

1. *Wikipedia*, s.v. "*Deseret News*," last edited September 9, 2017, https://en.wikipedia.org/wiki/Deseret_News (accessed September 22, 2017).

2. "1957 Pulitzer Prizes," Pulitzer.org, http://www.pulitzer.org/prize-winners-by-year/1957 (accessed September 22, 2017).

3. John W. Gallivan, publisher emeritus, *Salt Lake Tribune*, memo to John Malone, Liberty Media Group, June 14, 1999.

4. Lucinda Fleeson, "The Battle of Salt Lake," *American Journalism Review* (March 2001), http://ajrarchive.org/article.asp?id=335 (accessed September 9, 2016).

5. Michelle Celarier, "Vulture in Distress," *New York Post*, July 26, 2012, http://nypost.com/2012/07/26/vulture-in-distress/ (accessed August 22, 2016).

6. Anonymous JOA source, in discussion with the author, October 2016.

7. Paul Rolly and Tom Harvey, in discussions with the author, 2014–2015.

8. Terry Orme, in discussion with the author, April 7, 2014.

9. "A Brief History of *Salt Lake Tribune* since Its Birth—with Photos of the Paper through the Years," April 21, 2016, http://archive.sltrib.com/article.php?id=3799788&itype=CMSID (accessed September 22, 2017).

10. Orme, in discussion with the author, May 8, 2014.

11. O. N. Malmquist, *The First 100 Years: A History of the* Salt Lake Tribune, *1871–1971* (Salt Lake City: Utah State Historical Society, 1971), 373–81.

12. Michael D. Gallivan, in discussion with the author July 10, 2014.

13. R. Gary Gomm to Steven Garfinkel, "The Quest No. 26," Utah Newspaper Project: Citizens for Two Voices, http://www.utahnewspaperproject.org/ (accessed August 22, 2016).

14. Fleeson, "Battle of Salt Lake."

15. Anonymous, in discussion with the author, June 17, 2014.

CHAPTER 2: DEEP AND HISTORICAL RESENTMENTS

1. Peggy Fletcher Stack, "A Daughter Steps into the Light out of the Shadows," *Salt Lake Tribune*, August 3, 2006, http://archive.sltrib.com/article.php?id=4133935&itype=NGPSID (accessed September 11, 2016).

2. Will Bagley, *Blood of the Prophets: Brigham Young and the Massacre at Mountain Meadows* (Norman: University of Oklahoma Press, 2002), p. xviii.

3. Whitney R. Cross, *The Burned-Over District: The Social and Intellectual History of Enthusiastic Religion in Western New York, 1800–1850* (Ithaca, NY: Cornell University Press, 1950); *Wikipedia*, s.v. "Second Great Awakening," last updated August 5, 2017, https://en.wikipedia.org/wiki/Second_Great_Awakening (accessed August 23, 2017).

4. Richard Lyman Bushman, *Joseph Smith: Rough Stone Rolling* (New York: Vintage, 2007), pp. 37–39.

5. Peggy Fletcher Stack, "New Scholarship Coming to Mormon Lessons, but Will Instructors Really Teach It?" *Salt Lake Tribune*, December 1, 2016, http://archive.sltrib.com/article.php?id=4654869&itype=CMSID (accessed August 23, 2017).

6. Bushman, *Joseph Smith*, pp. 48–49.

7. Ibid., p. 72.

8. Ibid.

9. Ibid., p. 60.

10. Ibid., p. 58.

11. Ibid., p. 59.

12. Fawn McKay Brodie, *No Man Knows My History: The Life of Joseph Smith* (New York: First Vintage Books Edition, 1995), pp. 51–52.

13. Ibid., p. 54.

14. Ibid., pp. 55–63.

15. Ibid., pp. 77–79.

16. Ibid., p. 78.

17. Ibid., pp. 82–88.

18. Ibid., p. 99.

19. Ibid., pp. 95–106.

20. Ibid.

21. Bushman, *Joseph Smith*, pp. 181–82.

22. Brodie, *No Man Knows*, pp. 195–207.

CHAPTER 3: MISSOURI MASSACRE

1. John Hamer, *Northeast of Eden: A Historical Atlas of Missouri's Mormon County* (Caldwell County, MO: Far West Cultural Center, 2004); *Wikipedia*, s.v. "Far West, Missouri," last updated June 12, 2017, https://en.wikipedia.org/wiki/Far_West,_Missouri (accessed August 23, 2017).

2. Fawn McKay Brodie, *No Man Knows My History: The Life of Joseph Smith* (New York: First Vintage Books Edition, 1995), p. 130.

3. "Section 127: The Nauvoo Temple and Baptism for the Dead," in *Doctrine and Covenants Student Manual* (Church of Jesus Christ of Latter-day Saints, 2002), pp. 314–15, https://www.lds.org/manual/doctrine-and-covenants-student-manual/sections-122-131/section-127-the-nauvoo-temple-and-baptism-for-the-dead?lang=eng (accessed August 4, 2016).

4. Bernard DeVoto, *The Year of Decision 1846* (New York: St. Martin's Griffin, 2000), pp. 82–86; *Wikipedia*, s.v. "Missouri Executive Order 44," last updated August 10, 2017, https://en.wikipedia.org/wiki/Missouri_Executive_Order_44 (accessed August 23, 2017).

5. Brodie, *No Man Knows*, pp. 254–55.

6. Richard Lyman Bushman, *Joseph Smith: Rough Stone Rolling* (New York: First Vintage Books Edition, 2007), pp. 365–66.

7. Ibid., pp. 342–55.

8. Brodie, *No Man Knows*, pp. 323–24.

9. Bushman, *Joseph Smith*, pp. 349–55.

CHAPTER 4: GOLDEN PLATES AGAIN

1. Milan D. Smith Jr., "That Is the Handwriting of Abraham," *Dialogue, a Journal of Mormon Thought* 23, no. 4 (Winter 1990): 167–69, https://www.dialoguejournal.com/wp-content/uploads/sbi/articles/Dialogue_V23N04_169.pdf (accessed August 30, 2016).

2. Fawn McKay Brodie, *No Man Knows My History: The Life of Joseph Smith* (New York: First Vintage Books Edition, 1995), p. 170.

3. Report of the committee appointed by the Philomathean Society (1858) of the University of Pennsylvania to translate the inscription on the Rosetta Stone, Philadelphia; *Wikipedia*, s.v. "Philomathean Society," last updated June 26, 2017, https://en.wikipedia.org/wiki/Philomathean_Society (accessed August 23, 2017).

4. Brodie, *No Man Knows*, pp. 174–75; Richard Lyman Bushman, *Joseph Smith: Rough Stone Rolling* (New York: First Vintage Books Edition, 2007), p. 291.

5. "The Book of Abraham," in *The Pearl of Great Price Student Manual* (Church of Jesus Christ of Latter-day Saints, 2000), pp. 28–41, https://www.lds.org/manual/the-pearl-of-great-price-student-manual/the-book-of-abraham?lang=eng (accessed August 4, 2016).

6. "Translation and Historicity of the Book of Abraham," Church of Jesus Christ of Latter-day Saints, https://www.lds.org/topics/translation-and-historicity-of-the-book-of-abraham?lang=eng (accessed August 4, 2016).

7. Bushman, *Joseph Smith*, p. xxii.

CHAPTER 5: POLYGAMY AND BAPTISM FOR THE DEAD

1. Fawn McKay Brodie, *No Man Knows My History: The Life of Joseph Smith* (New York: First Vintage Books Edition, 1995), p. 137.

2. Ibid., p. 256.

3. Richard Lyman Bushman, *Joseph Smith: Rough Stone Rolling* (New York: First Vintage Books Edition, 2007), p. 403.

4. *Wikipedia*, s.v. "Nauvoo, Illinois," last updated August 21, 2017, https://en.wikipedia.org/wiki/Nauvoo,_Illinois (accessed August 23, 2017).

5. Ibid., pp. 410–12.

6. Ibid., pp. 423–24.

7. Ibid., pp. 437–77.

8. *Wikipedia*, s.v. "List of Joseph Smith's Wives," last updated August 3, 2017, https://en.wikipedia.org/wiki/List_of_Joseph_Smith%27s_wives (accessed August 23, 2017).

9. Bushman, *Joseph Smith*, pp. 421–23.

10. "Prominent People Mormons Have Baptized by Proxy," Mormonism Research Ministry, http://www.mrm.org/prominent-people-baptized-by-proxy (accessed August 23, 2017); Jordan Teicher and Richa Naik, "Here Are 10 People Posthumously Baptized by Mormons," *Business Insider*, March 2, 2012, http://www.businessinsider.com/here-are-10-people-posthumously-baptized-by-mormons-2012-3 (accessed July 27, 2016).

11. Brodie, *No Man Knows*, p. 364.

12. Ibid., pp. 362–66.

13. Bushman, *Joseph Smith*, pp. 522–25.

14. Polly Aird, Jeff Nichols, and Will Bagley, ed., "Voices of Dissent in the Mormon West," in *Kingdom of the West*, vol. 8 (Norman, OK: Arthur H. Clark, University of Oklahoma Press, 2011), p. 14.

CHAPTER 6: A PRESS DESTROYED AND PERIL TO THE PROPHET

1. Fawn McKay Brodie, *No Man Knows My History: The Life of Joseph Smith* (New York: First Vintage Books Edition, 1995), p. 368.

2. Ibid.

3. Ibid., p. 369.

4. Ibid., p. 370.

5. Ibid., p. 372.

6. Richard Lyman Bushman, *Joseph Smith: Rough Stone Rolling* (New York: First Vintage Books Edition, 2007), pp. 539–41.

7. Brodie, *No Man Knows*, pp. 374–75.

8. Ibid., p. 377.

9. Ibid.

10. Lavina Fielding Anderson and Irene M. Bates, ed., *Lucy's Book: A Critical Edition of Lucy Mack Smith's Family Memoir* (Salt Lake City: Signature, 2001).

11. Brodie, *No Man Knows*, p. 377.

12. Ibid.

13. Ibid., p. 378.

14. Ibid., pp. 378–79.

15. David E. Campbell, John C. Green, and J. Quinn Monson, *Seeking the Promised Land: Mormons and American Politics* (New York: Cambridge University Press, 2014), pp. 30–31.

16. Brodie, *No Man Knows*, p. 382.

17. Ibid., p. 386.

18. Ibid., p. 387.

19. Ibid., p. 388.

20. Ibid., p. 389.

21. Ibid.

22. Ibid.

23. Ibid., p. 391.

24. Ibid., p. 392.

25. Ibid., p. 393.

26. Ibid.

27. Ibid., p. 394.

28. Ibid.

29. Ibid.

30. Ibid.

31. Ibid., p. 396.

32. Bushman, *Joseph Smith*, p. xx.

33. Brigham Young, "Necessity of Building Temples—the Endowment" (April 6, 1853), reported by G. D. Watt, in *Journal of Discourses* (Liverpool: F. D. & S. W. Richards, 1855), p. 29–33; *Wikipedia*, s.v. "Oath of Vengeance," last updated July 13, 2017, https://en.wikipedia.org/wiki/Oath_of_vengeance #CITEREFYoung1853 (accessed August 23, 2017). For an expanded contextual view, see John Krakauer, *Under the Banner of Heaven: A Story of Violent Faith* (New York: Doubleday, 2003).

34. Young, "Necessity of Building Temples," pp. 29–33.

35. Lowell M. Snow, "Blood Atonement" (paper; Provo, UT: Brigham Young University, 1992), http://eom.byu.edu/index.php/Blood_Atonement (accessed December 5, 2016).

36. Will Bagley, *Blood of the Prophets: Brigham Young and the Massacre at Mountain Meadows,* 1st paperback ed. (Norman: University of Oklahoma Press, 2004), p. 51.

CHAPTER 7: BRIGHAM YOUNG TAKES THE REINS OF A CHURCH IN CHAOS

1. John G. Turner, *Brigham Young: Pioneer Prophet* (Cambridge: Harvard University Press, 2012), p. 111.

2. Ibid., p. 114–15.

3. Ibid., p. 111.

4. Ibid.

5. Ibid., pp. 121–22.

6. Will Bagley, *Blood of the Prophets: Brigham Young and the Massacre at Mountain Meadows* 1st paperback ed. (Norman: University of Oklahoma Press, 2004), p. 19.

7. Turner, *Brigham Young,* p. 125.

8. Ibid., p. 126.

9. Ibid., p. 123.

10. Ibid., pp. 114–21.

11. Ibid., pp. 126–28.

12. Ibid., p. 130.

13. Ibid., p. 440n42, quoting general church minutes, April 20, 1845.

14. Ibid., p. 130.

15. Ibid., p. 131.

16. Jeffrey Ogden Johnson, "Determining and Defining 'Wife'—the Brigham Young Households," *Dialogue, a Journal of Mormon Thought* 20, no. 3

(Fall 1987): 57–70; *Wikipedia*, s.v. "List of Brigham Young's Wives," last updated February 23, 2017, https://en.wikipedia.org/wiki/List_of_Brigham _Young%27s_wives (accessed August 23, 2017).

17. Turner, *Brigham Young*, p. 134.

18. Ibid., p. 136.

19. Bagley, *Blood of the Prophets*, pp. 19–21.

CHAPTER 8: WESTWARD HO

1. John G. Turner, *Brigham Young: Pioneer Prophet* (Cambridge: Harvard University Press, 2012), p. 143.

2. Ibid., p. 145.

3. Ibid., pp. 142–47.

4. Ibid., p. 144.

5. Ibid.

6. Ibid., p. 145.

7. Ibid.

8. Ibid.

9. Ibid., pp. 145–47.

10. Ibid.

11. Ibid., pp. 147–48.

12. Ibid., p. 152.

13. Ibid., p. 150.

14. Ibid., pp. 150–51.

15. Ibid., pp. 148–55.

16. Ibid., p. 151.

17. Ibid., p. 155.

18. Ibid., pp. 88–98.

19. Ibid., p. 162.

20. Ibid., p. 165.

21. Ibid.

22. Ibid., p. 166.

23. Ibid., p. 167.

24. Ibid.

25. Ibid.

26. Ibid.

27. Ibid., p. 168.

28. Ibid.

29. Ibid.

30. Ibid., pp. 172–73.

31. Ibid., p. 173.

32. Ibid., p. 175.

33. Will Bagley, *Blood of the Prophets: Brigham Young and the Massacre at Mountain Meadows*, 1st paperback ed. (Norman: University of Oklahoma Press, 2004), p. 23.

34. Turner, *Brigham Young*, p. 176.

35. Ibid., p. 181.

CHAPTER 9: PAIUTE INDIANS

1. Howard Christy, "Open Hand and Mailed Fist: Mormon-Indian Relations in Utah, 1847–52," *Utah Historical Quarterly* 46, no. 3 (1978), http://content.lib.utah.edu/cdm/ref/collection/uaida/id/18090 (accessed July 28, 2016).

2. Ibid.

3. Will Bagley, *Blood of the Prophets: Brigham Young and the Massacre at Mountain Meadows*, 1st paperback ed. (Norman: University of Oklahoma Press, 2004), p. 24n2.

4. Bill McKeever and Eric Johnson, "White and Delightsome or Pure and Delightsome? A Look at 2 Nephi 30:6," Mormon Curtain, January 4, 2005, http://www.mormoncurtain.com/topic_whiteanddelightsome.html (accessed December 5, 2016).

5. Bagley, *Blood of the Prophets*, p. 25.

6. Ibid., p. 24.

7. Ibid., p. 25.

8. Ibid.

9. Ibid.

10. Ibid., p. 26.

11. Ibid., p. 27.

12. Ibid., p. 28.

13. Ibid., p. 29.

14. Ibid.

15. Ibid., p. 28.

16. Ibid., p. 28.

17. Ibid., p. 29.

18. Ibid., p. 30.

19. J. Cecil Alter, *Utah the Storied Domain: A Documentary History of Utah's Eventful Career*, vol. 1 (Chicago and New York: American Historical Society, 1932), p. 142.

20. Bagley, *Blood of the Prophets*, pp. 33–34.
21. Ibid.
22. Ibid., p. 30.
23. Ibid.
24. Ibid.
25. Ibid.
26. Ibid., p. 31.
27. Ibid.
28. Ibid.
29. Ibid., pp. 31–32.
30. Ibid., pp. 33–34.
31. Ibid., p. 34.
32. Ibid., p. 20.
33. Ibid.
34. Ibid.
35. Ibid., pp. 19–21.
36. Ibid., p. 20.
37. Ibid.
38. Ibid., p. 19.
39. Ibid., p. 21.
40. Ibid.
41. Ibid.
42. Ibid.
43. Ibid.
44. Ibid.
45. Ibid.
46. Ibid., p. 35.
47. Alter, *Utah the Storied Domain*, p. 140.
48. Bagley, *Blood of the Prophets*, p. 35.
49. Ibid., p. 35.
50. Ibid., p. 36.
51. Ibid.
52. Ibid., pp. 36–37.
53. Ibid., p. 36.
54. Ibid., p. 37.

CHAPTER 10: A NEW MORMON NEWSPAPER

1. J. Cecil Alter, *Utah the Storied Domain: A Documentary History of Utah's Eventful Career*, vol. 1 (Chicago and New York: American Historical Society, 1932), p. 116.

2. Wendell J. Ashton, *Voice in the West: Biography of a Pioneer Newspaper* (New York: Duell, Sloan, & Pearce, 1950); *Wikipedia*, s.v. "*Deseret News*," last updated July 8, 2017, https://en.wikipedia.org/wiki/Deseret_News (accessed August 23, 2017).

3. *Wikipedia*, s.v. "Deseret (Book of Mormon)," last updated June 30, 2017, https://en.wikipedia.org/wiki/Deseret_(Book_of_Mormon) (accessed August 23, 2017).

4. Ashton, *Voice in the West*; *Wikipedia*, s.v. "*Deseret News.*"

5. Ibid.

6. John G. Turner, *Brigham Young: Pioneer Prophet* (Cambridge: Harvard University Press, 2012), p 185.

7. Will Bagley, *Blood of the Prophets: Brigham Young and the Massacre at Mountain Meadows*, 1st paperback ed. (Norman: University of Oklahoma Press, 2004), p. 23.

8. Turner, *Brigham Young*, p. 180.

9. Ibid.

10. Alter, *Utah the Storied Domain*, pp. 115–42.

11. Ibid., pp. 301–304.

12. Paul H. Peterson and Ronald Walker, "Brigham Young's Word of Wisdom Legacy," *BYU Studies* 42, nos. 3–4 (2003), https://byustudies.byu.edu/content/brigham-youngs-word-wisdom-legacy (accessed September 3, 2016).

13. *Wikipedia*, s.v. "Walkara," last updated July 20, 2017, https://en.wikipedia.org/wiki/Walkara (accessed August 23, 2017).

14. *Wikipedia*, s.v. "John Williams Gunnison," last updated July 23, 2017, https://en.wikipedia.org/wiki/John_Williams_Gunnison (accessed August 23, 2017).

15. Ibid.

16. Turner, *Brigham Young*, p. 231.

CHAPTER 11: SCAPEGOATING

1. John G. Turner, *Brigham Young: Pioneer Prophet* (Cambridge: Harvard University Press, 2012), p. 249.

2. Steve Pratt, *1856–60, Handcarts: Construction Plans* (Salt Lake City:

Heritage Gateways, Utah State Office of Education and Utah System of Higher Education, 2016); *Wikipedia*, s.v. "Mormon Handcart Pioneers," last updated August 14, 2017, https://en.wikipedia.org/wiki/Mormon_handcart_pioneers (accessed August 23, 2017).

3. LeRoy R. Hafen and Ann W. Hafen, *Handcarts to Zion: The Story of a Unique Western Migration, 1856–1860*, paperback ed. (Glendale, CA: Arthur Clarke, 1981; Lincoln: University of Nebraska Press, 1992), pp. 119–25; *Wikipedia*, s.v. "Mormon Handcart Pioneers."

4. Hafen and Hafen, *Handcarts to Zion*, pp. 119–25.

5. Ibid.

6. Ibid.

7. Ibid.

8. J. Cecil Alter, *Utah the Storied Domain: A Documentary History of Utah's Eventful Career*, vol. 1 (Chicago and New York: American Historical Society, 1932), p. 230.

9. Hafen and Hafen, *Handcarts to Zion*, pp. 134–38; *Wikipedia*, s.v. "Mormon Handcart Pioneers."

10. Ibid.

11. Wallace Stegner, *Gathering of Zion* (Lincoln: Bison, University of Nebraska Press, 1992), p. 222; *Wikipedia*, s.v. "Mormon Handcart Pioneers."

12. Alter, *Utah the Storied Domain*, p. 228.

13. Ann Eliza Young, *Wife No. 19: The Story of a Life in Bondage, Being a Complete Exposé of Mormonism, and Revealing the Sorrows, Sacrifices and Sufferings of Women in Polygamy* (Hartford, CT: Dustin, Gilman, 1876), pp. 204–205; Wikipedia, s.v. "Mormon Handcart Pioneers."

14. *Encyclopedia of Mormonism*, s.v. "Handcart Pioneers," Brigham Young University, Harold B. Lee Library, 1992; *Wikipedia*, s.v. "Mormon Handcart Pioneers."

15. Turner, *Brigham Young*, p. 334.

CHAPTER 12: BRIGHAM'S FURY AT THE FEDS AND CARPETBAGGERS

1. John G. Turner, *Brigham Young: Pioneer Prophet* (Cambridge: Harvard University Press, 2012), p. 185.

2. Ibid., p. 187.

3. Ibid.

4. Ibid., p. 186.

5. Ibid., p. 187.

6. Ibid., p. 188.

7. Ibid., p. 185.

8. Ibid., p. 196.

9. Ibid.

10. Ibid., p. 197.

11. Ibid., pp. 197–99.

12. Ibid., p. 199.

13. Ibid., p. 200.

14. Ibid., pp. 200–201.

15. Ibid.

16. Ibid.

17. Ibid., pp. 199–201.

18. Ibid., p. 201.

19. Ibid., p. 202.

20. Ibid., pp. 200–203.

21. Will Bagley, *Blood of the Prophets: Brigham Young and the Massacre at Mountain Meadows*, 1st paperback ed. (Norman: University of Oklahoma Press, 2004), p. 41.

22. Ibid., p. 42.

23. Ibid.

24. Ibid., p. 42, quoting D. Michael Quinn; *Mormon Hierarchy: Extensions of Power* (Salt Lake City: Signature, 1997), pp. 226, 260.

25. Ibid.

26. "Minutes of Conference: A Special Conference of the Elders of the Church of Jesus Christ of Latter-Day Saints Assembled in the Tabernacle, Great Salt Lake City, August 28th, 1852, 10 o'clock, a.m., Pursuant to Public Notice," *Deseret News Extra*, September 14, 1852, p. 14.

27. Matthew Bowman, *The Mormon People* (New York: Random House, 2012), p. 125.

28. Bagley, *Blood of the Prophets*, pp. 42–43.

29. Ibid.

30. Ibid., p. 43.

31. Turner, *Brigham Young*, p. 246.

32. Ibid., p. 246.

33. Bagley, *Blood of the Prophets*, p. 47.

34. Ibid.

35. Ibid., p. 46.

36. Ibid., p. 47.

37. Hurt was a non-Mormon Indian agent and one of the first to learn that Mormons had been involved in the Mountain Meadows Massacre, not

just Indians. Ibid., pp. 162–63. He would later barely escape with his life as Mormons sought to capture and probably kill him to prevent him from telling what he knew. Ibid., pp. 179.

38. Ibid., p. 49.

39. Ibid.

40. Ibid.

41. Ibid., p. 50.

42. Ibid.

43. Turner, *Brigham Young*, p. 375.

44. J. Cecil Alter, *Utah the Storied Domain: A Documentary History of Utah's Eventful Career*, vol. 1 (Chicago and New York: American Historical Society, 1932), p. 233.

45. Ibid.

46. Ibid.

47. Ibid., p. 236.

48. Turner, *Brigham Young*, p. 273.

49. Bagley, *Blood of the Prophets*, pp. 75–77.

50. Alter, *Utah the Storied Domain*, p. 236.

51. Turner, *Brigham Young*, p. 271.

52. Ibid., p. 268.

53. Bagley, *Blood of the Prophets*, p. 80.

54. Ibid., p. 81.

55. Ibid., p. 89.

56. Ibid., p. 84.

CHAPTER 13: THE MASSACRE AT MOUNTAIN MEADOWS

1. Will Bagley, *Blood of the Prophets: Brigham Young and the Massacre at Mountain Meadows*, 1st paperback ed. (Norman: University of Oklahoma Press, 2004), p. 173.

2. Ibid.

3. Will Bagley, in discussion with the author, July 2, 2014.

4. Bagley, *Blood of the Prophets*, p. 4.

5. John G. Turner, *Brigham Young: Pioneer Prophet* (Cambridge: Harvard University Press, 2012), p. 279.

6. Bagley, *Blood of the Prophets*, p. xv.

7. Ibid., pp. 54–68.

8. Ibid., pp. 68–72.

9. Ibid., p. 99.

10. Ibid., p. 111.
11. Ibid., p. 101.
12. Ibid., pp. 105–10.
13. Ibid., p. 115.
14. Ibid., p. 120.
15. Ibid., p. 119.
16. Ibid., p. 120.
17. Ibid., p. 119.
18. Ibid., p. 122.
19. Ibid., p. 123.
20. Ibid.
21. Ibid., pp. 122–24.
22. Ibid., p. 125.
23. Ibid.
24. Ibid., pp. 133–34.
25. Ibid., p. 133.
26. Ibid., p. 134.
27. Ibid., p. 136.
28. Ibid., pp. 136–37.
29. Turner, *Brigham Young*, p. 277.
30. Ibid., p. 177.
31. Bagley, *Blood of the Prophets*, p. 140.
32. Ibid., p. 141.
33. Ibid.
34. Ibid., p. 119.
35. Ibid., p. 141.
36. Ibid., p. 142.
37. Ibid., p. 144.
38. Ibid., p. 145.
39. Ibid., p. 146.
40. Ibid., p. 147.
41. Ibid., pp. 148–49.
42. Ibid., p. 149.
43. Ibid., p. 150.
44. Ibid., pp. 150–51.
45. Ibid., p. 151.
46. Ibid.
47. Ibid.
48. Ibid.
49. Ibid.

50. Ibid.
51. Ibid.
52. Ibid., p. 153.
53. Ibid.
54. Ibid.
55. Ibid., p. 154.
56. Ibid.
57. Ibid., p. 156.
58. Ibid.
59. Ibid.
60. Ibid., pp. 156–57.
61. Ibid.
62. Ibid., p. 158.
63. Ibid.
64. Ibid., p. 133.
65. Ibid., pp. 156–61.
66. Ibid., p. 177.

CHAPTER 14: THE WAR THAT ALMOST WAS

1. Will Bagley, *Blood of the Prophets: Brigham Young and the Massacre at Mountain Meadows*, 1st paperback ed. (Norman: University of Oklahoma Press, 2004), pp. 179–80.
2. Ibid., p. 181.
3. Ibid.
4. Ibid.
5. Ibid.
6. Ibid., p. 182.
7. Ibid., pp. 182–83.
8. Ibid., pp. 195–96.
9. John G. Turner, *Brigham Young: Pioneer Prophet* (Cambridge: Harvard University Press, 2012), p. 287.
10. Bagley, *Blood of the Prophets*, pp. 174–75.
11. Ibid., p. 175.
12. Ibid.
13. Ibid., p. 188.
14. Ibid., p. 189.
15. Ibid.
16. Ibid., p. 190.

17. Ibid., p. 191.
18. Ibid., p. 184.
19. Turner, *Brigham Young*, p. 290.
20. Bagley, *Blood of the Prophets*, p. 186.
21. Ibid.
22. Ibid.
23. Ibid.
24. Ibid., p. 185.
25. Ibid., p. 197.
26. Ibid., p. 202.
27. Ibid., pp. 198–202.
28. Ibid., p. 202.
29. Turner, *Brigham Young*, p. 293.
30. Ibid., p. 294.
31. Ibid.
32. Ibid.
33. Ibid., p. 295.
34. Ibid.
35. Ibid.
36. Ibid.
37. Ibid.
38. Ibid.
39. Ibid.
40. Ibid.
41. Ibid., p. 296.
42. Ibid., p. 297.
43. Ibid., p. 295.
44. Ibid., p. 298.
45. Ibid.
46. Ibid.
47. Bagley, *Blood of the Prophets*, p. 206.
48. Turner, *Brigham Young*, p. 307.
49. Ibid., pp. 307–308.
50. Bagley, *Blood of the Prophets*, p. 225.
51. Ibid., pp. 226–27.
52. Ibid., p. 227.
53. Ibid., pp. 228–29.
54. Ibid., p. 228.
55. Ibid., p. 229.
56. Ibid., p. 230.

57. Turner, *Brigham Young*, p. 317.

58. Ibid., p. 297.

CHAPTER 15: "FANATICS AND WHORES"

1. John G. Turner, *Brigham Young: Pioneer Prophet* (Cambridge: Harvard University Press, 2012), p. 313.

2. Ibid., p. 314.

3. Ibid., pp. 314–16.

4. Ibid., p. 315.

5. Ibid., p. 317.

6. Ibid., 317–18.

7. *Wikipedia*, s.v. "White Horse Prophecy," last updated August 1, 2017, https://en.wikipedia.org/wiki/White_Horse_Prophecy (accessed August 23, 2017.).

8. Turner, *Brigham Young*, p. 320.

9. Ibid., p. 321.

10. Ibid.

11. Ibid.

12. Ibid.

13. Ibid., pp. 324–25.

14. Ibid., p. 322.

15. Ibid.

16. Ibid., p. 323.

17. Ibid.

18. Ibid.

19. Ibid., p. 328.

20. Utah Digital Newspapers, https://digitalnewspapers.org/newspaper/?paper=Union+Vedette (accessed September 27, 2017).

21. Ibid.

22. Turner, *Brigham Young*, pp. 328–39.

23. Ibid., p. 337.

24. J. Cecil Alter, *Utah the Storied Domain: A Documentary History of Utah's Eventful Career*, vol. 1 (Chicago and New York: American Historical Society, 1932), pp. 351–59.

25. Plaque at Fort Douglas Military Museum, visited by the author on September 6, 2016.

26. "Virtual Jewish World: Utah, United States," Jewish Virtual Library, http://www.jewishvirtuallibrary.org/jsource/vjw/Utah.html (accessed September 6, 2016).

27. Alter, *Utah the Storied Domain*, p. 359.

28. William Fox, "Patrick Edward Connor, 'Father' of Utah Mining" (thesis, Brigham Young University, 1966), http://scholarsarchive.byu.edu/cgi/viewcontent.cgi?article=5695&context=etd (accessed September 27, 2017).

29. Alter, *Utah the Storied Domain*, p. 359.

30. Turner, *Brigham Young*, p. 349.

31. Michael D. Brasfield, "Squire Newton Brassfield," Brasfield-Brassfield Genealogies, 2008, http://www.brasfield.net/histories/Squire%20Newton%20Brassfield.htm (accessed August 3, 2016).

32. Turner, *Brigham Young*, p. 349.

33. Ibid., pp. 349–50.

34. Ibid., p. 349.

35. Ibid., p. 350.

36. Ibid.

37. Ibid.

38. Ibid., p. 362.

39. Ibid.

CHAPTER 16: THE *TRIBUNE* AND ZCMI ARE BORN

1. Utah Digital Newspapers, https://newspapers.lib.utah.edu/search?facet_paper=%22Union+Vedette%22&facet_type=issue&rows=50 (accessed September 30, 2017).

2. O. N. Malmquist, *The First 100 Years: A History of the Salt Lake Tribune, 1871–1971* (Salt Lake City: Utah State Historical Society, 1971).

3. Ibid., p. 9.

4. John G. Turner, *Brigham Young: Pioneer Prophet* (Cambridge: Harvard University Press, 2012), p. 354.

5. Ibid.

6. Ibid.

7. Ibid.

8. Ibid., pp. 355–56.

9. Ibid., p. 356.

10. Malmquist, *First 100 Years*, p. 9.

11. Turner, *Brigham Young*, p. 357.

12. Ibid.

13. Ibid.

14. Malmquist, *First 100 Years*, p. 10.

15. Ibid., p. 11.

16. Turner, *Brigham Young*, p. 358.
17. Malmquist, *First 100 Years*, p. 12.
18. Turner, *Brigham Young*, p. 358.
19. Malmquist, *First 100 Years*, p. 14.
20. Ibid., p. 17.
21. Ibid., pp. 17–18.
22. Ibid.
23. Ibid., p. 16–17.

CHAPTER 17: THE GREAT DIVIDE AND THE BORDER RUFFIANS

1. O. N. Malmquist, *The First 100 Years: A History of the* Salt Lake Tribune, *1871–1971* (Salt Lake City: Utah State Historical Society, 1971), p. 20.
2. Ibid., pp. 20–21.
3. Ibid.
4. Ibid.
5. Ibid., p. 24.
6. Ibid., pp. 24–25.
7. Ibid., pp. 27–28.
8. Ibid.
9. Ibid.
10. Ibid.
11. Will Bagley, in discussion with the author, July 2, 2014.
12. Malmquist, *First 100 Years*, pp. 152, 275, 325, 374, 262, 316–317.
13. Ibid., p. 320.
14. Ibid., p. 33.
15. Ibid., p. 35.
16. Ibid., p. 33.
17. Ibid., pp. 31–35.
18. Lucinda Fleeson, "The Battle of Salt Lake," *American Journalism Review* (March 2001), http://ajrarchive.org/article.asp?id=335 (accessed September 9, 2016).
19. Malmquist, *First 100 Years*, p. 41.
20. John G. Turner, *Brigham Young: Pioneer Prophet* (Cambridge: Harvard University Press, 2012), pp. 364–66.
21. Ibid., p. 369.
22. Malmquist, *First 100 Years*, p. 36.
23. Ibid., p. 37.

24. Ibid.
25. Ibid., pp. 31–33.
26. Turner, *Brigham Young*, p. 375.
27. Ibid.
28. Ibid., p. 386.
29. Ibid.
30. Ibid.
31. Ibid.
32. Ibid.
33. Ibid.
34. Ibid.
35. Ibid., p. 388.
36. Ibid., p. 289.
37. Ibid.
38. Ibid., p. 288.
39. Ibid., p. 389.
40. Ibid.
41. Ibid.
42. Ibid., pp. 375–89.

CHAPTER 18: MOUNTAIN MEADOWS: BRIGHAM YOUNG'S SCAPEGOAT

1. John G. Turner, *Brigham Young: Pioneer Prophet* (Cambridge: Harvard University Press, 2012), p. 389.
2. Will Bagley, *Blood of the Prophets: Brigham Young and the Massacre at Mountain Meadows*, 1st paperback ed. (Norman: University of Oklahoma Press, 2004), p. 268.
3. Bruce C. Hafen, "Disciplinary Procedures," *Encyclopedia of Mormonism* (Provo, UT: Harold B. Lee Library, Brigham Young University, 1992).
4. Bagley, *Blood of the Prophets*, p. 269.
5. Ibid.
6. Ibid.
7. Ibid.
8. Ibid.
9. Ibid.
10. Ibid.
11. Ibid., p. 41.
12. Ibid., p. 270.

13. Ibid.

14. Ibid.

15. Ibid., p. 259.

16. Turner, *Brigham Young*, p. 390.

17. Ibid., pp. 390–91; Bagley, *Blood of the Prophets*, pp. 258–61.

18. Bagley, *Blood of the Prophets*, p. 261.

19. Ibid., p. 271.

20. Ibid.

21. "Utah Legends: Mountain Meadows Massacre," Legends of America, http://www.legendsofamerica.com/ut-mountainmeadows.html (accessed August 23, 2017).

22. Bagley, *Blood of the Prophets*, p. 271.

23. Ibid.

24. Ibid., pp. 271–72.

25. Ibid., p. 273.

26. Ibid., p. 361.

27. Ibid., p. 273.

28. Ibid.

29. Ibid.

30. At least five well-regarded historians—Juanita Brooks, Dale Morgan, Wallace Stegner, John G. Turner, David Bigler, and Will Bagley affirm Brigham Young's ordering the massacre. Will Bagley, in an email to the author, December 15, 2016.

31. Bagley, *Blood of the Prophets*, p. 273.

32. Ibid.

33. Ibid., p. 274.

34. Ibid.

35. Ibid.

36. Ibid., pp. 274–75.

37. Ibid., p. 275.

38. Ibid.

39. Ibid.

40. Ibid.

41. Ibid., pp. 275–76.

42. Ibid., p. 276.

43. Ibid.

44. Ibid.

45. Ibid., p. 277.

46. Ibid.

47. Ibid.

48. Ibid., p. 278.

49. Ibid.
50. Ibid.
51. Ibid., p. 279.
52. Turner, *Brigham Young*, p. 391.
53. Bagley, *Blood of the Prophets*, p. 289.
54. Ibid.
55. Ibid., p. 290.
56. Ibid., p. 291.
57. Ibid.
58. Ibid., p. 291.
59. Ibid.
60. Ibid.
61. Ibid.
62. Ibid., pp. 289–92.
63. Ibid., p. 292.
64. Ibid., p. 325.
65. Ibid., p. 326.
66. Ibid., p. 293.
67. Ibid.
68. Ibid., p. 294.
69. Ibid., pp. 294–99.
70. Ibid., p. 296.
71. Ibid., p. 297.
72. Ibid.
73. Ibid.
74. Ibid.
75. Ibid., p. 298.
76. Ibid., p. 299.
77. Ibid., p. 300.
78. Ibid., p. 301.
79. Ibid.
80. Ibid., p. 302.
81. Ibid.
82. Ibid., pp. 303–304.
83. Ibid.
84. Ibid., p. 305.
85. Ibid., p. 303.
86. Ibid.
87. Ibid., p. 306.
88. Ibid., p. 307.

89. Ibid.

90. Ibid.

91. Ibid., p. 315.

92. Ibid., pp. 315–16.

93. Ibid., p. 315.

94. Ibid.

95. Ibid., p. 316.

96. Ibid.

97. Ibid.

98. Ibid., pp. 315–19.

99. Ibid., p. 317.

100. Ibid., p. 333.

101. Ibid., p. 329.

102. Ibid., p. 325.

103. Ibid., p. 318.

104. Ibid., p. 319.

105. Ibid., p. 322.

106. O. N. Malmquist, *The First 100 Years: A History of the* Salt Lake Tribune, *1871–1971* (Salt Lake City: Utah State Historical Society, 1971), p. 46.

107. Turner, *Brigham Young*, p. 409.

108. Malmquist, *First 100 Years*, p. 48.

109. Turner, *Brigham Young*, p. 413.

110. Bagley, *Blood of the Prophets*, p. 330.

CHAPTER 19: THE DEVIL IN THE FORM OF C. C. GOODWIN

1. O. N. Malmquist, *The First 100 Years: A History of the* Salt Lake Tribune, *1871–1971* (Salt Lake City: Utah State Historical Society, 1971), p. 53.

2. Ibid., p. 57.

3. Ibid.

4. Ibid., p. 59.

5. Ibid., pp. 56–61.

6. Ibid., p. 62.

7. Ibid., p. 74.

8. Ibid., p. 76.

9. Ibid.

10. Ibid., p. 80.

11. Harold Schindler, "Early *Tribune, Deseret News* Made Trash Talk an Art Form: *Tribune, Deseret News* Took off Gloves," *Salt Lake Tribune*, April 14, 1996,

http://historytogo.utah.gov/salt_lake_tribune/in_another_time/041496.html (accessed August 3, 2016).

12. *Wikipedia*, s.v. "Edmunds Act," last updated March 26, 2017, https:// en.wikipedia.org/wiki/Edmunds_Act (accessed August 23, 2017); *Wikipedia*, s.v. "Edmunds-Tucker Act," last updated July 26, 2017, https://en.wikipedia .org/wiki/Edmunds%E2%80%93Tucker_Act (accessed August 23, 2017).

13. Ibid.

14. Malmquist, *First 100 Years*, p. 81.

15. Ibid.

16. Ibid., p. 99.

17. Ibid.

18. Ibid., pp. 98–102.

19. Ibid., pp. 117–20.

20. Ibid., p. 138.

21. Ibid., p. 140.

22. Ibid., pp. 143–50.

CHAPTER 20: ENTER THOMAS KEARNS

1. O. N. Malmquist, *The First 100 Years: A History of the* Salt Lake Tribune, *1871–1971* (Salt Lake City: Utah State Historical Society, 1971), p. 186.

2. Ibid., p. 189.

3. Ibid., p. 178.

4. Ibid., p. 183.

5. Ibid., p. 193.

6. Ibid., p. 183.

7. Ibid., p. 207.

8. Ibid., p. 195.

9. Ibid., pp. 178–84.

10. Ibid., p. 218.

11. Michael D. Gallivan, in personal discussion with the author, August 4, 2014.

12. Malmquist, *First 100 Years*, p. 231.

13. Ibid., p. 238; W. Paul Reeve, "A Utahn, George Sutherland, Served on the US Supreme Court," January 1995, http://historytogo.utah.gov/utah _chapters/from_war_to_war/georgesutherland.html (accessed Sept. 13, 2016).

14. Malmquist, *First 100 Years*, p. 140.

15. Ibid., pp. 178–266.

16. Ibid., p. 269.

17. Ibid., p. 275.

18. Ibid., pp. 282–83.

19. Ibid., p. 293.

20. Ibid., p. 314.

21. Ibid., p. 324.

22. Ibid., p. 329.

23. Ibid., pp. 354–57.

24. Ibid., p. 332.

25. Ibid., p. 333.

26. Ibid., pp. 332–34.

27. Ibid., pp. 363–66.

28. Ibid., p. 366.

29. Gallivan, in discussion with the author, August 14, 2014.

30. Malmquist, *First 100 Years*, p. 368.

31. Ibid., p. 367.

32. Ibid., pp. 363–72.

33. Gallivan, in discussion with the author, April 27, 2015.

34. Gallivan, in discussion with the author, July 10, 2014.

35. Malmquist, *First 100 Years*, pp. 373–81.

36. Ibid., p. 362.

37. Ibid., pp. 373–81.

38. Salt Lake Tribune Publishing Company, LLC, v. AT&T Corporation & AT&T Broadband, LLC, and Media News Group, memorandum in Support of Plaintiff's Motion for Temporary Restraining Order and Preliminary Injunction, U.S. District Court for Utah, Civil No. 2:00CV936C, January 8, 2001. Copy in possession of the author.

39. *Wikipedia*, s.v. "Newspaper Preservation Act of 1970," last updated June 5, 2017, https://en.wikipedia.org/wiki/Newspaper_Preservation_Act_of_1970 (accessed August 23, 2017).

40. John W. Gallivan, "*Deseret News* vs. Facts" (unpublished manuscript, December 21, 2000). Response to *Deseret News* claims. Courtesy of Michael D. Gallivan, July 10, 2014.

41. Malmquist, *First 100 Years*, pp. 386–87.

42. Gallivan, in discussion with the author, July 10, 2014.

43. John W. Gallivan Sr., in discussion with the author, July 2011; Michael D. Gallivan, in discussion with the author, 2014 and 2015; personal papers of John W. Gallivan Sr. provided by Michael D. Gallivan; James E. Shelledy, Mike Korologos, and H. Devereaux Jennings, in discussion with the author on numerous dates.

44. Malmquist, *First 100 Years*, p. 391.

45. Ibid., p. 397.

CHAPTER 21: BATTLE ROYAL FOR THE *TRIBUNE*

1. Rod Decker, KUTV Channel 2 (Salt Lake City) television reporter, in discussion with the author, January 20, 2017.

2. Salt Lake Tribune Publishing Company, LLC, v. AT&T Corporation & AT&T Broadband, LLC, Deseret News Publishing Company and Media News Group, memorandum in Support of Plaintiff's Motion for Temporary Restraining Order and Preliminary Injunction, U.S. District Court for Utah, Civil No. 2:00CV936C, January 8, 2001. Copy in possession of the author.

3. Michael Scherer, "The News in Mormon Country," *Columbia Journalism Review* 41, no. 6 (March–April 2003): 42, http://connection.ebscohost.com/c/articles/9213052/news-mormon-country (accessed September 16, 2016).

4. John W. Gallivan, memo to John Malone, Liberty Media Group, June 14, 1999. Courtesy Michael D. Gallivan.

5. James "Deseret Jim" Mortimer (1932–2010), publisher of the *Deseret News* (1985–2000), in discussion with the author, 1990.

6. John W. Gallivan, "*Deseret News* vs. Facts" (unpublished manuscript, December 21, 2000), p. 6. Response to *Deseret News* claims. Courtesy of Michael D. Gallivan, July 10, 2014.

7. Gallivan, memo to Malone. Courtesy Michael D. Gallivan.

8. John W. Gallivan, memo to Jon Huntsman Sr., October 22, 2001. Courtesy Michael D. Gallivan.

9. Gallivan, "*Deseret News* vs. Facts," p. 12.

10. Ibid., p. 3.

11. Ibid.

12. Ibid., pp. 4–5.

13. Decker, in discussion with the author.

14. Lucinda Fleeson, "The Battle of Salt Lake," *American Journalism Review* (March 2001), http://ajrarchive.org/article.asp?id=335 (accessed August 11, 2016).

15. Mike Korologos, in discussion with the author, August 1, 2016.

16. Author's term.

17. Fleeson, "Battle of Salt Lake."

18. Ibid.

19. Ibid.

20. Michael Vigh, Elizabeth Neff, and Kristen Moulton, "Paper Chase: How the *Tribune* Slipped Away from a Family and Why the D-News Took Advantage: The *Tribune* Faces Uncertainty; Option Ruled Valid; So Now What?" *Salt Lake Tribune*, June 9, 2002, http://archive.sltrib.com/article.php?id=500448&itype=id (accessed September 16, 2016).

21. Philip McCarthey and Tom McCarthey, in discussion with the author, July 8, 2014.

22. Michael D. Gallivan, in discussion with the author, August 17, 2016.

23. Dominic Welch, in discussion with the author, October 21, 2015.

24. Scherer, "News in Mormon Country."

25. Gallivan, in discussion with the author.

26. Ibid.

27. Philip McCarthey and Tom McCarthey, in discussion with the author, October 19, 2016.

28. Vigh, Neff, and Moulton, "Paper Chase."

29. McCarthey and McCarthey, in discussions with the author, 2015 and 2016.

30. Peter Waldman, "AT&T's Plan to Sell Newspaper Adds Fuel to a Salt Lake Feud," *Wall Street Journal*, October 6, 2000, http://www.wsj.com/articles/SB970793627452042902 (accessed September 15, 2016).

31. Vigh, Neff, and Moulton, "Paper Chase."

32. Ibid.

33. Tom McCarthey, in discussions with the author, May 26, 2016.

34. Fleeson, "Battle of Salt Lake."

35. Ibid.

36. Vigh, Neff, and Moulton, "Paper Chase."

37. James E. Shelledy, in discussion with the author, September 26, 2016.

38. Ibid.

39. Philip McCarthey and Tom McCarthey, in discussion with the author, July 8, 2014.

40. Vigh, Neff, and Moulton, "Paper Chase."

41. Ibid.

42. *Wikipedia*, s.v. "Leo Hindery," last updated August 8, 2017, https://en.wikipedia.org/wiki/Leo_Hindery (accessed August 24, 2017).

43. Fleeson, "Battle of Salt Lake."

44. John W. Gallivan, "Mock Story," p. 6, September 12, 2000. In possession of author. Courtesy of Michael D. Gallivan.

45. John W. "Jack" Gallivan to Leo Hindery, "Personal and Confidential Memo," July 7, 1999. Courtesy of Michael D. Gallivan.

46. Fleeson, "Battle of Salt Lake."

47. Glen Snarr, memo to Leo Hindery, "The Quest No. 4," Utah Newspaper Project/Citizens for Two Voices, November 19, 1997, http://www.utahnewspaperproject.org/The-Quest (accessed September 16, 2016).

48. Scherer, "News from Mormon Country."

49. Glen Snarr and Gary Gomm to the First Presidency, "The Quest No.

5," Utah Newspaper Project, http://www.utahnewspaperproject.org/The
-Quest (accessed September 16, 2016).

50. Jerry D. Spangler, Angie Welling, and Maria Titze, "20 Questions:
Trying to Make Sense of the Salt Lake Newspaper War," *Deseret News,* June 30,
2002, https://www.deseretnews.com/article/405015041/20-questions-Trying
-to-make-sense-of-the-Salt-Lake-Newspaper-war.html (accessed December 7,
2016).

51. Waldman, "AT&T's Plan."

52. Ibid.

53. Ibid.

54. Snarr, memo to Hindery.

55. Dominic Welch, in discussion with the author, October 21, 2015.

56. Phone calls and emails made to Leo Hindery in 2015–2016 were not
answered. He is currently listed as being a partner of Intermedia, a New York–
based media industry private equity fund.

57. Scherer, "News in Mormon Country."

58. Michael P. Huseby, vice president and CFO, AT&T Broadband, to
Dominic A. Welch, "Strictly Private and Confidential" letter, June 22, 2000.
Copy courtesy of Michael D. Gallivan.

59. Shelledy, in discussion with the author, September 26, 2016.

60. Carrie A. Moore, "What's Changed at Tabernacle?" *Deseret Morning
News,* March 27, 2007; *Wikipedia,* s.v. "Salt Lake Tabernacle," last updated
March 8, 2017, https://en.wikipedia.org/wiki/Salt_Lake_Tabernacle
(accessed August 23, 2017).

61. "Salt Lake City, UT," Oscar Wilde in America, http://oscarwildein
america.org/lectures-1882/april/0410-salt-lake-city.html (accessed August 5,
2016).

62. Scherer, "News in Mormon Country."

63. R. Gary Gomm to Steven Garfinkel, "The Quest No. 26," Utah
Newspaper Project, http://www.utahnewspaperproject.org/ (accessed August
5, 2016).

64. Jim Woolf, in discussion with the author, July 7, 2015.

65. Patty Henetz, in discussion with the author, July 13, 2015, and
October 8, 2015.

66. James E. Shelledy, in discussion with the author, October 6, 2014, and
June 30, 2015.

67. Shelledy, in discussion with the author, September 26, 2016.

68. Woolf, in discussion with the author.

69. Ibid.

CHAPTER 22: MORMONS VS. THE OUTSIDE WORLD

1. James E. Shelledy, in discussions with the author, October 6, 2014, and June 30, 2015.

2. Ibid.

3. Stan Bowman, in discussion with the author, 1962.

4. O. N. Malmquist, *The First 100 Years: A History of the* Salt Lake Tribune, *1871–1971* (Salt Lake City: Utah State Historical Society, 1971), p. 397.

5. Ibid.

6. Raymond E. Beckham, "Utah Newspaper War of 1968: Liquor-by-the-Drink" (thesis; Provo, UT: Brigham Young University, Department of Communication, August 1969), http://scholarsarchive.byu.edu/cgi/viewcontent.cgi?article=5514&context=etd (accessed September 17, 2016).

7. Ibid.

8. Shelledy, in discussion with the author, October 6, 2014.

9. Church of Jesus Christ of Latter-day Saints, "Spencer W. Kimball," https://www.lds.org/churchhistory/presidents/controllers/potcController.jsp?leader=12&topic=facts (accessed September 29, 2017).

10. "President Ezra Taft Benson: A Sure Voice of Faith," Church of Jesus Christ of Latter-day Saints, https://www.lds.org/ensign/1994/07/president-ezra-taft-benson-a-sure-voice-of-faith?lang=eng&_r=1 (accessed August 14, 2016).

11. "Gordon B. Hinckley, 15th President of the Church," Church of Jesus Christ of Latter-day Saints, 2004, https://www.lds.org/churchhistory/presidents/controllers/potcController.jsp?topic=facts&leader=15 (accessed August 13, 2016).

12. Robert Lindsey, *A Gathering of Saints: A True Story of Monday, Murder, and Deceit* (New York: Simon and Schuster, 1988), p. 41; *Wikipedia*, s.v. "Mark Hofmann," last updated August 2, 2017, https://en.wikipedia.org/wiki/Mark_Hofmann (accessed August 23, 2017).

13. Ibid.

14. Ibid.

15. Lindsey, *Gathering of Saints*, pp. 68–69.

16. Ibid., pp. 66–69.

17. Richard N. Ostling and Joan K. Ostling, *Mormon America: The Power and the Promise* (San Francisco: HarperSanFrancisco, 1999), p. 253; *Wikipedia*, s.v. "Mark Hofmann."

18. Ibid.

19. Lindsey, *Gathering of Saints*, pp. 80–81.

20. Ibid., pp. 118–19.

21. Ibid., pp. 95, 98.

22. Ibid., pp. 100–106.

23. Ibid., p. 377.

24. Brian Innes, *Fakes and Forgeries: The True Crime Stories of History's Greatest Deceptions* (Pleasantville, NY: Readers Digest, 2005), pp. 132–34.

25. Lindsey, *Gathering of Saints*, p. 147.

26. Ibid., pp. 179–82.

27. Ibid.

28. Ibid., p. 21.

29. Jim Woolf, in discussion with the author, January 9, 2015.

30. Woolf, in discussion with the author, April 11, 2015; Mike Carter, in discussion with the author, December 7, 2015.

31. *Wikipedia*, s.v. "Mark Hofmann."

32. Dallin H. Oaks, "Recent Events Involving Church History and Forged Documents" (talk, Brigham Young University, August 6, 1987), https://www.lds.org/ensign/1987/10/recent-events-involving-church-history-and-forged-documents?lang=eng&_r=1 (accessed August 8, 2016).

33. Richard E. Turley, *Victims: The LDS Church and the Mark Hofmann Case* (Urbana, IL: University of Illinois, 1992); *Wikipedia*, s.v. "Mark Hofmann."

34. Ostling and Ostling, *Mormon America*, p. 252.

35. Lindsey, *Gathering of Saints*, pp. 372–73.

36. Ibid.

CHAPTER 23: MOUNTAIN MEADOWS REDUX

1. James E. Shelledy, in discussion with the author, September 26, 2016.

2. This and the following information and quotes from Christopher Smith, "Unearthing Mountain Meadows Secrets: Backhoe at a S. Utah Killing Field Rips Open 142-Year-Old Wound," *Salt Lake Tribune*, March 12, 2000, http://www.cesnur.org/testi/morm_01.htm (accessed August 23, 2017). Original text courtesy of Will Bagley, 2014.

3. This and the following information and quotes from Christopher Smith, "Voices of the Dead," *Salt Lake Tribune*, March 13, 2000, http://www.cesnur.org/testi/morm_01.htm (accessed August 23, 2017). Original text courtesy of Will Bagley, 2014.

4. This and the following information and quotes from Christopher Smith, "Mountain Meadows Massacre: The Dilemma of Blame," *Salt Lake Tribune*, March 14, 2000, http://www.cesnur.org/testi/morm_01.htm (accessed August 23, 2017). Original text courtesy of Will Bagley, 2014.

5. Dominic Welch, in discussion with the author, October 21, 2015.

6. Ibid.

7. Peter Waldman, "AT&T's Plan to Sell Newspaper Adds Fuel to a Salt Lake Feud," *Wall Street Journal*, October 6, 2000, http://www.wsj.com/articles/SB970793627452042902 (accessed December 20, 2016).

8. Welch, in discussion with the author.

9. Ibid.

10. Ibid.

11. Ibid.

12. Waldman, "AT&T's Plan."

13. Shelledy, in discussion with the author.

CHAPTER 24: MEDIANEWS GROUP BUYS THE *TRIBUNE*

1. Kearns *Tribune* Meeting, "The Quest No. 14," Utah Newspaper Project/Two Voices, October 21, 1998, http://www.utahnewspaperproject.org/The-Quest (accessed August 8, 2016).

2. Dominic Welch, in discussion with the author, October 21, 2015.

3. "Robert Gary Gomm," American Cancer Society, http://main.acsevents.org/site/TR?pg=fund&fr_id=9910&pxfid=1041457 (accessed August 16, 2016).

4. John W. Gallivan, "*Deseret News* vs. Facts" (unpublished manuscript, December 21, 2000). Response to *Deseret News* claims. Courtesy of Michael D. Gallivan, July 10, 2014.

5. Ibid.

6. Glen Snarr and Gary Gomm to the First Presidency, "The Quest No. 5," Utah Newspaper Project/Citizens for Two Voices, February 24, 1998, http://www.utahnewspaperproject.org/The-Quest (accessed August 8, 2016).

7. John W. Gallivan "Personal and Confidential" letter to Leo Hindery, July 7, 1999. Courtesy of Michael D. Gallivan.

8. Lucinda Fleeson, "The Battle of Salt Lake," *American Journalism Review* (March 2001), http://ajrarchive.org/article.asp?id=335 (accessed August 24, 2017. Hard copy in possession of author courtesy of Will Bagley.

9. Peter Waldman, "AT&T's Plan to Sell Newspaper Adds Fuel to Salt Lake Feud," *Wall Street Journal*, October 6, 2000, http://www.wsj.com/articles/SB970793627452042902 (accessed August 11, 2016).

10. Fleeson, "Battle of Salt Lake."

11. "AT&T Inc.: Recipients among Federal Candidates, 2000 Cycle," OpenSecrets.org, https://www.opensecrets.org/orgs/recips.php?id=D0000000

76&chamber=S&party=R&cycle=2000&state=UT&sort=A (accessed August 12, 2016).

12. Michael Vigh, Elizabeth Neff, and Kristen Moulton, "Paper Chase: How the *Tribune* Slipped Away from a Family and Why the D-News Took Advantage: The *Tribune* Faces Uncertainty; Option Ruled Valid; So Now What?" *Salt Lake Tribune*, June 9, 2002, http://archive.sltrib.com/article.php ?id=500448&itype=id (accessed August 8, 2016).

13. Philip McCarthey and Tom McCarthey, in discussion with the author, October 19, 2016.

14. Fleeson, "Battle of Salt Lake."

15. Ibid.

16. Ibid.

17. Ibid.

18. Patty Henetz, in discussion with the author, October 8, 2015.

19. Vigh, Neff, and Moulton, "Paper Chase."

20. Michael Scherer, "The News in Mormon Country," *Columbia Journalism Review* 41, no. 6 (March–April 2003): 42, http://connection.ebscohost.com/ c/articles/9213052/news-mormon-country (accessed August 24, 2017). Printout of article provided by Will Bagley, July 7, 2014.

21. Ibid.

22. Waldman, "AT&T's Plan."

23. Fleeson, "Battle of Salt Lake."

24. Ibid.

25. Felicity Barringer, "Media Talk: Managers of Utah Paper Attempt to Block Its Sale," *New York Times*, December 4, 2000, http://www.nytimes.com/ 2000/12/04/business/mediatalk-managers-of-utah-paper-attempt-to-block-its -sale.html?_r=0 (accessed August 12, 2016).

26. Philip McCarthey and Tom McCarthey, in discussion with the author, July 8, 2014.

27. Ibid.

28. Welch, in discussion with the author.

29. Fleeson, "Battle of Salt Lake."

30. Welch, in discussion with the author.

31. Vigh, Neff, and Moulton, "Paper Chase."

32. Pat Bagley, in discussion with the author, November 4, 2016.

33. Ibid.

34. John W. Gallivan, *The* Salt Lake Tribune*: Guide for Publishers, Editors, Writers, Reporters, Columnists, and all Editorial Contributors* (Salt Lake City: Salt Lake Tribune, 1983), pp. 8–9, courtesy Michael D. Gallivan.

35. James E. Shelledy, in discussion with the author, September 26, 2016.

36. Peter Waldman, "Salt Lake Paper Control Shifts in Big Victory for Mormons," *Wall Street Journal*, August 1, 2000, http://www.wsj.com/articles/ SB1028140095328962480 (accessed August 11, 2016). See "Timeline."

37. Natalia Vislyeva, "Huntsman Meets Putin as New U.S. Envoy to Russia," *Salt Lake Tribune*, October 4, 2017, http://saltlaketribune.ut.news memory.com/?token=4506d18d362782c235b2650c6a1ba525_59d50496_42e 7a4e&selDate=20171004 (accessed October 4, 2017).

38. John W. Gallivan, memo to Jon Huntsman, October 22, 2001. Courtesy of Michael D. Gallivan.

39. Scherer, "News in Mormon Country."

40. Vigh, Neff, and Moulton, "Paper Chase."

41. Fleeson, "Battle of Salt Lake."

CHAPTER 25: THE *TRIBUNE*'S BUY-BACK OPTION

1. Michael Scherer, "The News in Mormon Country," *Columbia Journalism Review* 41, no. 6 (March–April 2003): 42, http://connection.ebscohost.com/ c/articles/9213052/news-mormon-country (accessed August 24, 2017). Hard copy courtesy of Will Bagley, July 7, 2014.

2. Kearns *Tribune* Meeting, "The Quest No. 14," Utah Newspaper Project/Two Voices, October 21, 1998, http://www.utahnewspaperproject .org/The-Quest (accessed August 8, 2016).

3. Scherer, "News from Mormon Country."

4. Ibid.

5. Ariel Hart, "Singleton Wins? Not So Fast," *Columbia Journalism Review*, May–June 2003.

6. Memorandum in Support of Plaintiff's Motion for Temporary Restraining Order and Preliminary Injunction, Civil No. 2:00CV936 C, United States Court for the District of Utah, p 29.

7. Philip McCarthey and Tom McCarthey, in discussion with the author, July 8, 2014.

8. *Wikipedia*, s.v. "Ted Stewart," last updated July 19, 2017, https:// en.wikipedia.org/wiki/Ted_Stewart (accessed August 24, 2017).

9. Joan O'Brien, in discussion with the author, November 12, 2015.

10. Philip McCarthey and Tom McCarthey, in discussion with the author, July 8, 2014.

11. Anonymous attorney, in discussion with the author, August 14, 2016.

12. Anonymous attorney, in discussion with the author, March 9, 2016.

13. Philip McCarthey and Tom McCarthey, in discussion with the author, July 8, 2014.

14. Ibid.

15. Michael Vigh, Elizabeth Neff, and Kristen Moulton, "Paper Chase: How the *Tribune* Slipped Away from a Family and Why the D-News Took Advantage: The *Tribune* Faces Uncertainty; Option Ruled Valid; So Now What?" *Salt Lake Tribune*, June 9, 2002, http://archive.sltrib.com/article.php?id=500448&itype=id (accessed August 8, 2016).

16. O'Brien, in discussion with the author.

17. Ibid.

18. Ibid.

19. Gordon B. Hinckley, Thomas Monson, and James E. Faust to John W. Gallivan; Mark R. Peterson to George L. Nelson, "The Quest No. 2," Utah Newspaper Project, http://www.utahnewspaperproject.org/The-Quest (accessed August 14, 2016).

20. Michael D. Gallivan, 2015, typed, undated note to author.

21. Philip McCarthey and Tom McCarthey, in discussion with the author, October 19, 2016.

CHAPTER 26: SINGLETON BANKRUPT, ALDEN GLOBAL CAPITAL SWOOPS IN

1. Philip McCarthey and Tom McCarthey, in discussion with the author, October 19, 2016.

2. Lucinda Dillion Kinkead, "Trib Editor Quits amid Enquirer Imbroglio," *Deseret News*, May 2, 2003, http://www.deseretnews.com/article/980667/Trib-editor-quits-amid-Enquirer-imbroglio.html?pg=all (accessed August 14, 2016).

3. Author's observations, *Salt Lake Tribune*, http://www.sltrib.com/ (accessed September 19, 2016).

4. James E. Shelledy, in discussion with the author, September 26, 2016.

5. Michael Roberts, "Dean Singleton Interview about Stepping Down as CEO of MediaNews Group," *Westword*, January 19, 2011, http://www.westword.com/news/dean-singleton-interview-about-stepping-down-as-ceo-of-medianews-group-5887595 (accessed September 19, 2016).

6. Mike Spector and Shira Ovide, "Media News Holding Company to Seek Bankruptcy Protection," *Wall Street Journal*, January 15, 2010, http://www.wsj.com/articles/SB10001424052748703657604575005813195786280 (accessed December 22, 2016).

7. Thomas and Philip McCarthey, in discussion with author, July 8, 2014.

8. Author's personal observation over many years; "Peggy Fletcher Stack," Christian Century, https://www.christiancentury.org/contributor/peggy-fletcher-stack (accessed October 3, 2017).

9. James E. Shelledy, in discussion with the author, October 6, 2014.

10. Former and present *Salt Lake Tribune* staff members, in informal discussions with the author, 2015–2016.

11. Renee McGaw, "MediaNews Group Parent Emerges from Chapter 11," *Denver Business Journal,* March 19, 2010, http://www.bizjournals.com/denver/stories/2010/03/15/daily69.html (accessed August 14, 2016).

12. A *Salt Lake Tribune* insider who requested anonymity in conversation with the author, April 12, 2016.

13. *Wikipedia*, s.v. "MediaNews Group," last updated August 23, 2017, https://en.wikipedia.org/wiki/MediaNews_Group (accessed August 23, 2017).

14. Arvid Keeson, "*Deseret News* Moves to Extradite Demise of *Salt Lake Tribune*," Utah Stories, May 27, 2014, http://www.utahstories.com/2014/05/salt-lake-tribune-likely-closure/ (accessed August 12, 2016).

15. A *Salt Lake Tribune* editor who requested anonymity in discussion and emails with the author, January 12, 2017.

CHAPTER 27: THE NOTE AND ITS CONSEQUENCES

1. Tom Harvey, email exchanges with the author, August 15–16, 2016.

2. Tom Harvey, "*Tribune* Sells Interest in Printing Plant to Rival," *Salt Lake Tribune,* October 21, 2013, http://archive.sltrib.com/article.php?id=57026770&itype=CMSID (accessed August 23, 2017).

3. Ibid.

4. Tony Semerad, "Feds Scrutinize Salt Lake Newspapers Deal," *Salt Lake Tribune,* April 10, 2014, http://archive.sltrib.com/article.php?id=57791269&itype=CMSID (accessed August 23, 2017).

5. Anonymous source close to JOA provided figures in discussion with the author, 2016.

6. Tony Semerad, "*Deseret News* CEO: New Deal Protects *Tribune* Independence," *Salt Lake Tribune,* April 22, 2014, reporting on KUER's "Radio West" broadcast of April 20, 2014, http://archive.sltrib.com/article.php?id=57846152&itype=CMSID (accessed August 23, 2017).

7. Joan O'Brien, speech to the First Unitarian Church of Salt Lake City, June 2016. Copy in author's possession.

8. Jay Shelledy, in conversation with the author, September 26, 2016.

9. Jill Lepore, "The Disruption Machine," *New Yorker,* June 23, 2014, http://www.newyorker.com/magazine/2014/06/23/the-disruption-machine (accessed August 14, 2016).

10. "Local Digital News Makes National Play," NetNewsCheck, April 9, 2012, http://www.netnewscheck.com/article/17993/local-deseret-makes -national-digital-play (accessed August 9, 2016).

11. *Clark Gilbert, "Dual Transformation," and the Sunday* Deseret News *National Edition* (Salt Lake City: Utah Newspaper Project, 2014), http://www .utahnewspaperproject.org/userfiles/file/Absolute%20final%20version%20 of%20national%20edition%20report.pdf (accessed December 22, 2016).

12. Anonymous, in discussion with the author, June 2016.

13. Keith McCord, "Layoffs, New Operating Model at *Deseret News,*" KSL .com, August 31, 2010, http://www.ksl.com/?nid=148&sid=12230812 (accessed December 22, 2016).

14. Scott D. Pierce, "May Sweeps: KUTV-Ch. 2 Remains No. 1 in Late-News Household Ratings," *Salt Lake Tribune,* May 27, 2016, http://archive .sltrib.com/article.php?id=3941019&itype=CMSID (accessed December 22, 2016).

15. Anonymous former LDS Church executive, in conversation with the author, October 25, 2016.

16. *Clark Gilbert, "Dual Transformation."*

17. Ibid.

18. Caroline Winter, "How the Mormons Make Money," *Bloomberg,* July 18, 2012, https://www.bloomberg.com/amp/news/articles/2012-07-18/how-the -mormons-make-money (accessed August 14, 2016).

19. Joseph Lichterman, "Religious but Not Mormon? The Church-Owned *Deseret News* Considers You a Growth Market," Nieman Lab, April 14, 2014, http://www.niemanlab.org/2014/04/religious-but-not-mormon-the-church -owned-deseret-news-considers-you-a-growth-market/ (accessed January 10, 2017).

20. *Clark Gilbert, "Dual Transformation."*

21. John W. Gallivan, "*Tribune* Sale—The Truth," December 21, 2000, unpublished response to *Deseret News* article of December 4, 2000. Courtesy of Michael D. Gallivan.

22. Media One representative, in discussion with the author, November 16, 2016.

23. Author's observations of *Deseret News* national edition, October 23, 2016.

24. Joan O'Brien, in discussion with the author, January 18, 2017.

25. James E. Shelledy, in discussion with the author, October 6, 2014.

26. Anonymous former LDS Church executive, in discussion with the author, February 1, 2017.

27. Anonymous former LDS Church executive, in conversation with the author, October 25, 2016.

28. James E. Shelledy in conversation with the author, September 26, 2016.

29. Terry Orme, in conversation with the author, November 2, 2016.

30. *Wikipedia*, s.v. "Demographics of Utah," last updated June 19, 2017, https://en.wikipedia.org/wiki/Demographics_of_Utah (accessed August16, 2016).

31. O'Brien, in discussion with the author, August 5, 2016.

32. Ibid.

33. Joan O'Brien et al., letter to John R. Read, US Department of Justice, October 28, 2013, http://www.utahnewspaperproject.org/userfiles/file/Justice%20letter%20redacted%20names%2C%20addr.pdf (accessed August 14, 2016).

34. Anonymous LDS Church insider, in conversation with the author, July 30, 2014.

35. Patty Henetz, in discussion with the author, July 13, 2015.

36. O'Brien, in discussion with the author, October 7, 2015.

37. Shelledy, in conversation with the author, September 26, 2016.

38. Ibid.

39. O'Brien, in discussion with the author, August 5, 2016.

40. Joan O'Brien, in letter to David Kully, US Department of Justice, February 28, 2014, http://www.utahnewspaperproject.org/userfiles/file/DOJ%202nd%20letter%20final.pdf (accessed August 12, 2016).

41. "Karra J. Porter," Lawyers.com, http://www.lawyers.com/salt-lake-city/utah/karra-j-porter-1716077-a/ (accessed August 7, 2016).

42. Karra J. Porter, in discussion with the author, December 20, 2016.

43. Ibid.

44. Patty Henetz, in conversation with the author, July 28, 2015.

45. Joan O'Brien, in conversation with the author, June 14, 2015.

46. Semerad, "*Deseret News* CEO."

47. Michael D. Gallivan, in discussion with the author, July 10, 2014.

48. Porter, in discussion with the author.

49. Arvid Keeson, "*Deseret News* Conspires to Expedite Demise of *Salt Lake Tribune*," Utah Stories, May 27, 2014, http://www.utahstories.com/2014/05/salt-lake-tribune-likely-closure/ (accessed August 24, 2017).

50. Semerad, "*Deseret News* CEO."

51. Phone calls and emails for interviews or comments went unanswered

or were deflected by the following individuals: Brent Low, chairman of the board, Newspaper Agency Corporation, aka Media One of Utah (JOA), telephone discussion, September 24, 2015; Eric D. Hawkins, senior media manager and spokesman for the presidency, Church of Jesus Christ of Latter-day Saints, email exchange, December 26, 2016; Kristen Howey, LDS Church spokeswoman, telephone conversation regarding photographs, July 26, 2016; Doug Wilks, editor, *Deseret News*, email requesting interview, December 26, 2016; Paul Edwards, former editor, *Deseret News*, phone calls on December 26, 2016; email, December 26, 2016; two subsequent phone calls, January 8, 2017, and January 13, 2017.

52. Email from author to Clark Gilbert, March 20, 2016. Clark Gilbert, in responding email to author, March 20, 2016, referred all questions to the current management of the *Deseret News*.

53. *Wikipedia*, s.v. "List of Presidents of the Church of Jesus Christ of Latter-day Saints," last updated August 24, 2017, https://en.wikipedia.org/wiki/List_of_presidents_of_The_Church_of_Jesus_Christ_of_Latter-day_Saints (accessed August 24, 2017).

54. Nancy Conway, "Declaration," June 15, 2014, http://www.utah newspaperproject.org/userfiles/file/Conway%20Declaration.pdf (accessed October 3, 2017).

55. Tony Semerad, "Suit Seeks to Block Utah Newspaper Deal, Argues It Dooms the *Tribune*," *Salt Lake Tribune*, June 16, 2014, http://archive.sltrib .com/article.php?id=58074486&itype=CMSID (accessed August 16, 2016).

56. Complaint for Injunctive and Declaratory Relief, Utah Newspaper Project dba Citizens for Two Voices, plaintiffs, vs. Deseret News Publishing Company and Kearns-Tribune LLC, defendants, U.S. District Court, District of Utah, July 28, 2014, http://www.utahnewspaperproject.org/userfiles/file/Amended%20complaint%20challenging%20JOA.pdf

57. Porter, in discussion with the author.

58. Ibid.

59. Ibid.

60. Ibid.

61. Author in attendance, September 8, 2014, personal observations.

62. Joan O'Brien, in conversation with the author, October 7, 2015.

63. A spokesman representing Justin Dempsey for the Department of Justice declined an interview with Dempsey on the basis of case confidentiality. Dempsey is a trial attorney for the Department of Justice's Litigation III Section, Anti-Trust Division. Department of Justice, in telephone conversation with the author, January 12, 2017.

64. Porter, in discussion with the author.

65. Tony Semerad, "Judge Won't' Dismiss Lawsuit against *Tribune-Deseret News* Deal," *Salt Lake Tribune*, September 8, 2014, http://archive.sltrib.com/article.php?id=58388987&itype=CMSID (accessed August 24, 2017).

66. O'Brien, in discussion with the author, April 19, 2015.

67. Porter, in discussion with the author.

68. Ibid.

69. Philip McCarthey and Tom McCarthey, in discussion with the author, July 8, 2014.

70. Ibid.

71. Anonymous former reporter for the *Salt Lake Tribune*, in conversation with the author, March 2015.

72. Anonymous former reporter for the *Salt Lake Tribune*, in conversation with the author, March 2015.

73. Tom McCarthey, in discussion with the author, April 26, 2016.

74. Ibid.

CHAPTER 28: ENTER AND REENTER THE HUNTSMAN FAMILY

1. Karra J. Porter, in discussion with the author, December 20, 2016.

2. Joan O'Brien, in discussion with the author, August 5, 2016.

3. Terry Orme, in discussion with the author, October 10, 2016.

4. Ibid.

5. Matt Canham and Thomas Burr, *Mormon Rivals: The Romneys, the Huntsmans, and the Pursuit of Power* (Salt Lake City: Salt Lake Tribune, 2015).

6. Orme, in discussion with the author.

7. Patty Henetz, in discussion with the author, October 8, 2015.

8. Ibid.

9. Orme, in discussion with the author.

10. Dominic Welch, in discussion with the author, October 5, 2016.

11. *Wikipedia*, s.v. "Jon Huntsman Sr.," last updated July 31, 2017, https://en.wikipedia.org/wiki/Jon_Huntsman_Sr. (accessed August 7, 2016).

12. Ibid.

13. *Wikipedia*, s.v. "Jon Huntsman Jr." last edited October 2, 2017, https://en.wikipedia.org/wiki/Jon_Huntsman_Jr. (accessed October 2, 2017).

14. Joyce E. Cutler, "An FBI Agent was Stabbed and Two 17-Year-Old . . ." UPI, December 9, 1987, http://www.upi.com/Archives/1987/12/09/An-FBI-agent-was-stabbed-and-and-two-17-year-old/1379566024400/?spt=su (accessed October 1, 2017).

15. "Abby Huntsman," Fox News, http://www.foxnews.com/person/h/abby-huntsman.html (accessed October 1, 2017).

16. "About Paul Huntsman, the Potential Next Owner of the *Tribune*," *Salt Lake Tribune*, April 20, 2016, http://archive.sltrib.com/article.php?id=3800481&itype=CMSID (accessed April 20, 2016).

17. Anonymous JOA source, in discussion with the author, August 2016.

18. O'Brien, in discussion with the author.

19. James E. Shelledy, in discussion with the author, September 26, 2016.

20. Joan O'Brien, reading from an internal *Tribune* memo (author unknown) in discussion with the author, August 5, 2016.

21. Calls and emails to Senator Dabakis in 2015 and 2016 went unanswered.

22. Robert Gehrke, "Modern Mormon's Culture Drives Them to GOP," *Salt Lake Tribune*, September 16, 2015, http://www.sltrib.com/info/staff/1576911–155/mormons-church-percent-political-republican-authors (accessed August 16, 2016).

23. Michael McFall, "Sen. Jim Dabakis Is One of the People Trying to Buy the *Salt Lake Tribune*," *Salt Lake Tribune*, April 5, 2016, http://www.sltrib.com/news/2016/04/06/sen-jim-dabakis-is-one-of-the-people-trying-to-buy-the-salt-lake-tribune/ (accessed August 16, 2016).

24. Henetz, in discussion with the author.

25. Jill Lepore, "The Disruption Machine," *New Yorker*, June 23, 2014, http://www.newyorker.com/magazine/2014/06/23/the-disruption-machine (accessed August 16, 2016).

26. Will Bagley, in discussion with the author, July 2, 2014.

27. Tony Semerad, "Huntsman Family Buying the *Salt Lake Tribune*, Hopes to Insure Independent Voice for Future Generations," *Salt Lake Tribune*, April 21, 2016, http://archive.sltrib.com/article.php?id=3799365&itype=CMSID (accessed August 18, 2016).

28. Ibid.

29. Ibid.

30. Matt Canham, "Prospective Owner of the *Tribune*. Ownership of Utah's Largest Paper Would Provide a Bullhorn—If He Wants to Use It," *Salt Lake Tribune*, May 13, 2016, http://www.sltrib.com/home/3832090–155/you-dont-know-paul-huntsman-owning (accessed August 18, 2016).

31. O'Brien, in discussion with the author, August 5, 2016.

32. Porter, in discussion with the author, December 21, 2016.

33. O'Brien in discussion with the author, August 5, 2016.

34. Associated Press, "The Latest: Huntsman Bought *Tribune* to Preserve Unique Voice," May 31, 2016, https://apnews.com/790691a66f804087b947d5

5034b28ea5/latest-huntsman-bought-tribune-preserve-unique-voice (accessed October 2, 2017).

35. Anonymous JOA source, in discussion with the author, October 2016.

36. Shelledy, in discussion with the author.

37. O'Brien, in discussion with the author, August 5, 2016.

38. Ibid.

39. Ibid.

40. Porter, in discussion with the author, December 20, 2016.

41. Paul Huntsman, "Letter from the *Salt Lake Tribune*'s New Publisher," *Salt Lake Tribune*, June 3, 2016, http://archive.sltrib.com/article .php?id=3951909&itype=CMSID (accessed August 24, 2017).

42. Ibid.

43. Tony Semerad, "*Salt Lake Tribune* Names New Top Managing Editor, Adds Columnist," *Salt Lake Tribune*, November 22, 2016, http://archive.sltrib .com/article.php?id=4621742&itype=CMSID (accessed November 20, 2016).

44. Bryan Schott, "Poll: Utahns Want the *Salt Lake Tribune* to Continue Publishing," *Utah Policy* (blog), May 26, 2016, http://utahpolicy.com/index .php/features/today-at-utah-policy/9641-poll-utahns-want-the-salt-lake-tribune -to-continue-publishing?tmpl=component&print=1&page (accessed August 19, 2016).

45. Michael D. Gallivan, in discussion with the author, August 17, 2016.

46. Shelledy, in discussion with the author, September 26, 2016.

47. Save the *Salt Lake Tribune*, Facebook post, April 24, 2016, 1:52 p.m., https://www.facebook.com/savethesaltlaketribune/posts/1206856989334709 ?comment_id=1206921075994967&comment_tracking=%7B%22tn%22%3A %22R%22%7D (accessed August 4, 2016).

48. Matt Canham, "Don't Know Paul Huntsman? His Ownership of the *Salt Lake Tribune* May Change That," *Salt Lake Tribune*, June 1, 2016, http:// archive.sltrib.com/article.php?id=3832090&itype=CMSID (accessed October 1, 2017).

49. Porter, in discussion with the author, December 20, 2016.

50. Ibid.

51. Telephone calls (July 9, 2016, and December 28, 2016), emails (May 17, 2016, and December 28, 2016), and requests via third parties (October 2016) went unanswered.

52. Canham, "Don't Know Paul Huntsman?"

53. Ibid.

54. Ibid.

55. Anonymous person close to the family in discussion with author, September 14, 2016.

56. Paul Huntsman, Facebook post, October 25, 2011, 9:09 a.m., https://www.facebook.com/paul.huntsman.3/posts/2551841353553 (accessed August 28, 2017); Paul Huntsman, Facebook post, November 5, 2012, 5:03 p.m., https://www.facebook.com/paul.huntsman.3/posts/4797426371775 (accessed August 28, 2017).

57. Orme, in discussion with the author, June 16, 2016.

58. Ibid.

59. Ibid.

60. Semerad, "Huntsman Family Buying the *Salt Lake Tribune*."

61. Jon M. Huntsman Sr., *Barefoot to Billionaire: Reflection on a Life's Work and a Promise to Cure Cancer* (New York: Overlook Duckworth 2014), pp. 185–86.

62. Anonymous *Salt Lake Tribune* employee in discussion with the author, August 23, 2016.

63. Semerad, "*Salt Lake Tribune* Names New Top Managing Editor."

64. Paul Rolly, in discussion with the author, August 5, 2016.

65. Orme, in discussion with the author, October 10, 2016.

66. Benjamin Wood, "*Salt Lake Tribune*'s New Editor, Napier-Pearce, Is Thrilled to Return to Paper, Praises Predecessor Orme," *Salt Lake Tribune*, July 29, 2016, http://archive.sltrib.com/article.php?id=4172798&itype=CMSID &pid=3467361 (accessed October 24, 2016).

67. Ibid.

68. O'Brien, in discussion with the author, November 29, 2016.

69. Anonymous *Salt Lake Tribune* employee in discussion with the author, August 23, 2016.

70. Shelledy, in discussion with the author, September 26, 2016.

71. Wood, "*Salt Lake Tribune*'s New Editor."

72. Semerad, "*Salt Lake Tribune* Names New Top Managing Editor."

73. Ibid.

74. A *Tribune* editor who requested anonymity, in discussion and emails with the author, January 12, 2017.

75. Jennifer Napier-Pearce, in discussion with the author, January 11, 2017.

76. Ibid.

77. "Mormon Leaks," YouTube video channel, posted by MormonLeaks, https://www.youtube.com/channel/UCJTIFO9JJWiXABNXHDUKj4A (accessed October 3, 2016).

78. Matt Canham, "Leaked Videos Show Mormon Apostles Discussing Political Influence, Gay Marriage, Marijuana, and More," *Salt Lake Tribune*, October 19, 2016, http://archive.sltrib.com/article.php?id =4423214&itype=CMSID (accessed August 25, 2017).

79. Personal observation by the author, November 9, 2016.

80. Napier-Pearce, in discussion with the author.

81. Ibid.

82. Benjamin Wood, "Huntsman Calls for 'Inept' U. Administrators to Be Fired over Cancer Institute's CEO's Termination," *Salt Lake Tribune*, April 21, 2017, http://archive.sltrib.com/article.php?id=5203352&itype=CMSID (accessed August 17, 2017).

83. Ibid.

84. "*Tribune* Editorial: It Is Time for New Leadership at the University of Utah and Its Health Sciences Colleges," *Salt Lake Tribune*, April 22, 2017, http://archive.sltrib.com/article.php?id=5195473&itype=CMSID (accessed August 17, 2017).

85. Alex Stuckey and Benjamin Wood, "University of Utah President Stepping Down; Successor will Pick Permanent Health Sciences V.P.," *Salt Lake Tribune*, May 3, 2017, http://archive.sltrib.com/article. php?id=5239033&itype=CMSID (accessed October 1, 2017).

86. Joan O'Brien, speech to the First Unitarian Church of Salt Lake City, June 2016.

CHAPTER 29: WHITHER THE LDS CHURCH?

1. Chuck Clark, "Op-Ed: An Inclusive Vision for Utah's Pioneer Day Parade," *Salt Lake Tribune*, July 24, 2016, http://archive.sltrib.com/article .php?id=4138189&itype=CMSID (accessed October 3, 2016).

2. Polly Aird, Jeff Nichols, and Will Bagley, *Playing with Shadows: Voices of Dissent in the Mormon West* (Norman, OK: Arthur H. Clark, 2011), p. 13.

3. Richard N. Ostling and Joan K. Ostling, *Mormon America: The Power and the Promise* (San Francisco: HarperSanFrancisco, 1999), p. 252; *Wikipedia*, s.v. "Mark Hofmann," last updated August 2, 2017, https://en.wikipedia.org/ wiki/Mark_Hofmann (accessed August 25, 2017).

4. Michael D. Gallivan, in conversation with the author, August 17, 2016.

5. Tad Walch, "More Expansive Boundaries, Not 'Bubbles' for LDS Church, Otterson Says," *Deseret News*, April 12, 2016, http://www.deseretnews .com/article/865652045/LDS-Church-boundaries-more-expansive-than -restrictive-Michael-Otterson-says-at-UVU.html?pg=all (accessed April 12, 2016).

6. Richard E. Turley Jr., "The Mountain Meadows Massacre," *Ensign*, September 2007, https://www.lds.org/ensign/2007/09/the-mountain -meadows-massacre?lang=eng (accessed August 25, 2017).

7. Peggy Fletcher Stack, "LDS Church Publishes Volume with a More Scholarly Approach to Mormon History," *Salt Lake Tribune,* December 21, 2016, http://archive.sltrib.com/article.php?id=4740751&itype=CMSID (accessed August 25, 2017).

8. Peggy Fletcher Stack, "Mass Exodus from LDS? Stats Paint a Different Picture," *Salt Lake Tribune,* November 17, 2016, http://archive.sltrib.com/article.php?id=4535962&itype=CMSID (accessed August 25, 2017).

9. Utah Lighthouse Ministry, "About Us," http://www.utlm.org/navaboutus.htm (accessed October 2, 2017).

10. Recovery from Mormonism, http://www.exmormon.org/ (accessed October 3, 2016); Mormon Curtain, http://www.mormoncurtain.com/ (accessed October 3, 2016).

11. *Wikipedia,* s.v. "Foundation for Ancient Research and Mormon Studies," last updated April 15, 2017, https://en.wikipedia.org/wiki/Foundation _for_Ancient_Research_and_Mormon_Studies (accessed October 3, 2016).

12. *Sunstone* homepage, https://www.sunstonemagazine.com/ (accessed October 3, 2016).

13. Dana Haight Cattani, "The Stubborn Ounces of My Weight," *Sunstone,* April 5, 2016, https://www.sunstonemagazine.com/the-stubborn-ounces-of -my-weight/ (accessed January 2, 2017).

14. Joan O'Brien, in discussion with the author, April 9, 2015.

15. Christy Money, "Those Who Leave the Church Deserve Unconditional Love," *Salt Lake Tribune,* December 4, 2016, http://saltlaketribune.ut.news memory.com/?token=b5409f4b3316270ed822043e7c01b79a_5844577b_42e7 a4e&selDate=20161204 (accessed December 4, 2016).

16. Ibid.

17. Anonymous, "Why I Can't 'Leave the Church Alone,'" *Zelph on the Shelf* (blog), http://zelphontheshelf.com/why-i-cant-leave-the-church-alone/ (accessed October 26, 2016).

18. Rod Decker, KUTV Ch. 2 (Salt Lake City) reporter, in discussion with the author, January 20, 2017.

19. Lee Davidson, "With Utah Legislature's Mormon Supermajority, Is It Representative of the People?" *Salt Lake Tribune,* December 12, 2016, http://archive.sltrib.com/article.php?id=4663941&itype=CMSID (accessed October 1, 2017).

20. Ibid.

21. Annie Knox, "One Answer to Utah's Teacher Shortage: Hire People Who Are Not Teachers," *Salt Lake Tribune,* June 15, 2016, http://archive.sltrib .com/article.php?id=4006906&itype=CMSID (accessed August 25, 2017).

22. Benjamin Wood, "Working Two Jobs Is Simple Math for Teachers,"

Salt Lake Tribune, November 27, 2016, http://saltlaketribune.ut.newsmemory
.com/?token=e533de8e9d857d64fffb702738197494_583b23a0_42e7a4e&sel
Date=20161127 (accessed November 27, 2016).

23. Editorial, "Our Schools Now: Need for School Money Is Real," *Salt
Lake Tribune,* January 8, 2017, http://saltlaketribune.ut.newsmemory.com/?tok
en=faac5004771cefafb46ff97f94a7535b_587280f1_42e7a4e&selDate=20170108
(accessed January 8, 2017).

24. Personal observation of the author, a consistent reader of the letters
to the editor.

25. American Lung Association, "State of the Air 2015: Salt Lake City-
Provo-Orem, UT," http://www.stateoftheair.org/2015/msas/salt-lake-city
-provo-orem-ut.html#pm24 (accessed October 4, 2015).

26. George Pyle, "Medicaid Expansion Rides Again," *Salt Lake Tribune,*
March 28, 2017 http://archive.sltrib.com/article.php?id=5111604
&itype=CMSID (accessed October 3, 2017); Bob Bernick, "Poll: Utahns
Want Larger Medicaid Expansion," Utah Policy.com, April 26, 2016, http://
utahpolicy.com/index.php/features/today-at-utah-policy/9290-poll-utahns
-want-larger-medicaid-expansion (accessed October 1, 2017).

27. Lindsay Whitehurst, "Report: Tourism Spending in Utah Grew to
Nearly $8 Billion," Associated Press, May 25, 2016, https://apnews.com/f2676
3ab48d448fa8974955a78f6ae1c/report-tourism-spending-utah-grew-nearly-8
-billion (accessed October 5, 2017).

28. Paul C. Burke, John Mackay, and Brett L. Tollman, "It's Okay to
Be Gay, and Utah Teachers Need to Be Able to Say It Is," *Salt Lake Tribune,*
November 6, 2016, http://archive.sltrib.com/article.php?id=4533227
&itype=CMSID (accessed August 25, 2017).

29. Carl Wimmer, "The Role of the LDS Church in Utah's Politics,"
Mormonism Research Ministry, http://www.mrm.org/utah-politics (accessed
August 25, 2017).

30. Peggy Fletcher Stack, "Mormon Conversions Lag behind Huge
Missionary Growth," *Salt Lake Tribune,* May 2, 2014, http://archive.sltrib.com/
article.php?id=57862203&itype=CMSID (accessed August 25, 2017).

31. Peggy Fletcher Stack, "How Much Do Top Mormon Leaders Make?
Leaked Pay Stubs May Surprise You," *Salt Lake Tribune,* January 9, 2017, http://
archive.sltrib.com/article.php?id=4800350&itype=CMSID (accessed August
25, 2017).

32. Peggy Fletcher Stack, "Two Years after an Excommunicated Kate Kelly
Sought a Giant Leap, Mormon Feminists Keep Making Small Steps toward
Equity'," *Salt Lake Tribune,* July 21, 2016, http://archive.sltrib.com/article
.php?id=4042513&itype=CMSID (accessed October 4, 2016).

33. Jennifer Napier-Pearce, "The *Salt Lake Tribune* Chooses Madi Barney, Who Pushed for Change at BYU, as Utahn of the Year," *Salt Lake Tribune*, January 10, 2017, http://archive.sltrib.com/article.php?id=4732048 &itype=CMSID (accessed August 25, 2017).

34. David Noyce, "*Salt Lake Tribune* Wins Pulitzer for Campus Rape Coverage, Praises Victims for Sharing Their Stories," *Salt Lake Tribune*, April 26, 2017, http://archive.sltrib.com/article.php?id=5161643&itype=CMSID (accessed April 10, 2017).

35. Peggy Fletcher Stack, "With Average Age of 80, Mormon Church Has Never Had Older Top Leaders," *Salt Lake Tribune*, March 3, 2015, http://archive.sltrib.com/article.php?id=2245029&itype=CMSID (accessed August 25, 2017).

36. Amy McDonald, "Who Will Be the Next Mormon Prophet? This Infographic Explains," *Salt Lake Tribune*, July 27, 2015, http://archive.sltrib.com/article.php?id=2705341&itype=CMSID (accessed August 25, 2017).

37. Peggy Fletcher Stack, "Mormon Videos Spur Question: Should Aging LDS Apostles Be Able to Retire?" *Salt Lake Tribune*, October 28, 2016, http://archive.sltrib.com/article.php?id=4440116&itype=CMSID (accessed January 7, 2017).

38. *Wikipedia*, s.v. "Black People and the Priesthood (LDS)," last edited September 27, 2017, https://en.wikipedia.org/wiki/Black_people_and _priesthood_(LDS) (accessed October 3, 2017).

39. Peggy Fletcher Stack, "Mormon Gay Policy Is 'Will of the Lord' through His Prophet, Senior Apostle Says," *Salt Lake Tribune*, February 3, 2016, http://archive.sltrib.com/article.php?id=3391057&itype=CMSID (accessed August 25, 2017).

40. "Where Are Our Leaders? A Mormon Catholic Comparison," *Nearing Kolob* (blog), http://www.nearingkolob.com/leaders-mormon-catholic -comparison/ (accessed October 3, 2017).

41. Ibid.

42. Jonathan Haidt, *The Righteous Mind: Why Good People Are Divided by Religion and Politics* (New York: Vintage, 2013), p. 107.

43. Polly Aird, Jeff Nichols, and Will Bagley, ed., "Voices of Dissent in the Mormon West," in *Kingdom of the West*, vol. 8 (Norman, OK: Arthur H. Clark, University of Oklahoma Press, 2011), p. 14.

CHAPTER 30: THE *TRIBUNE*'S FUTURE

1. Pat Bagley, in discussion with the author, November 4, 2016.

2. Jennifer Napier-Pearce, in discussion with the author, January 11, 2017.

3. Mamta Badkar, "Buffett Explains Why He Paid $344 Million for 28 Newspapers, and Thinks the Industry Still Has a Future," *Business Insider*, March 1, 2013, http://www.businessinsider.com/warren-buffett-buying -newspapers-2013-3 (accessed October 4, 2016).

4. Ibid.

5. Joan O'Brien, speech at the First Unitarian Church of Salt Lake City, June 2016. Copy of transcript in author's possession.

6. Kathleen Kingsbury, "Print as a Premium Offering," Nieman Labs Predictions for Journalism in 2017, December 19, 2016, http://www.nieman lab.org/2016/12/print-as-a-premium-offering/?utm_source=Daily+Lab +email+list&utm_campaign=793f78051b-dailylabemail3&utm_medium =email&utm_term=0_d68264fd5e-793f78051b-395990497 (accessed December 19, 2016).

7. Jennifer Napier-Pearce, *Salt Lake Tribune*, November 20, 2016, http:// saltlaketribune.ut.newsmemory.com/?token=a6920919b7087bc85e0c8b9e2c 35bfe8_5831e397_42e7a4e&selDate=20161120 (accessed November 20, 2016).

8. Marina Gomberg, "Optimistic Tales to Supplement Your Hard News Diet," *Salt Lake Tribune*, January 15, 2017, http://saltlaketribune.ut.news memory.com/?token=de91326c6750ebf20c8c026690410019_587bbeb6_42e7 a4e&selDate=20170115 (accessed January 17, 2017).

9. James E. Shelledy, in conversation with the author, August 25, 2016.

10. Napier-Pearce, in discussion with the author.

11. Terry Orme, in discussion with the author, October 10, 2016.

12. Brian Maffly, "Archeologist Says He's Found True Actual Mountain Meadows Massacre Graves; It's Not on LDS-Owned Land," *Salt Lake Tribune*, September 30, 2015, http://archive.sltrib.com/article .php?id=2961537&itype=CMSID (accessed August 25, 2017).

13. Everett Bassett, in discussion with the author, December 19, 2016.

APPENDIX: THREE *TRIBUNE* ARTICLES IN FULL ABOUT THE EXCAVATION AT THE MOUNTAIN MEADOWS MASSACRE SITE

1. Christopher Smith, "Unearthing Mountain Meadows Secrets: Backhoe at a S. Utah Killing Field Rips Open 142-Year-Old Wound," *Salt Lake Tribune*, March 124, 2000, http://www.cesnur.org/testi/morm_01.htm (accessed

August 23, 2017). Original text courtesy of Will Bagley, 2014. Reprinted with permission © *Salt Lake Tribune*. Includes slight variations from a previous version.

2. Christopher Smith, "Voices of the Dead," *Salt Lake Tribune*, March 13, 2000, http://www.cesnur.org/testi/morm_01.htm (accessed August 23, 2017). Original text courtesy of Will Bagley, 2014. Reprinted with permission © *Salt Lake Tribune*. Includes slight variations from a previous version.

3. Christopher Smith, "Mountain Meadows Massacre: The Dilemma of Blame," *Salt Lake Tribune*, March 12, 2000, http://www.cesnur.org/testi/morm_01.htm (accessed August 23, 2017). Original text courtesy of Will Bagley, 2014. Reprinted with permission © *Salt Lake Tribune*. Includes slight variations from a previous version.

INDEX